I0876692

Cozy Things to Draw

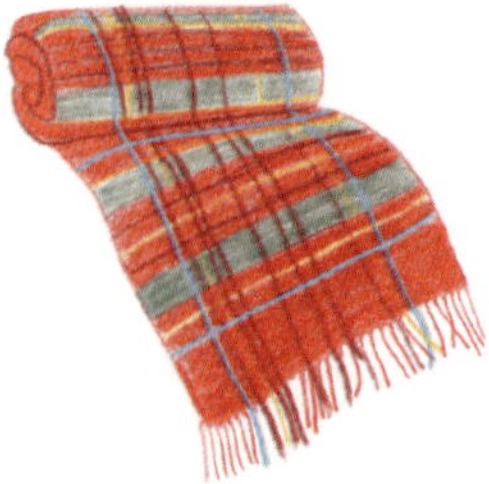
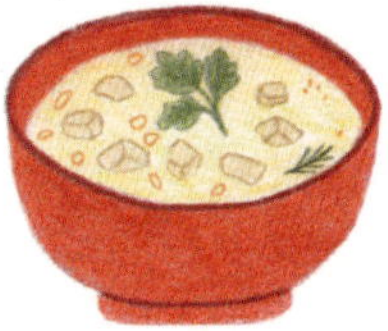
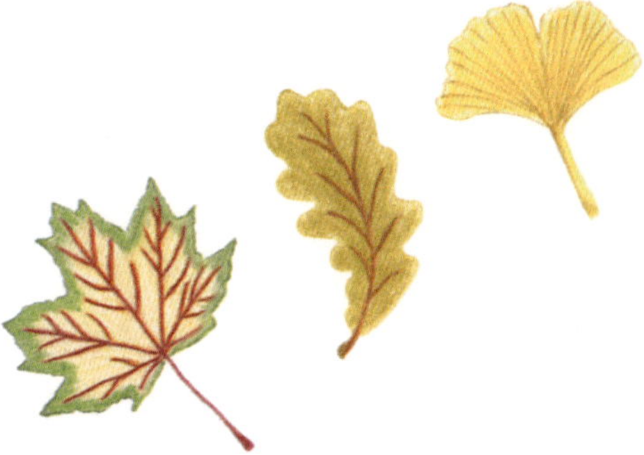
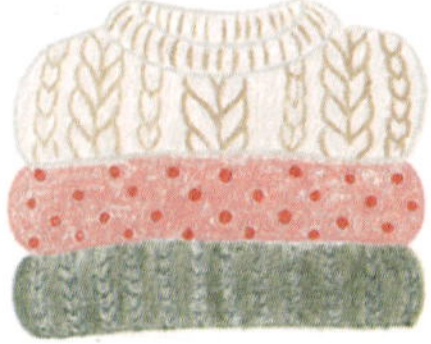
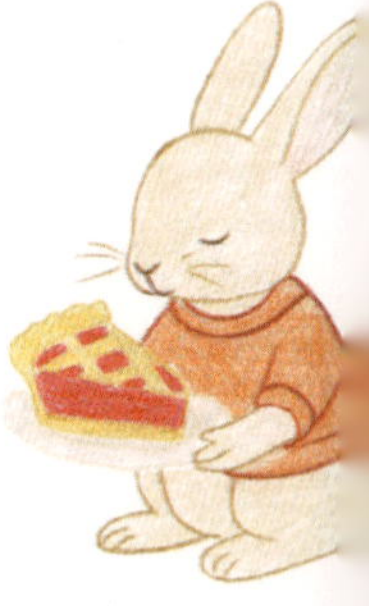

Cozy Things to Draw

Analía Fratti

Skittledog

CONTENTS

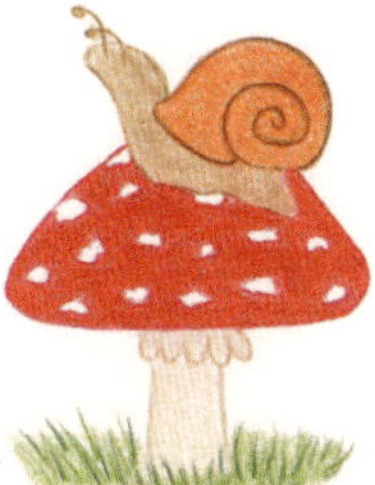

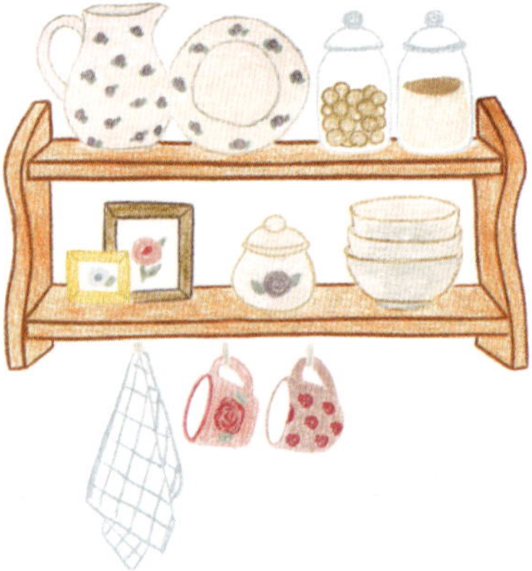

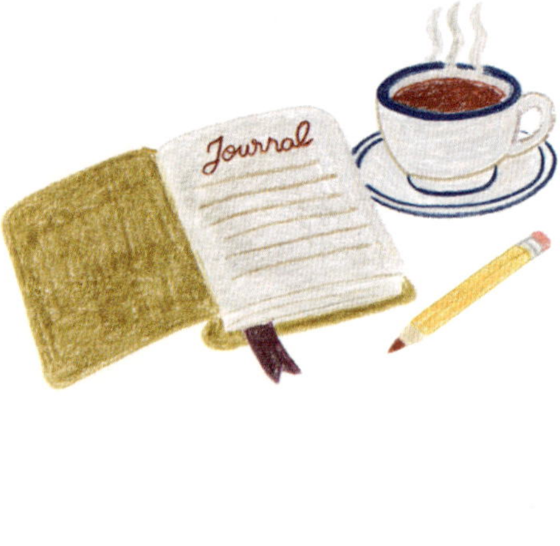
Journal

WELCOME!

This book has been designed as a calming space for you to slow down, pick up your pencils and enjoy drawing – without any pressure. You don't need to be an artist or to worry about getting anything 'right'. These pages are intended to feel comforting, familiar and easy to return to – like a warm cup of tea or a favourite corner in your home.

Inside, you'll discover simple coloured-pencil illustrations inspired by everyday moments, nature and the joy that can be found through slow living. Each project is broken down into clear, visual steps, allowing you to follow along at your own pace. The colour palette used is given at the top of each page to make it quick and easy to select the pencils you need.

Draw straight onto the pages: skip around, repeat and revisit the same illustration multiple times if you want to. Each one also appears as a simple outline so that you can practise the colour techniques before having a go at the complete drawing process.

There's no rush to finish, and you don't need to perfect every line. Small imperfections are part of what gives the drawings their warmth and personality. Some days, you may want to colour carefully and slowly; other days, you may prefer to keep things loose and light. Both approaches are completely valid here. Let this book be a place where drawing feels relaxing rather than demanding. Take your time, enjoy the process, and let your own style emerge naturally as you go along.

THINGS YOU'LL NEED

You don't need many drawing supplies to get started. A few simple materials used thoughtfully are all you need to complete each illustration.

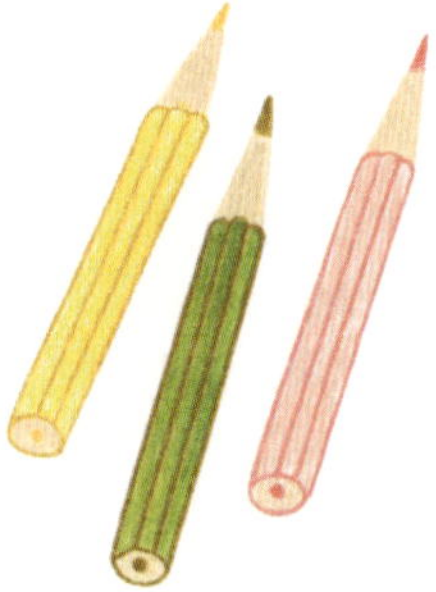

COLOURED PENCILS

Any coloured pencils will work for this book. You don't need professional or expensive supplies. Softer pencils blend more easily, but soft blends are possible with any pencils if you keep your pressure light. You'll often reuse the same colours, building depth through layering rather than constantly switching pencils.

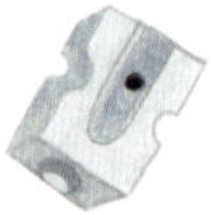

GOOD-QUALITY SHARPENER

Keeping your pencils sharp makes a noticeable difference, especially for small details, clean edges and fine patterns. Sharp tips give you more control and help keep illustrations crisp and readable.

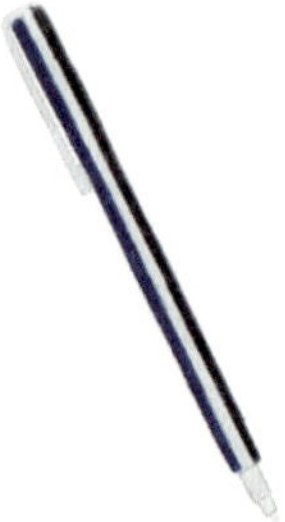

THIN-TIP ERASER

An eraser isn't only for correcting mistakes. A thin-tip eraser is especially useful for gently lifting colour to create highlights, soften edges or add small, light details. Many drawings in this book use erasing as part of the final look.

WARMING-UP EXERCISES

Before starting an illustration, warming up your hand can help you feel more comfortable and in control of your pencils. Copying the marks below will loosen your hand and help you understand how your pencil responds to different movements and pressure.

Think of this as a short transition into drawing. A few minutes of relaxed marks on some scrap paper can help steady your lines, soften your pressure and make the drawing process feel more natural. There's no goal to reach here – just an opportunity to get familiar with your tools and ease into the page.

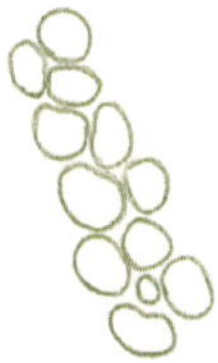

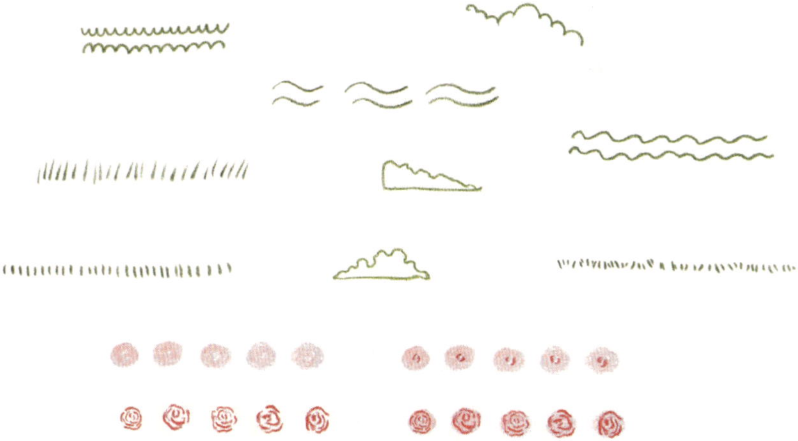

DRAWING TECHNIQUES

You'll notice the same techniques repeating throughout the projects. There's no need to memorize them – your hand will learn naturally as you draw along. These techniques recur throughout the book, gently guiding you as you draw. With each page, they'll become more familiar, until they feel natural and intuitive.

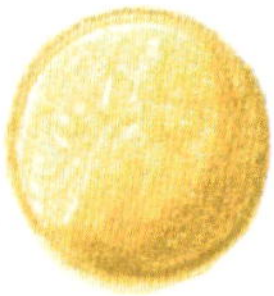

LAYERING COLOURS

Most illustrations are built by layering colour gradually. Start with the lightest tone first, then add darker tones on top to create depth. Beginning with lighter colours keeps the drawing soft and gives you more control as you build.

USING DIFFERENT TONES

You'll often use two or three shades of the same colour family. These aren't meant to be used all at once – layer them slowly, adding the darker tones only where you want form, weight or emphasis.

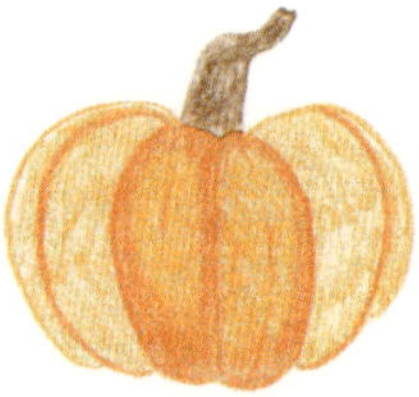

BLENDING THROUGH LAYERING

Blending in this book doesn't rely on heavy pressure or special tools. Instead, colours blend naturally as you layer light strokes on top of one another. Overlapping colours softly and building them up gradually creates smooth transitions without flattening the drawing.

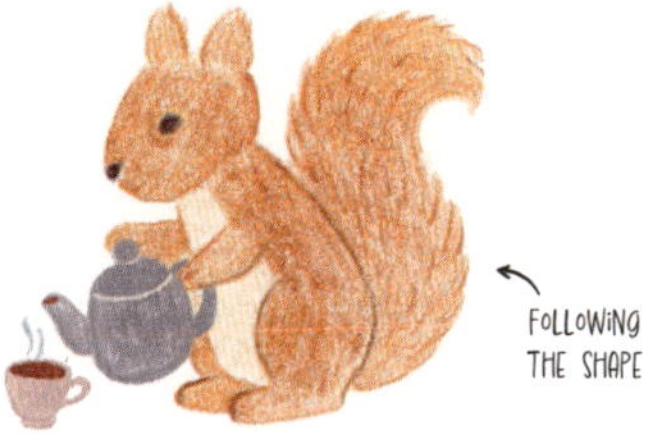

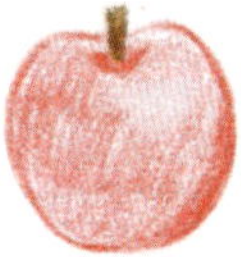

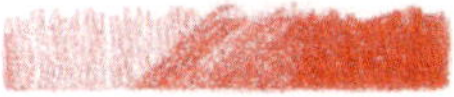

PRESSURE OVER OUTLINES

Rather than outlining everything heavily, depth is created by pressing a little harder in selected areas. The same colour can look very different depending on how much pressure you apply.

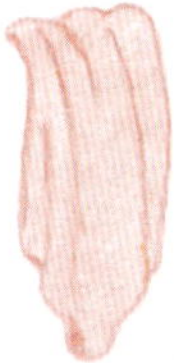

FOLLOWING THE SHAPE

Let your pencil strokes follow the form of what you're drawing. Curved strokes help round objects feel three-dimensional, while short strokes suggest texture in fabric, fur or wood.

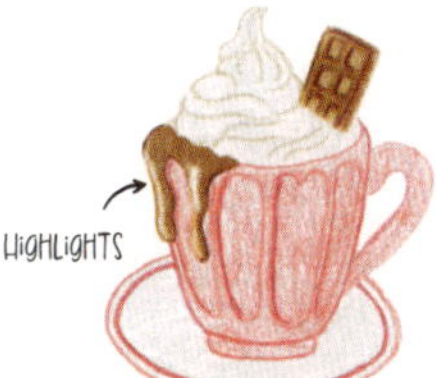

LIFTING HIGHLIGHTS

Use your eraser to lift colour where you want light to appear. Small, controlled erasing creates highlights and softens transitions without adding new colours.

EVERYDAY MOMENTS

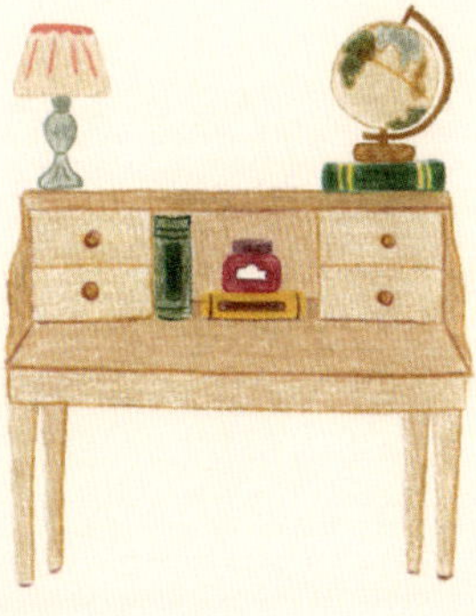

TEACUP

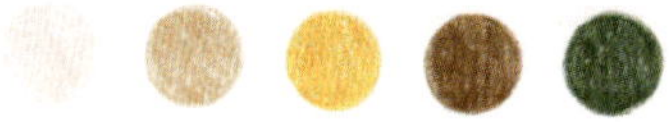

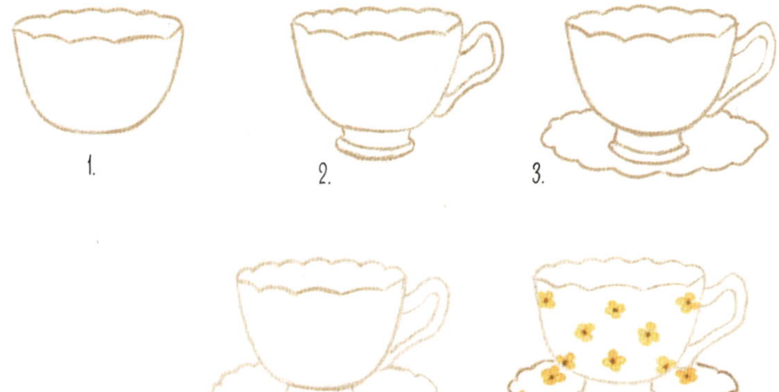
1.
2.
3.
4.
5.
6.
7.
ADD THE DARKER BROWN ALONG THE BORDERS FOR DEPTH AND DEFINITION.

JAM JAR

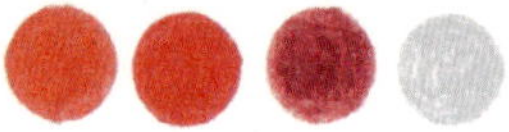

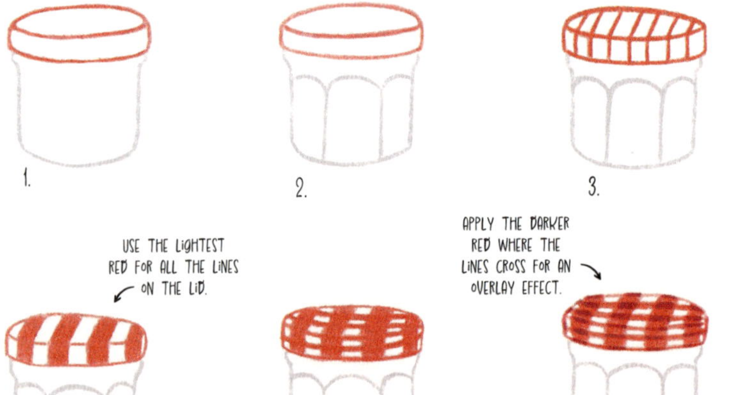
1.
2.
3.
USE THE LIGHTEST RED FOR ALL THE LINES ON THE LID.
APPLY THE DARKER RED WHERE THE LINES CROSS FOR AN OVERLAY EFFECT.
4.
5.
6.
7.
8.
USE THE DARKER SHADE OF RED ON THE OUTER 'ARCHES' TO CREATE DEPTH.

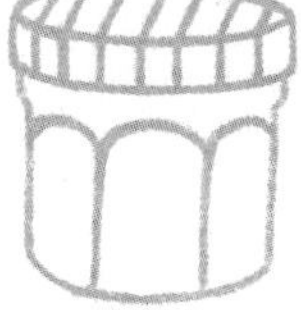

BOOKSHELF

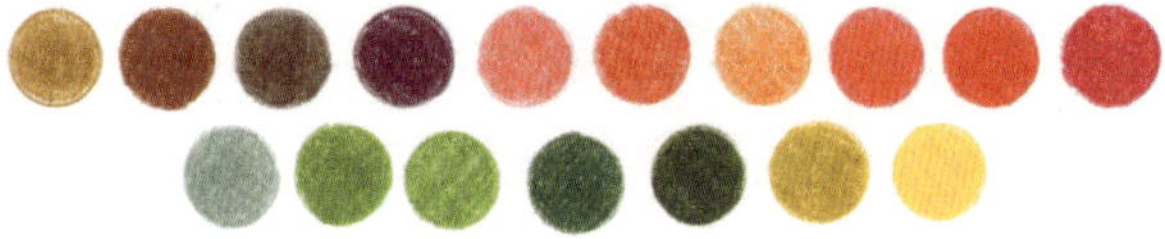

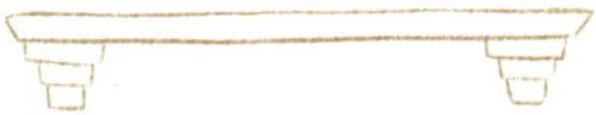

1.

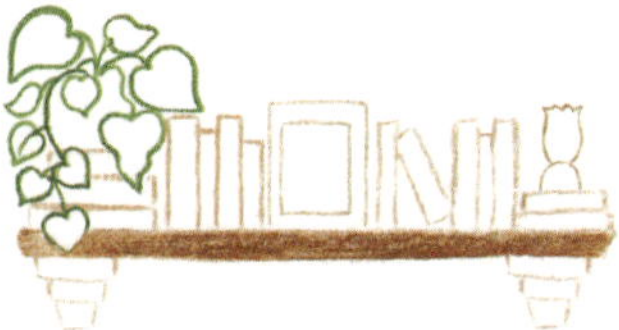

2.

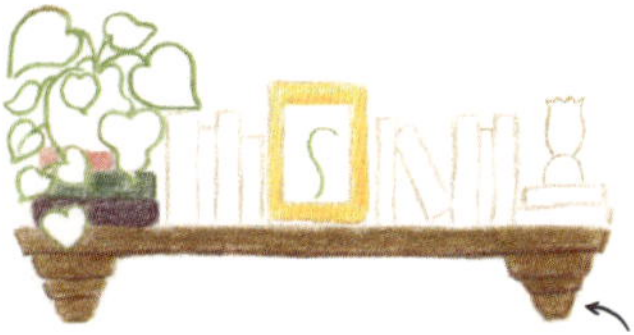

3.

CREATE DEFINITION BY USING A DARKER TONE OR BY ADDING MORE PRESSURE ALONG THE EDGES.

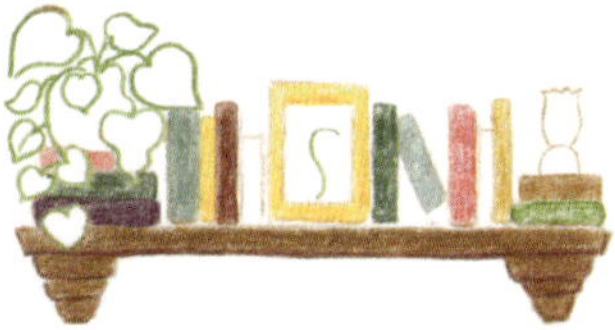

4.

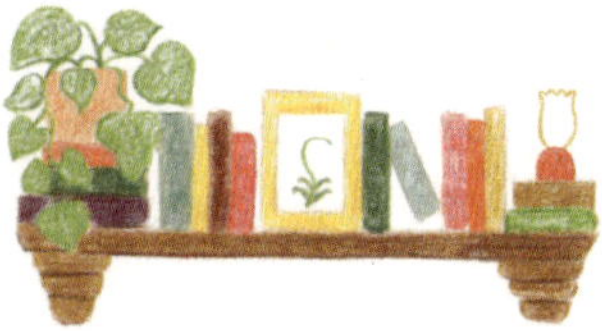

5.

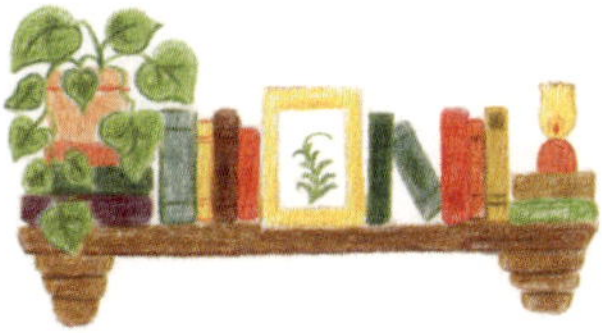

6.

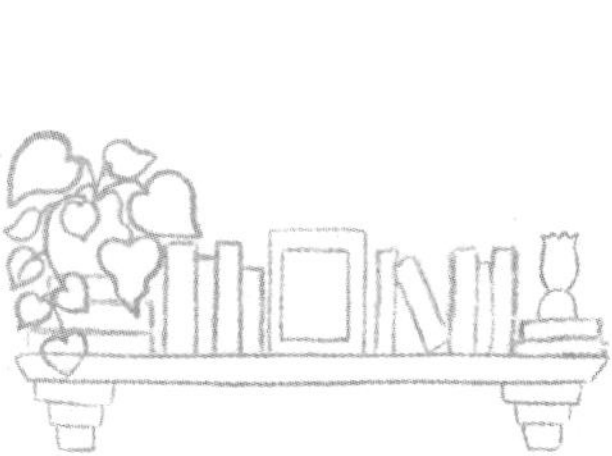

ARMCHAIR

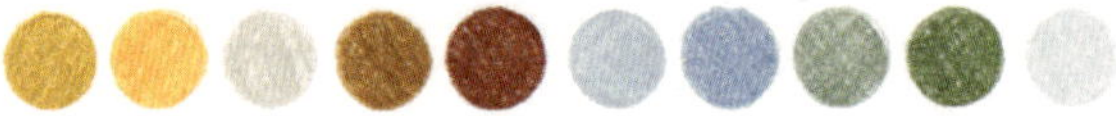

1.

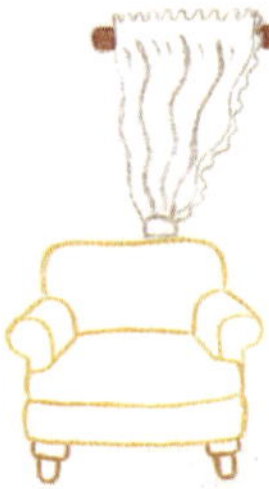

2.

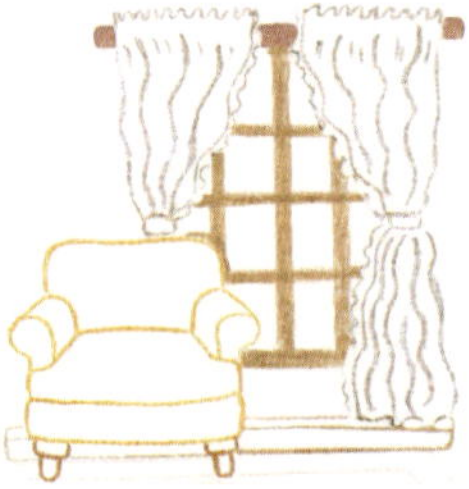

3.

DARKER AREAS ON THE CURTAINS GIVE THEM MOVEMENT.

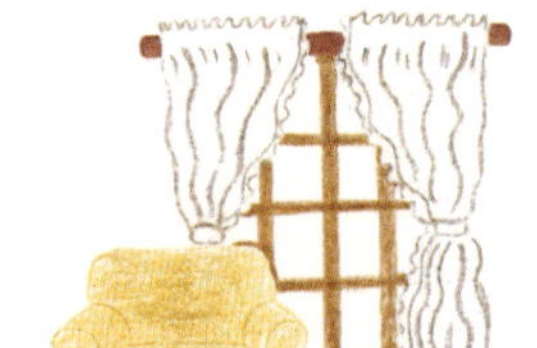

4.

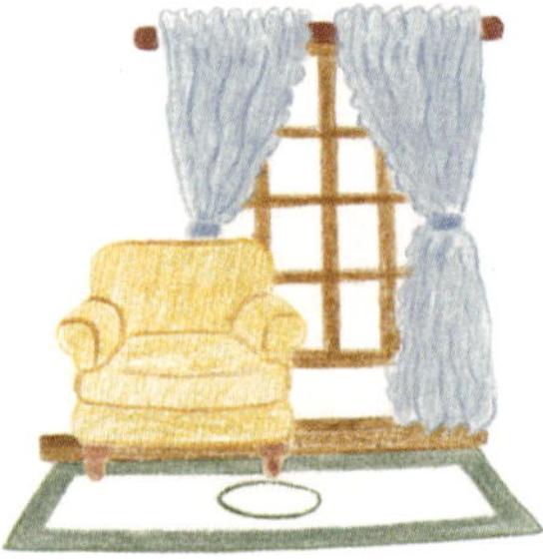

5.

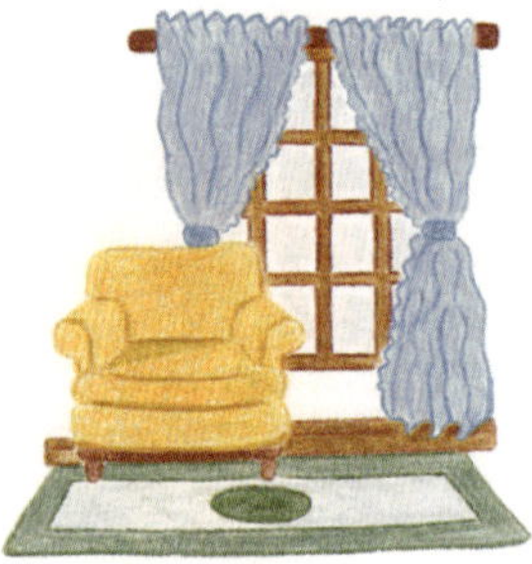

6.

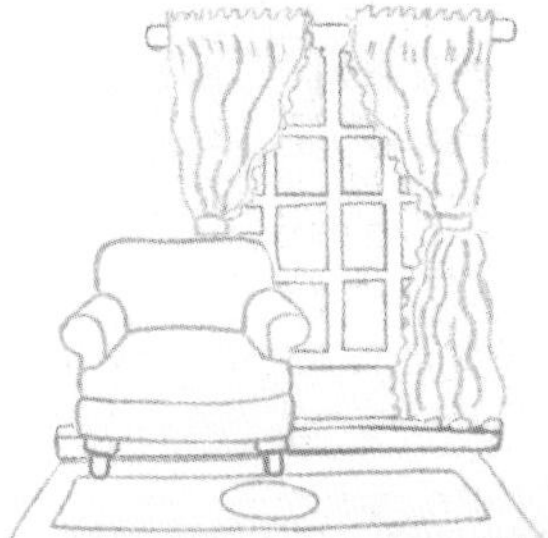

Mug of Cocoa

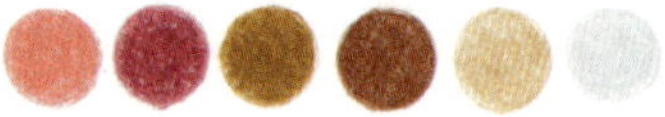

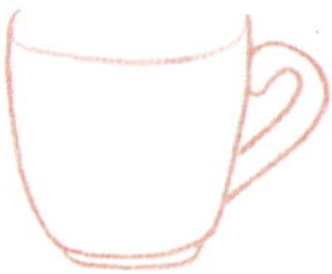

1.

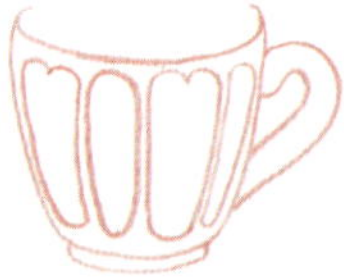

2.

3.

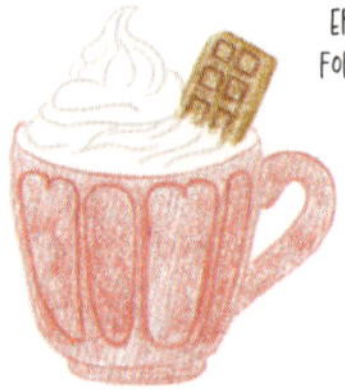

4.

REMOVE A BIT OF THE CUP WITH A THIN-TIP ERASER TO MAKE SPACE FOR THE CHOCOLATE DRIP.

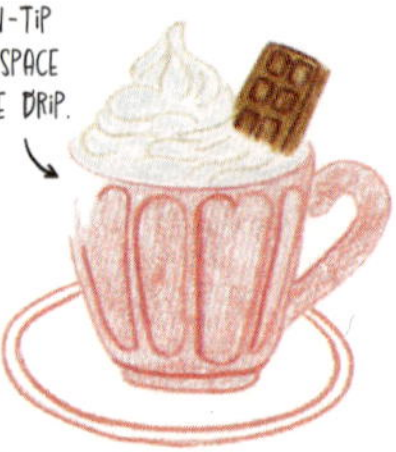

5.

CREATE HIGHLIGHTS WITH A THIN-TIP ERASER.

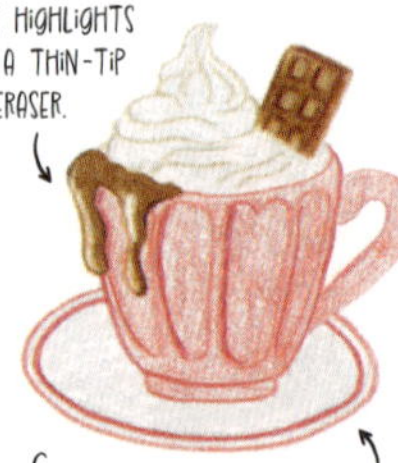

6.

APPLY STRONGER PRESSURE ON THE CREAM, CHOCOLATE AND CUP TO ADD DEPTH.

COZY DESK

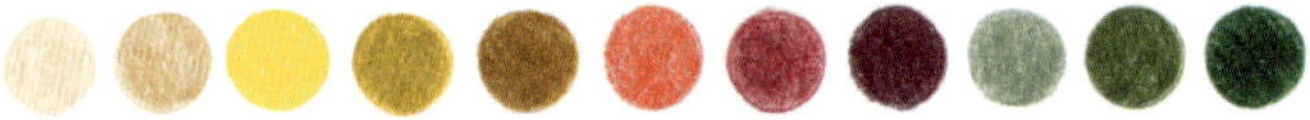

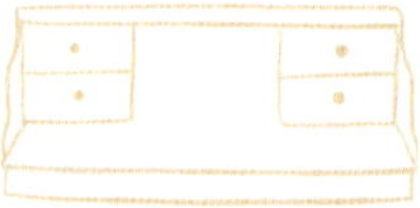

1.

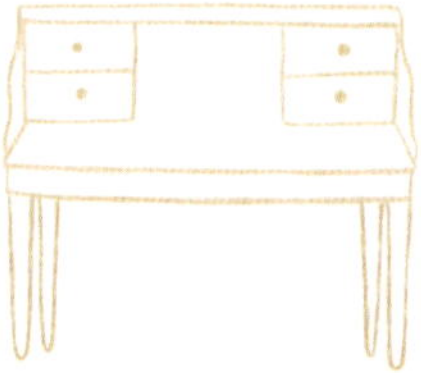

2.

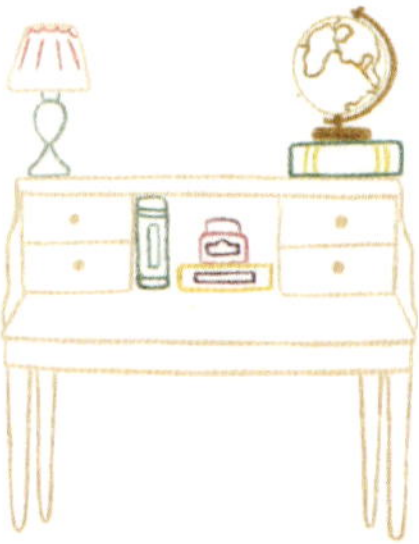

3.

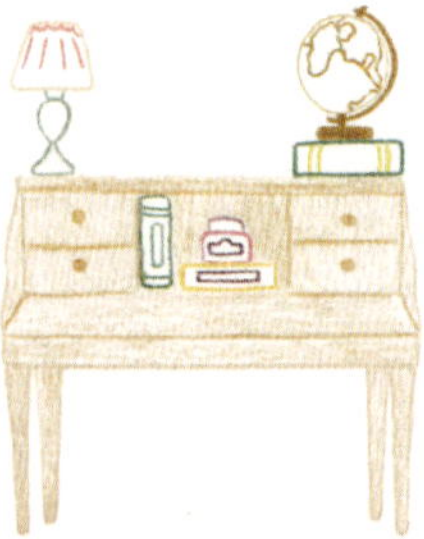

4.

ADD SOFT HIGHLIGHTS TO THE LAMP SHADE, GLOBE AND DRAWER EDGES WITH A THIN-TIP ERASER.

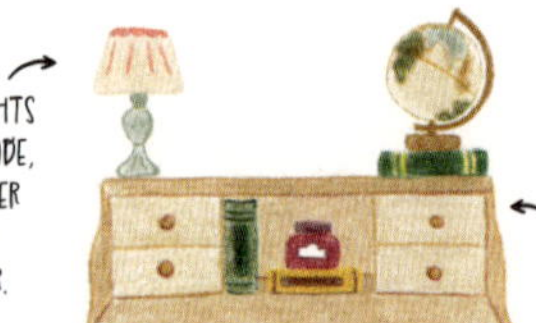

BUILD DEPTH BY INCREASING PRESSURE IN SELECTED AREAS OF THE WOOD, BOOKS AND GLOBE.

5.

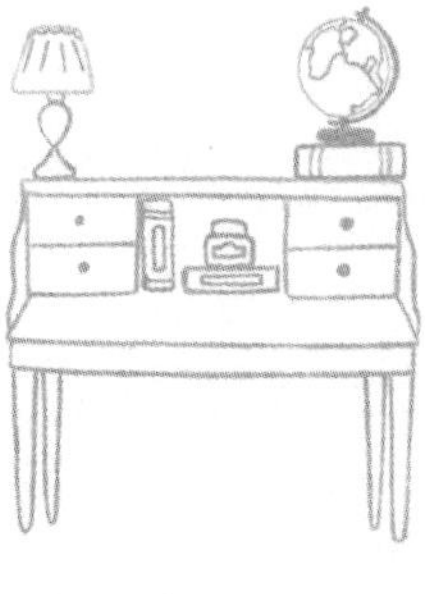

CUP OF COFFEE

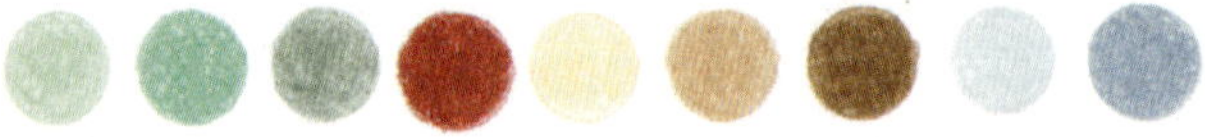

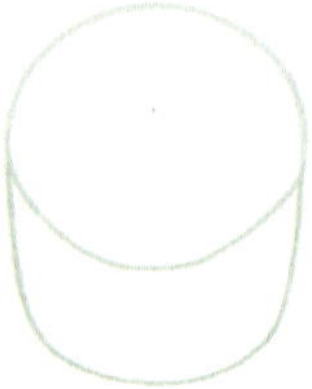

1.

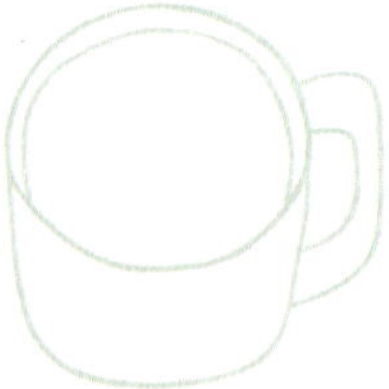

2.

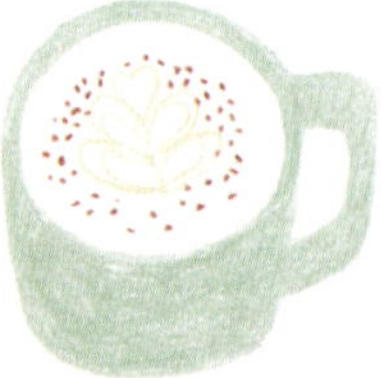

3.

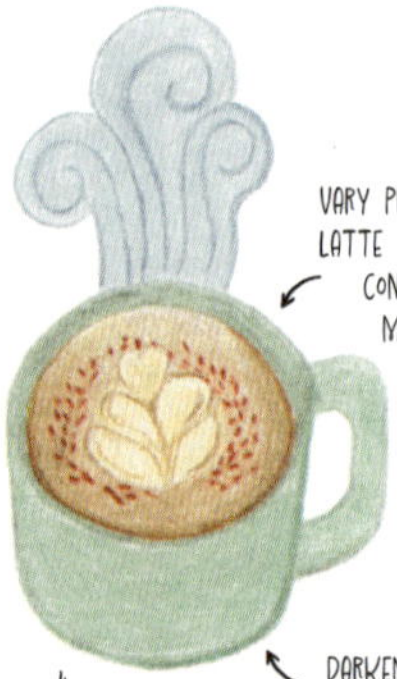

4.

VARY PRESSURE IN THE LATTE ART TO CREATE CONTRAST AND MOVEMENT.

DARKEN THE EDGE OF THE COFFEE AND THE CUP.

PUMPKIN SPICED LATTE

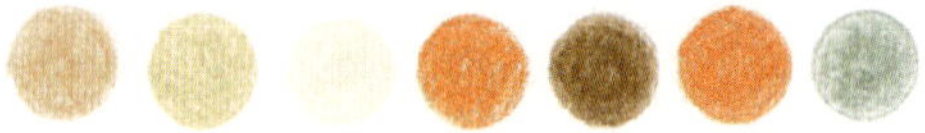

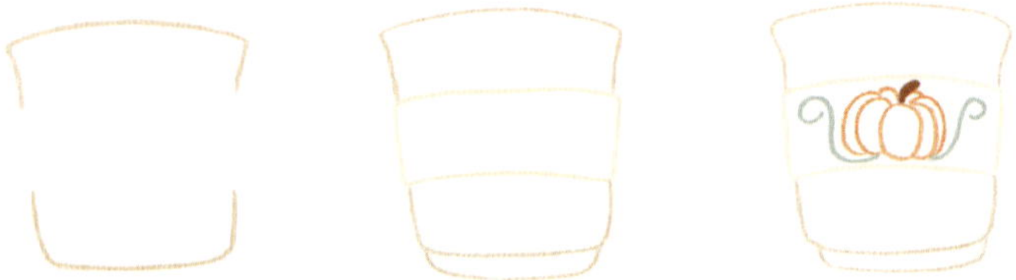

1. 2. 3.

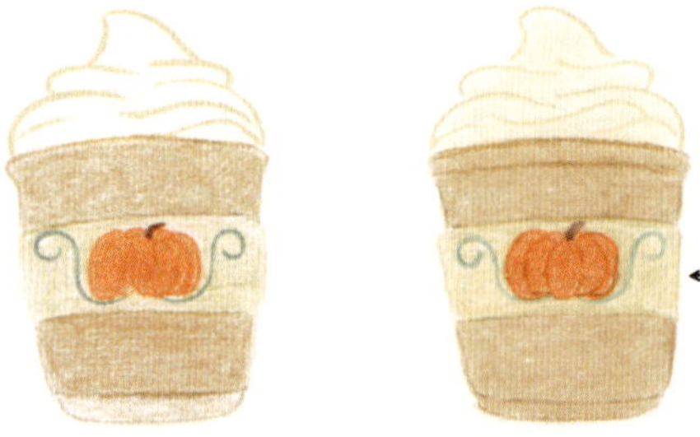

USE THE DARKER ORANGE ON THE PUMPKIN ACCENTS AND ADD PRESSURE SHADING FOR DEPTH.

4. 5.

COFFEE BEANS

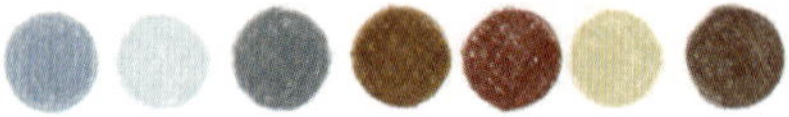

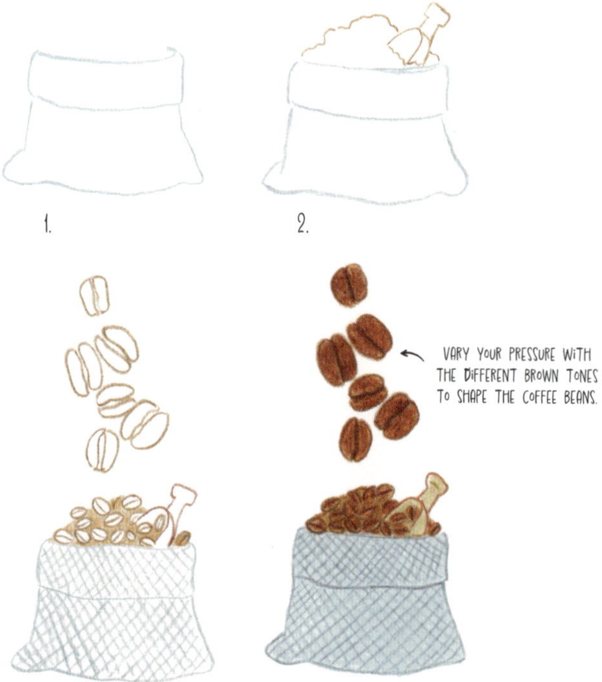

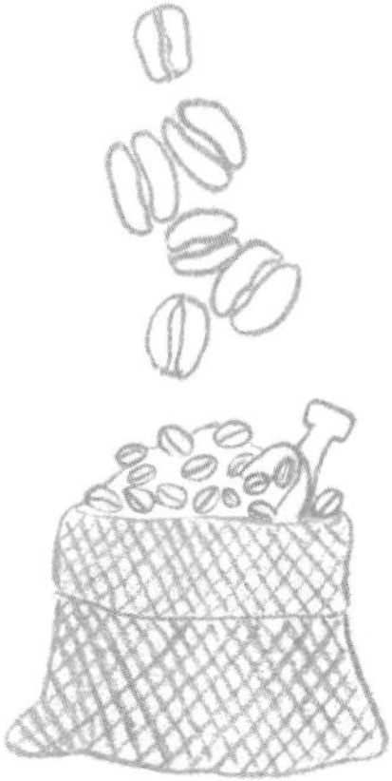

FLUFFY SLIPPERS

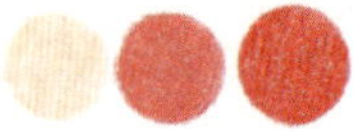

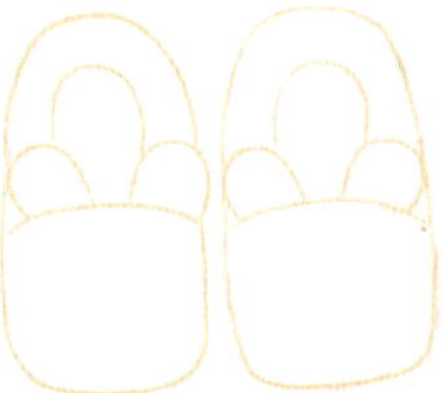

1.

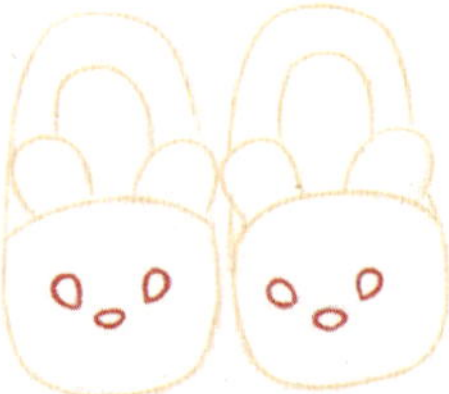

2.

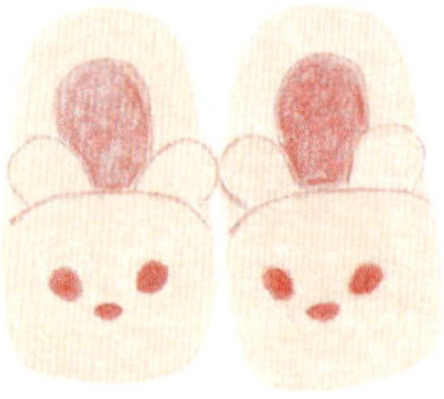

3.

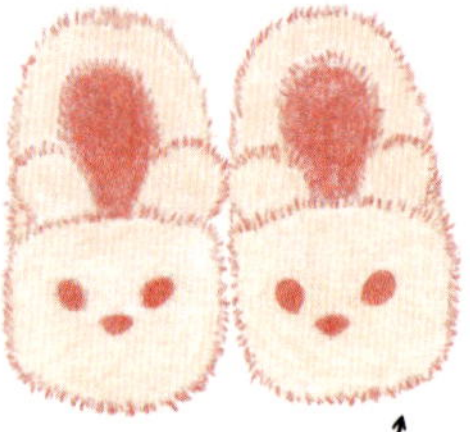

4.

BUILD THE FLUFFY TEXTURE WITH SHORT OUTWARD STROKES AND VARIED PRESSURE USING THE TWO PINK TONES.

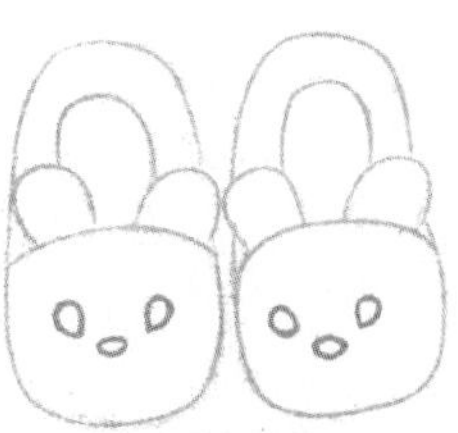

ALARM CLOCK

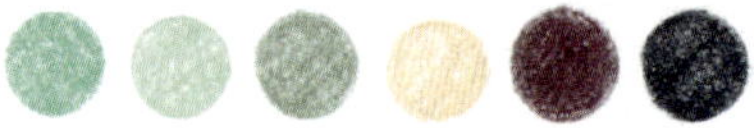

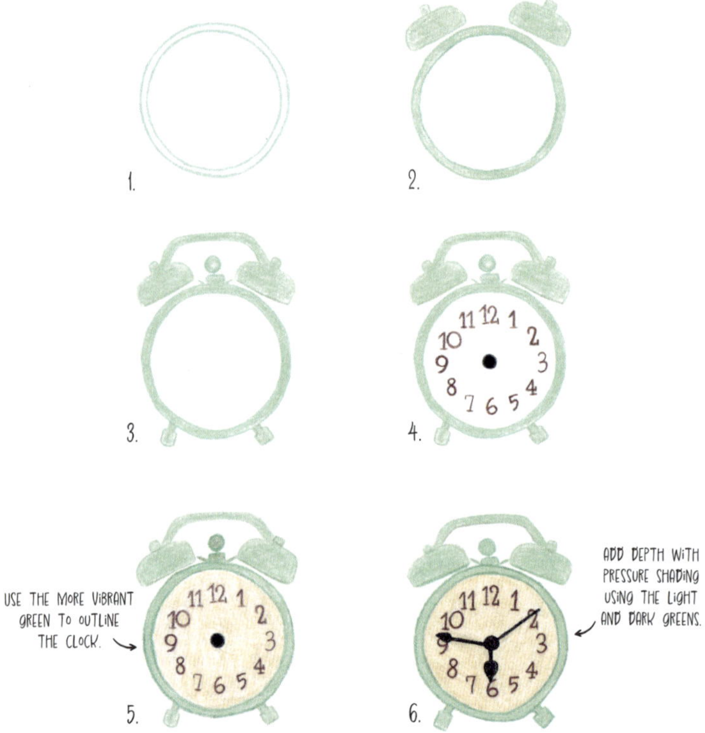

1.
2.
3.
4.
5.
USE THE MORE VIBRANT GREEN TO OUTLINE THE CLOCK.
6.
ADD DEPTH WITH PRESSURE SHADING USING THE LIGHT AND DARK GREENS.

TEA STRAINER

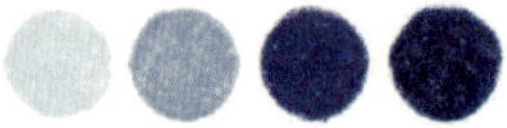

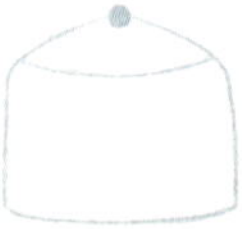

1.

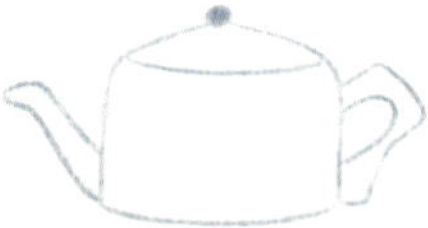

2.

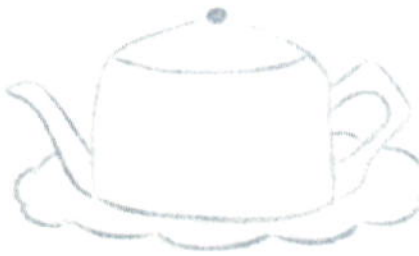

3.

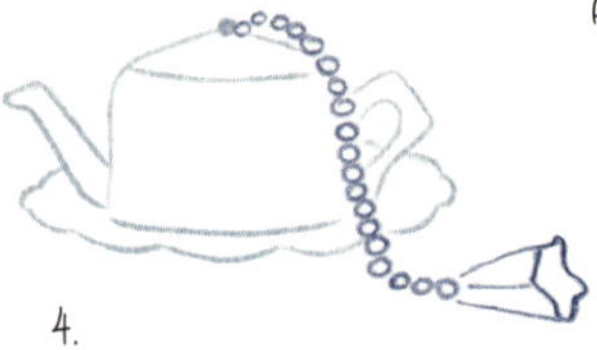

4.

SHADE THE METAL BODY WITH THE LIGHT AND DARK GREY.

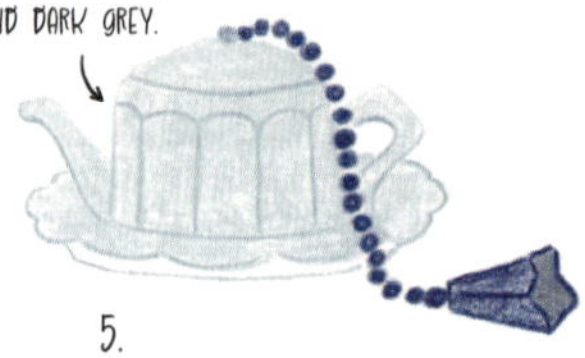

5.

EACH HOLE IS A GREY CIRCLE WITH A DARK-BLUE CENTRE. OUTLINE HALF THE EDGE WITH DARK BLUE.

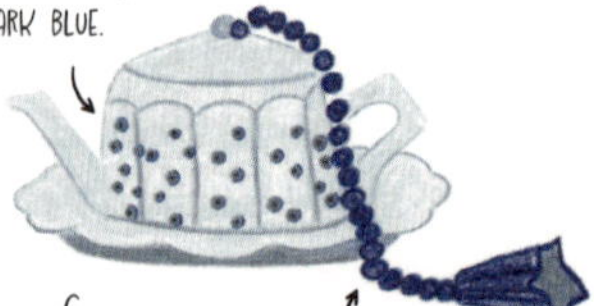

6.

SHAPE THE BEADS USING VARIED PRESSURE WITH THE DARK BLUE.

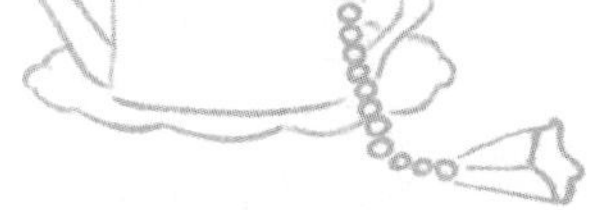

COFFEE PRESS

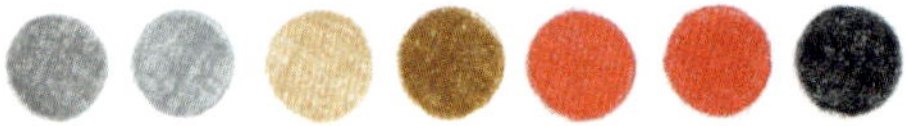

1.

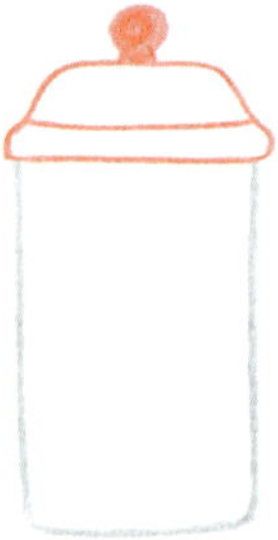

2.

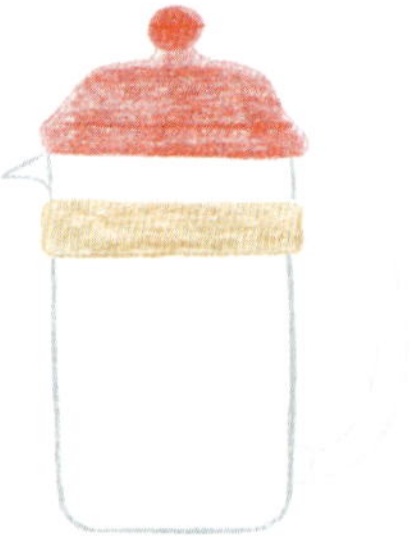

3.

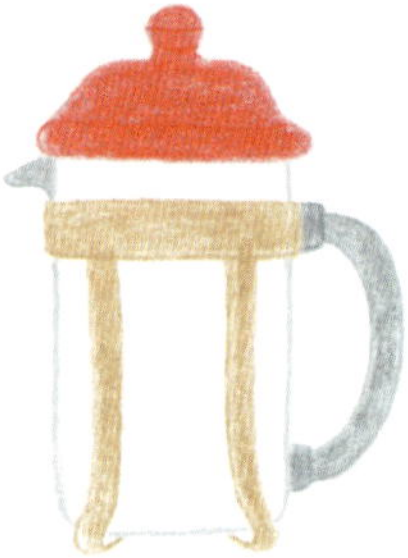

4.

USE THE DARKER RED FOR THE LID OUTLINES AND ACCENTS.

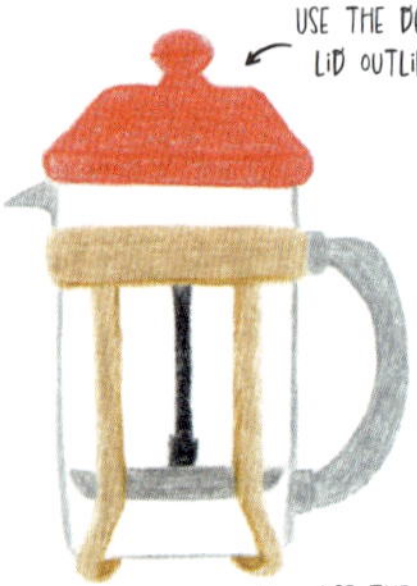

5.

USE THE DARKER GOLD FOR THE INLAY DETAILS.

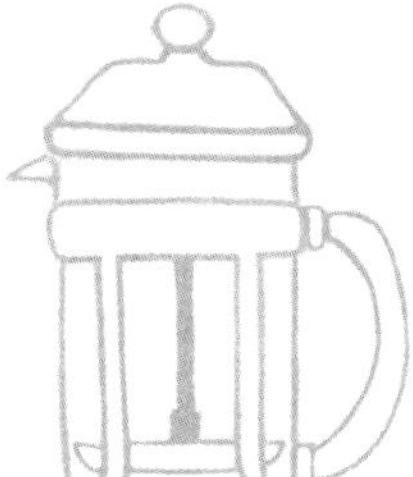

CROISSANT

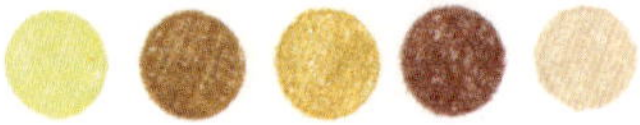

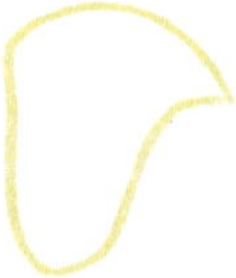

1.

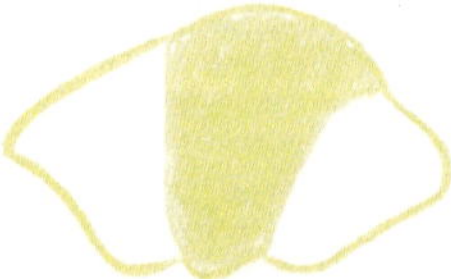

2.

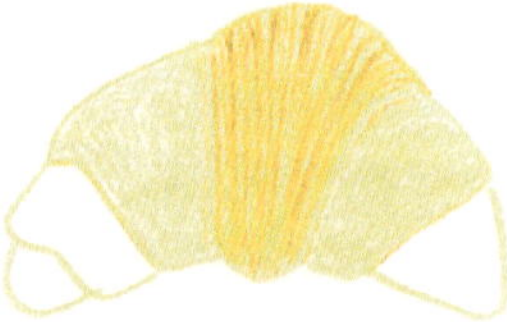

3.

START BUILDING UP PENCIL STROKES USING DARK YELLOW AND LIGHT BROWN.

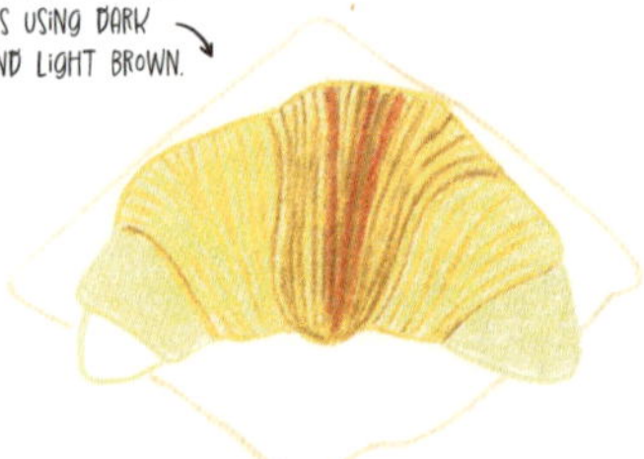

4.

ADD STROKES USING THE DARK BROWN TO CREATE THE FLUFFY PASTRY TEXTURE.

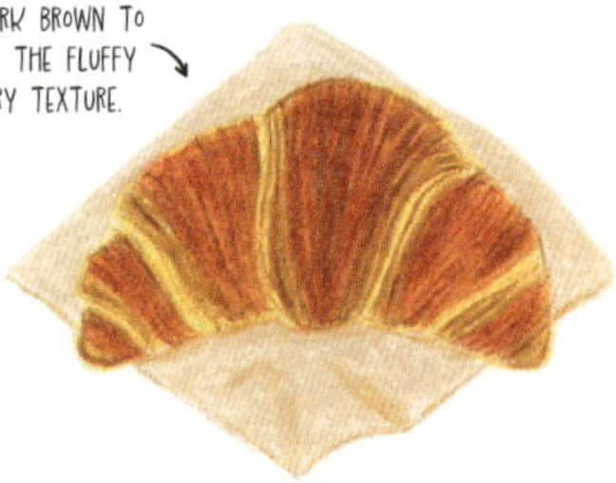

5.

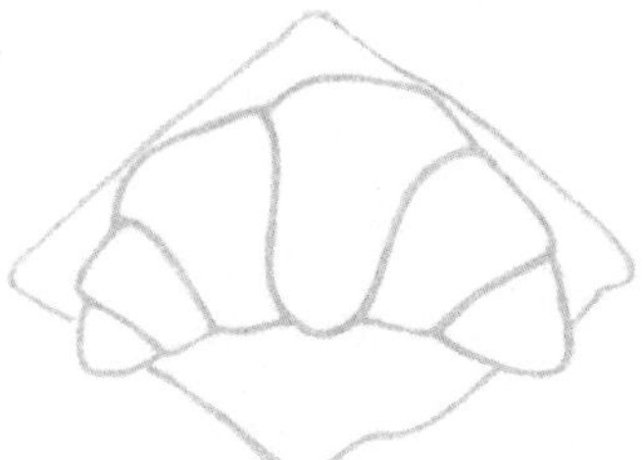

TEAPOT

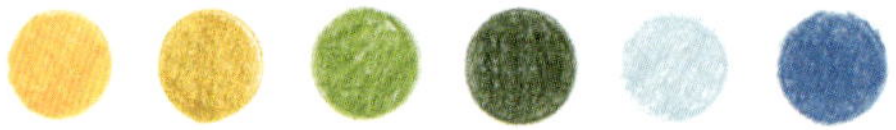

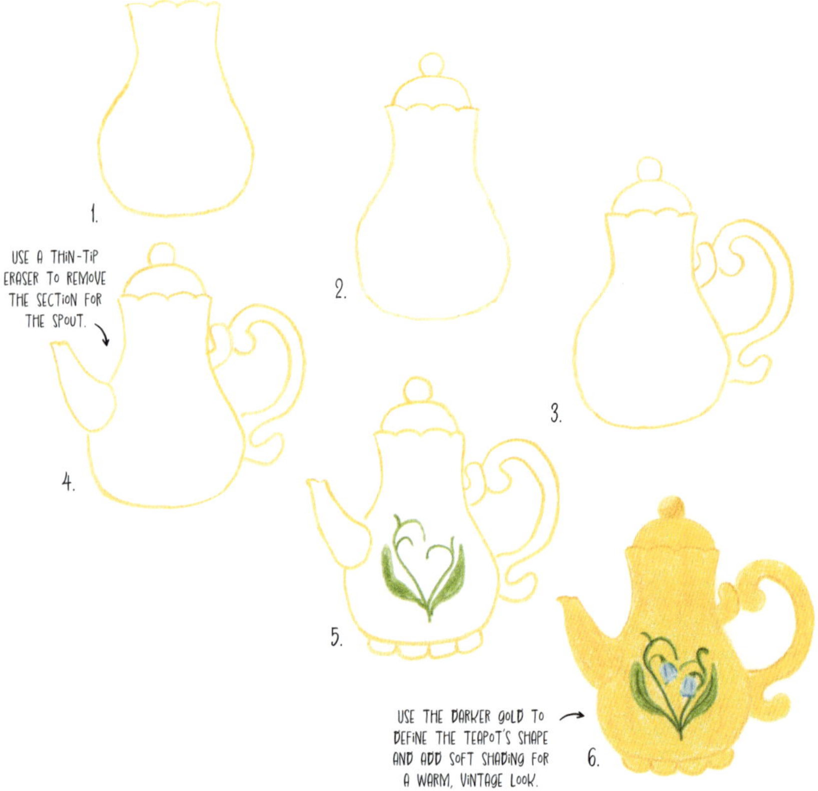
1.
2.
3.
USE A THIN-TIP ERASER TO REMOVE THE SECTION FOR THE SPOUT.
4.
5.
USE THE DARKER GOLD TO DEFINE THE TEAPOT'S SHAPE AND ADD SOFT SHADING FOR A WARM, VINTAGE LOOK.
6.

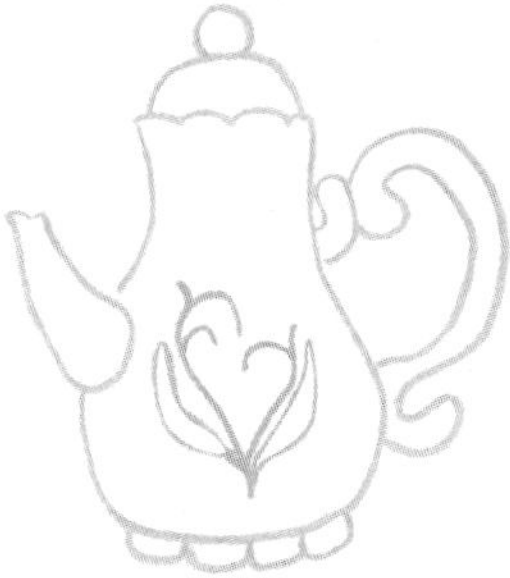

POLAROID PHOTOS

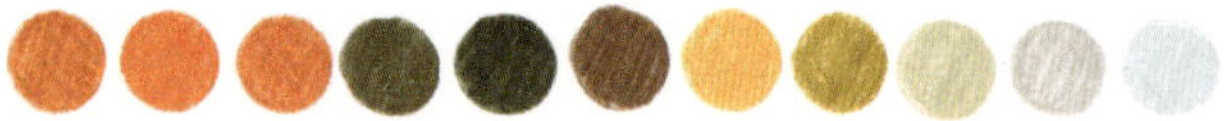

1.

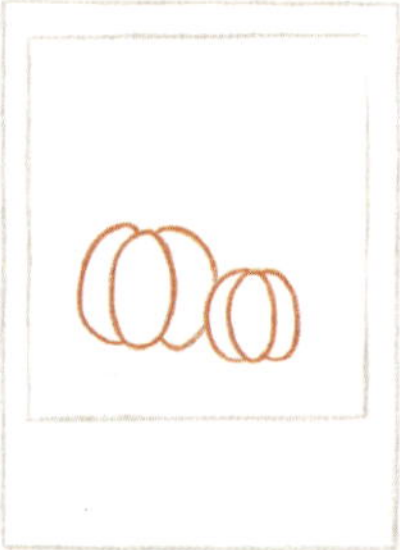

2.

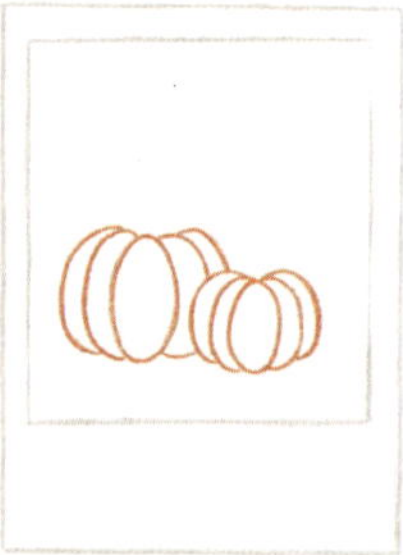

3.

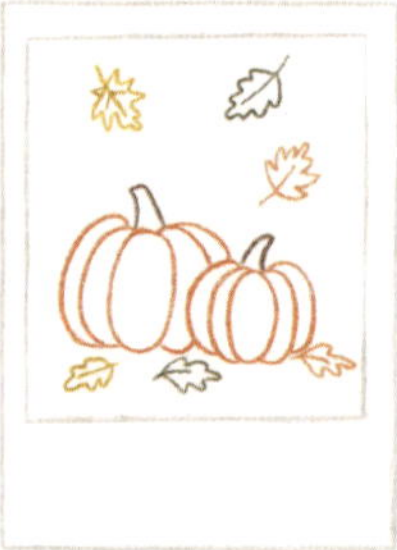

4.

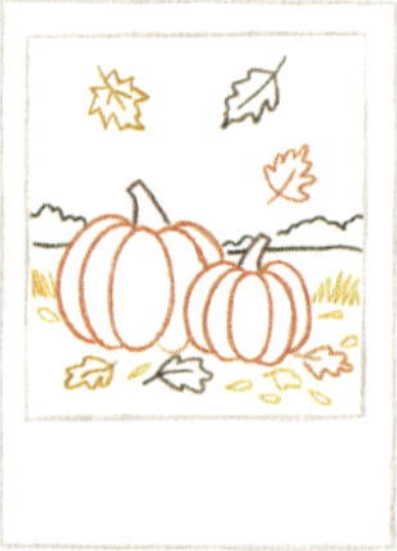

5.

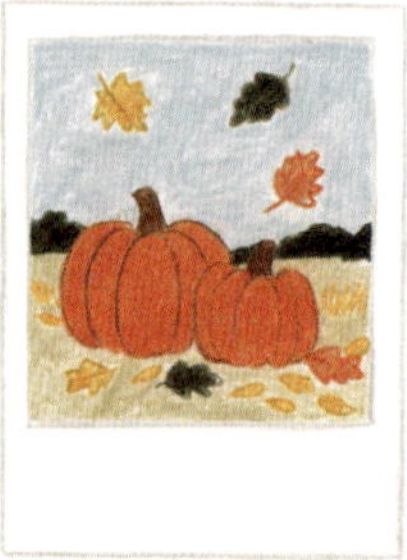

6.

BALANCE THE COLOURS BY KEEPING THE SKY PALE AND THE FOREGROUND WARMER.

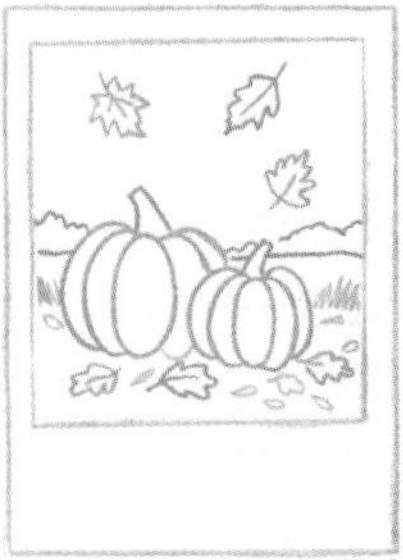

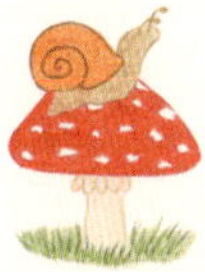

A LOVE OF NATURE

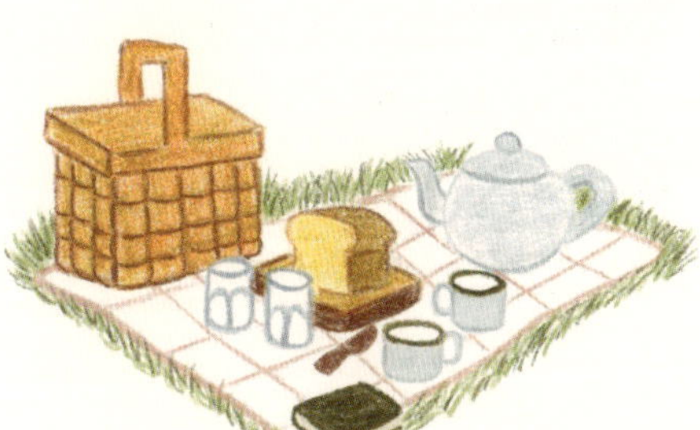

POTTED PLANTS

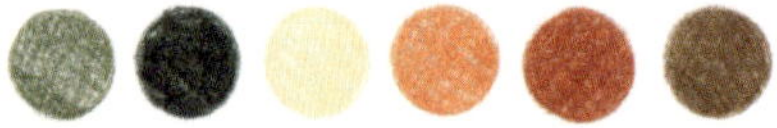

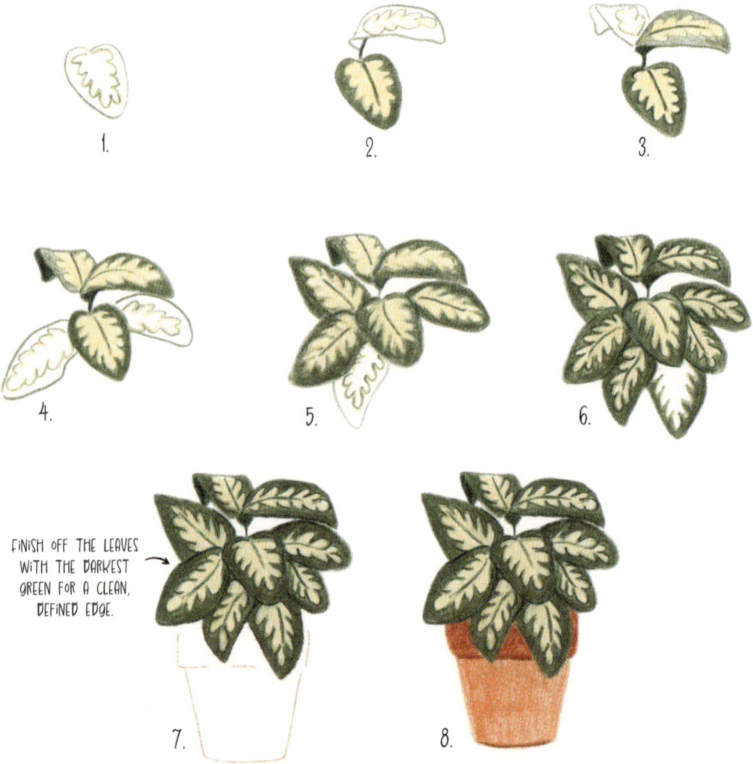

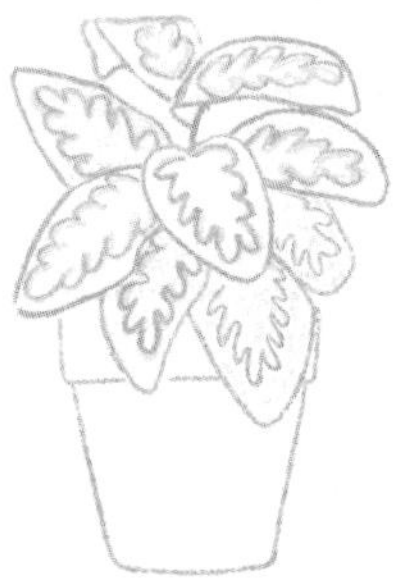

WILDFLOWERS

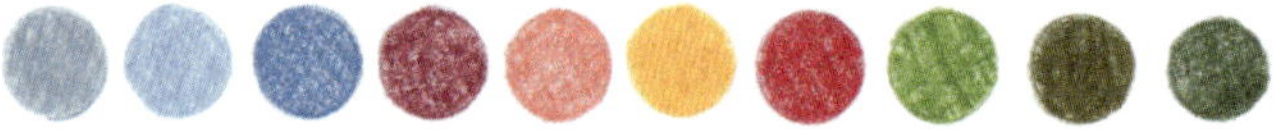

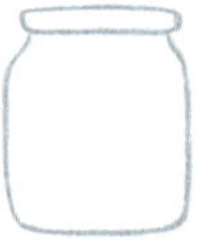

1.

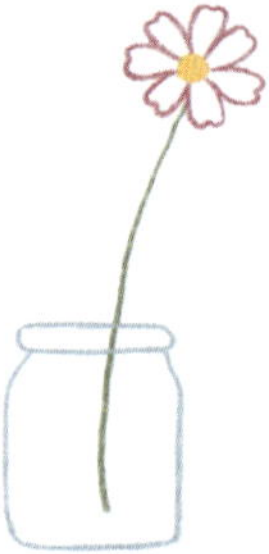

2.

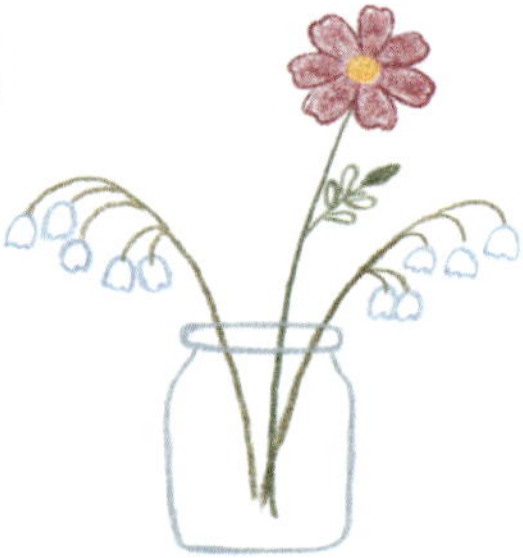

3.

USE SOFT PRESSURE FOR THE BASE COLOURS.

4.

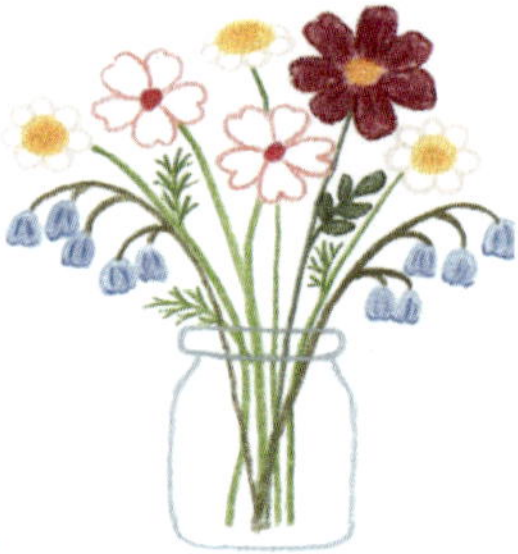

5.

DEEPEN THE ACCENTS AND DETAILS WITH MORE PRESSURE ON THE DARKER TONES.

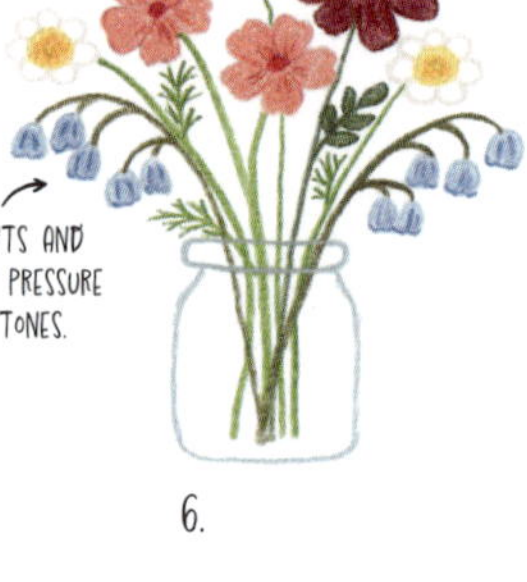

6.

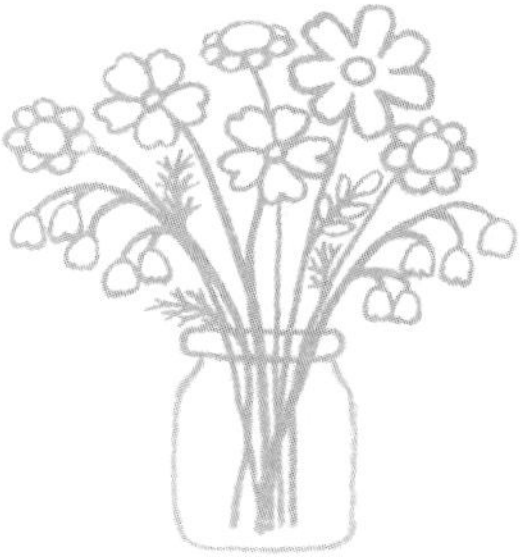

MUSHROOM AND SNAIL

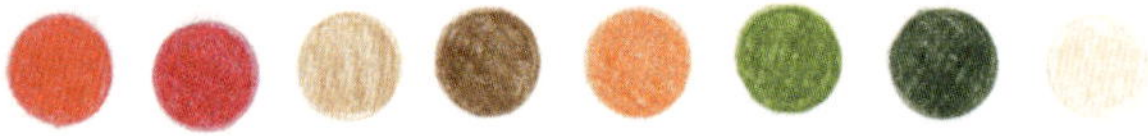

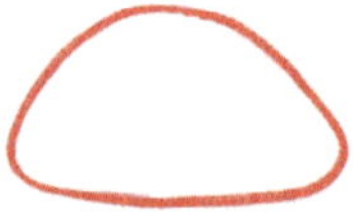

1.

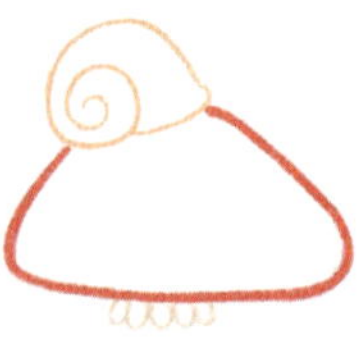

2.

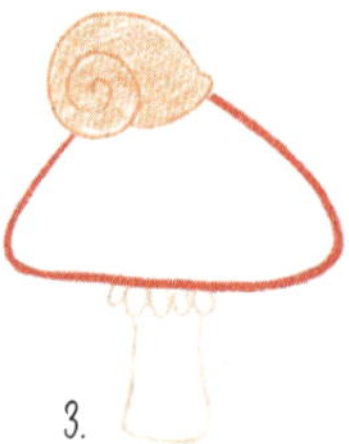

3.

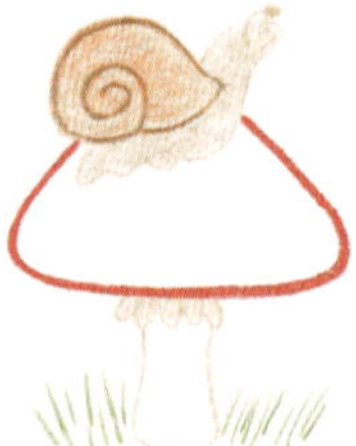

4.

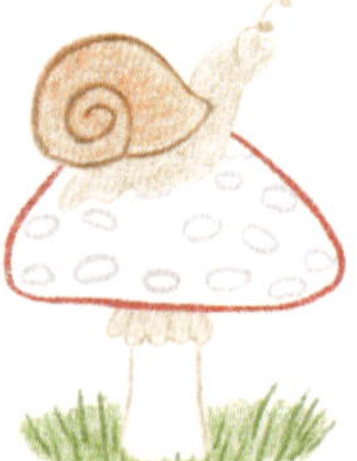

5.

VARY THE SIZE AND SPACING OF THE MUSHROOM SPOTS FOR A MORE NATURAL LOOK.

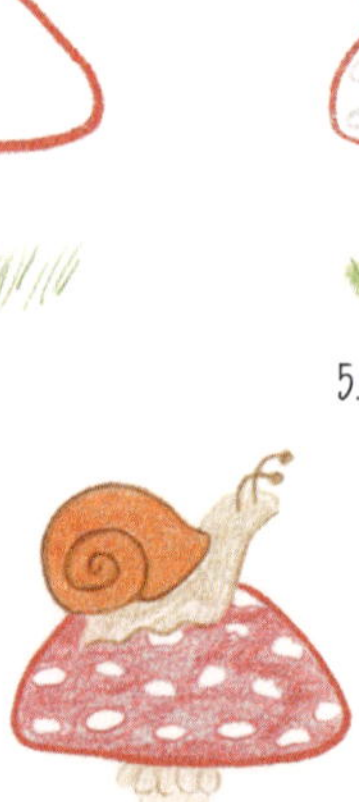

6.

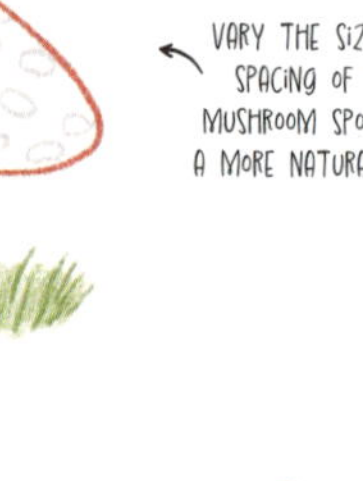

7.

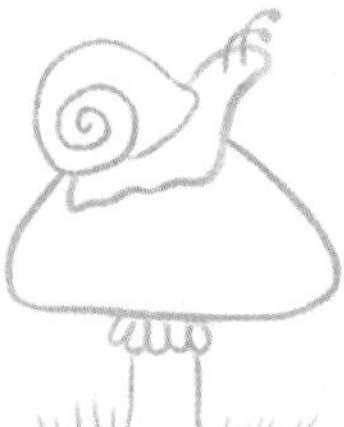

FALLEN LEAVES

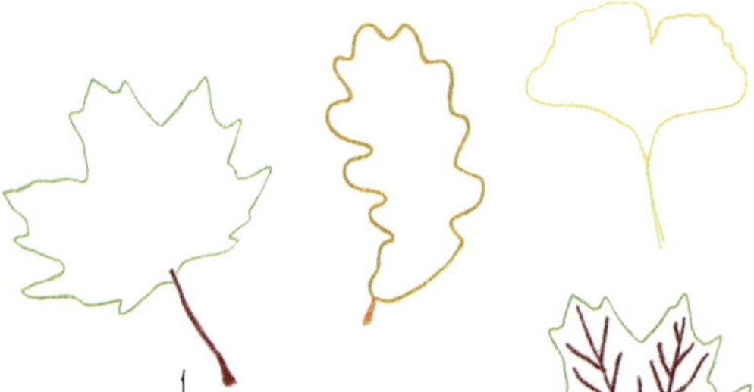

1.

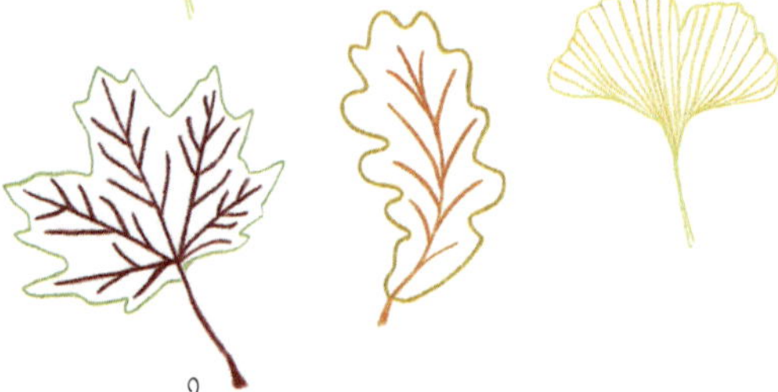

2.

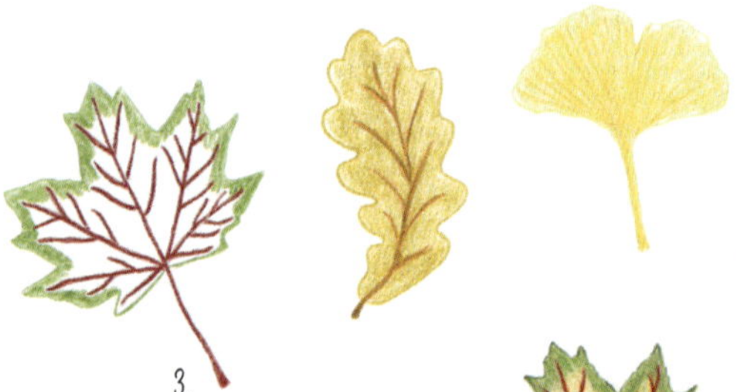

3.

LAYER THE COLOURS ON THE LEAVES AND AROUND THE VEINS TO BUILD THE RICH TONES.

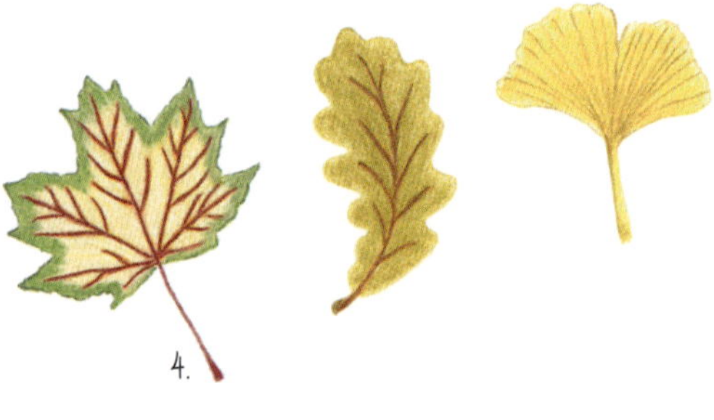

4.

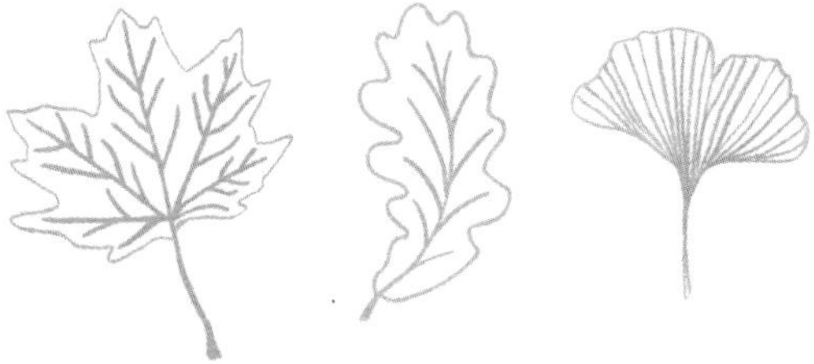

SUNFLOWERS

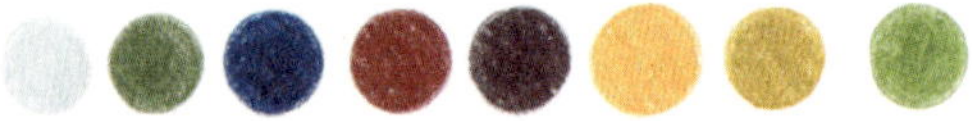

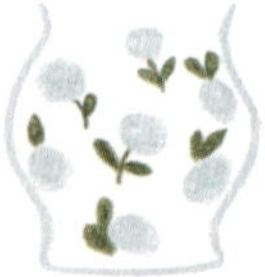

1.

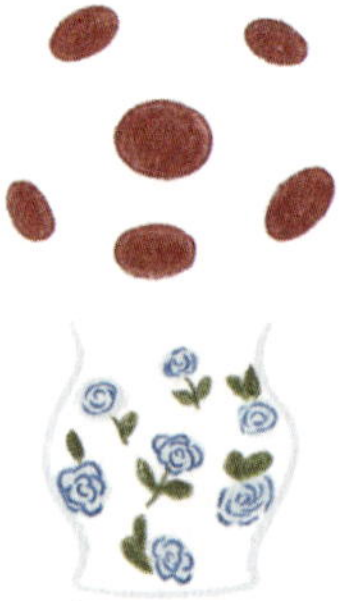

2.

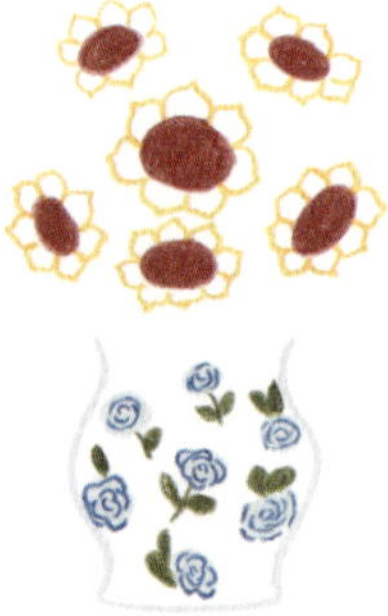

3.

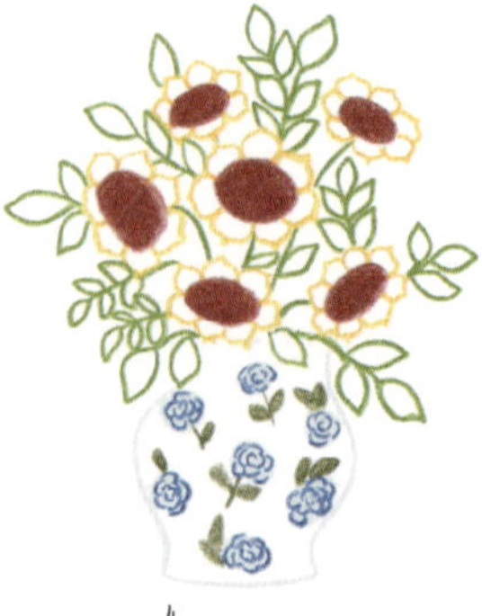

4.

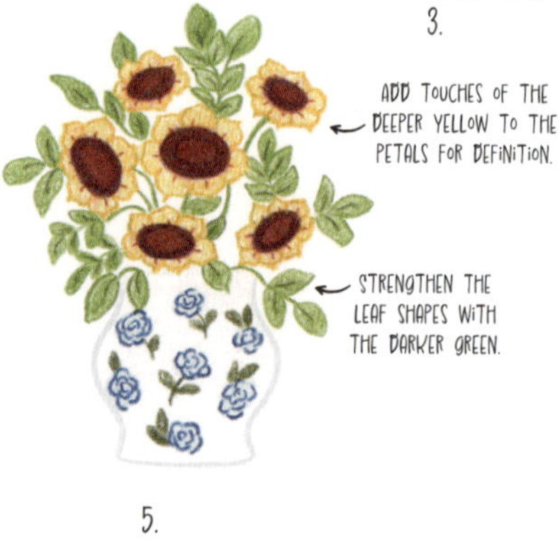

5.

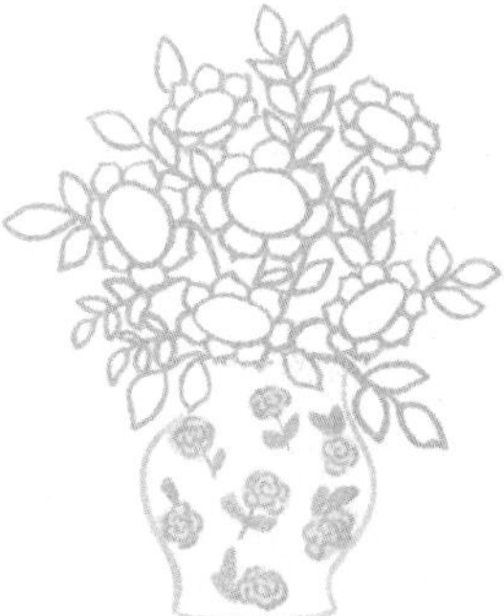

GARDEN BASKET

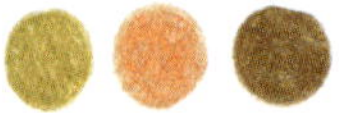

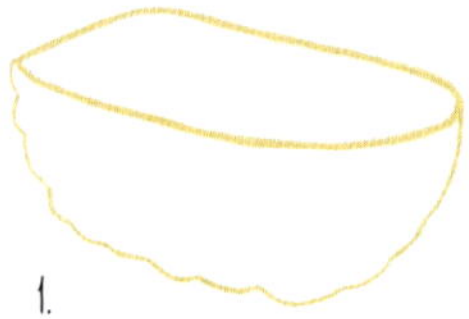

1.

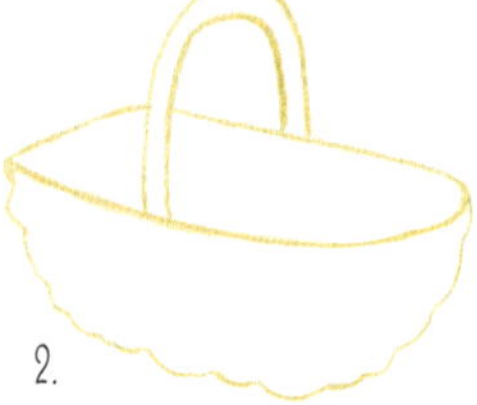

2.

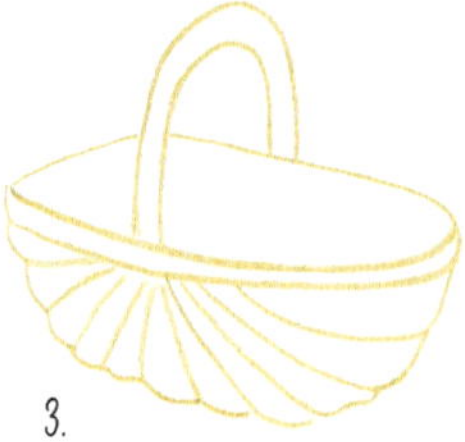

3.

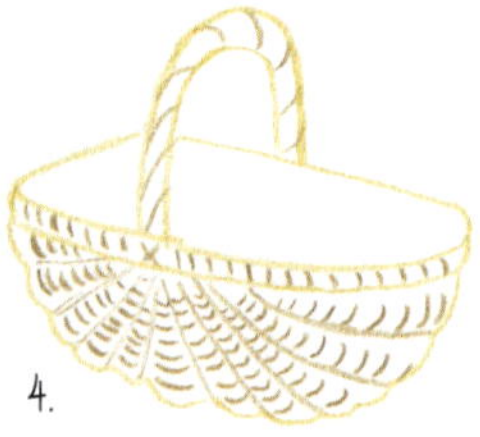

4.

USE THE DARKER BROWNS WITH A FIRMER PRESSURE TO BRING OUT THE WICKER TEXTURE AND DEEPEN THE WOVEN SHADOWS.

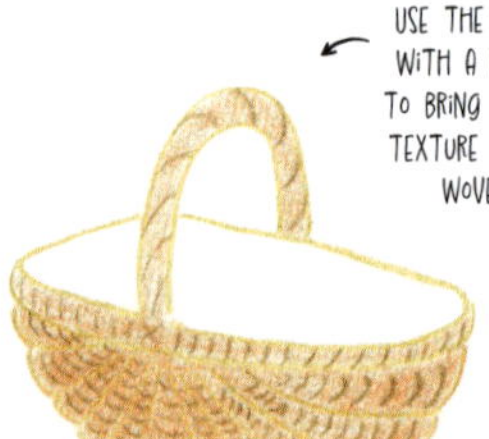

5.

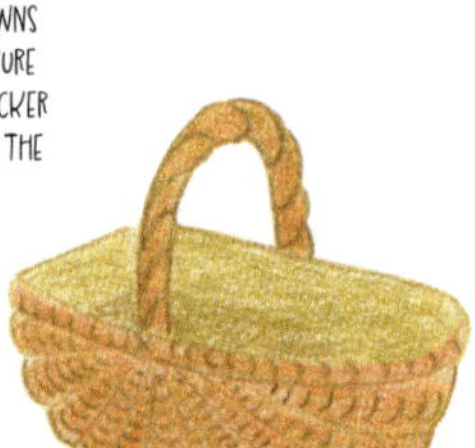

6.

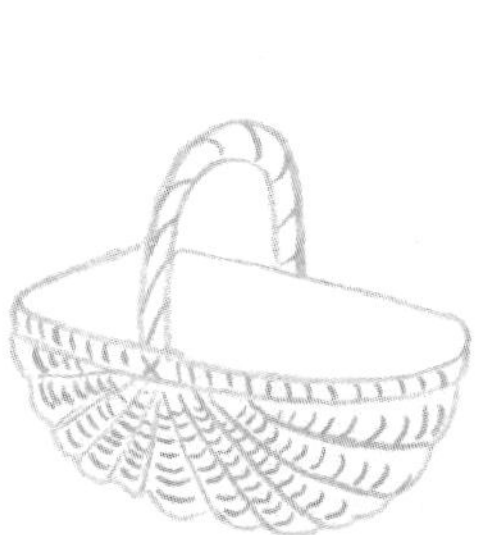

PiCNiC

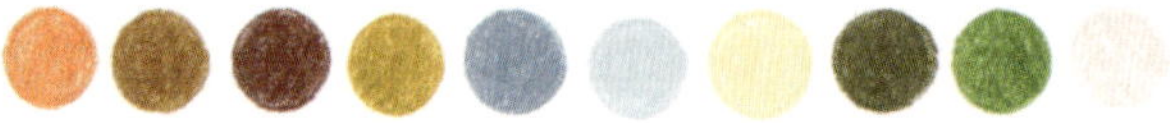

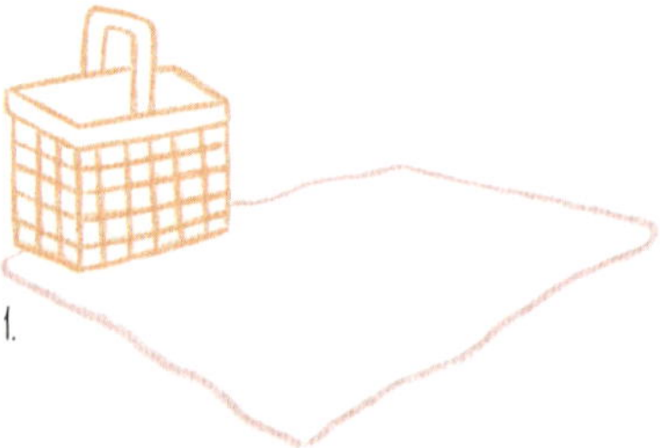

1.

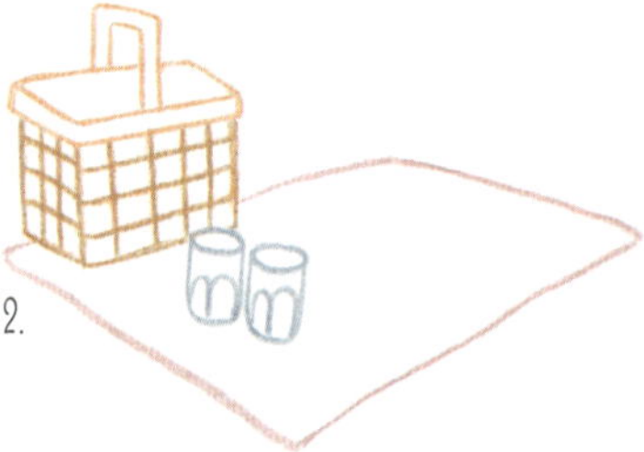

2.

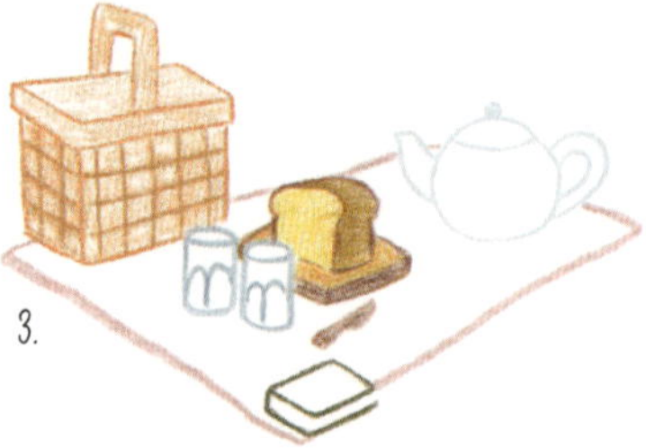

3.

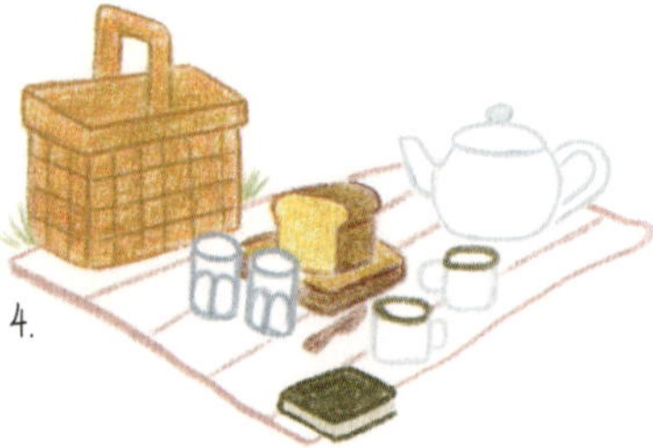

4.

USE SLIGHTLY RICHER BROWNS ON THE BASKET AND TOAST TO ADD WARMTH AND DEPTH.

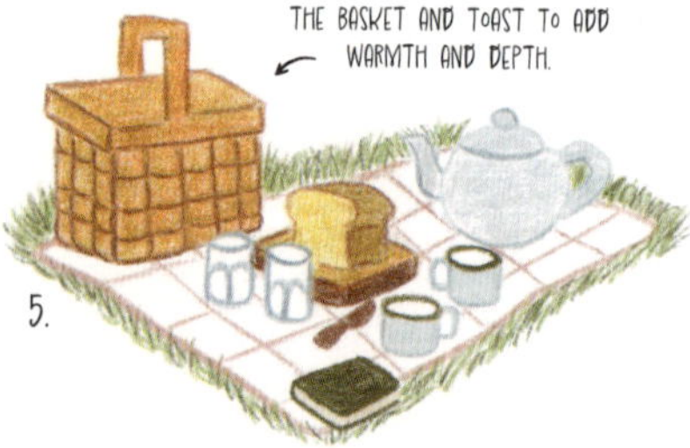

5.

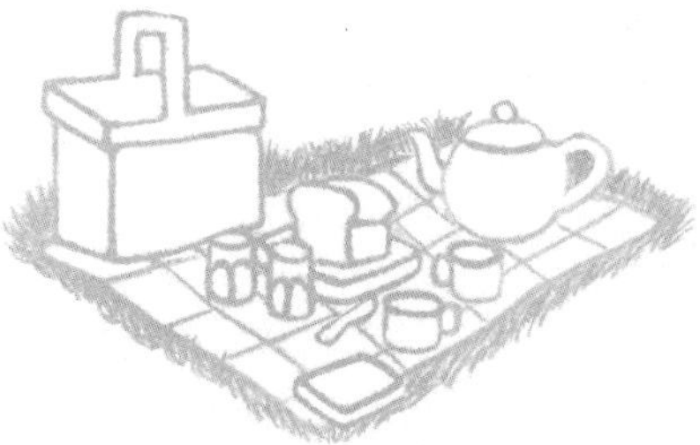

SQUIRREL

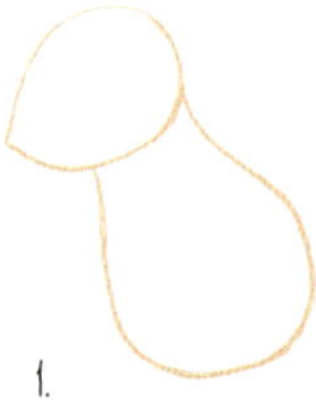

1.

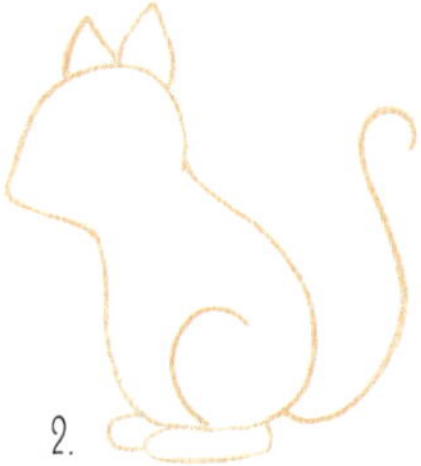

2.

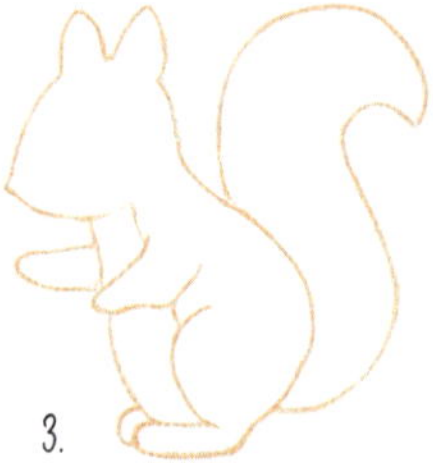

3.

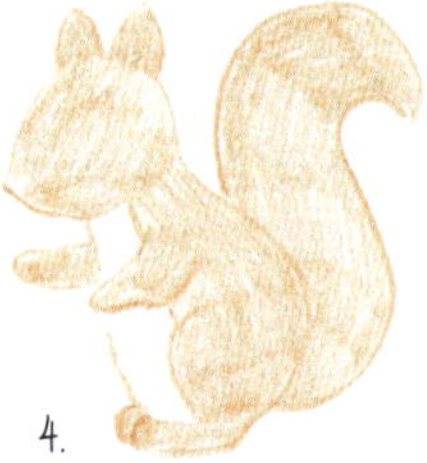

4.

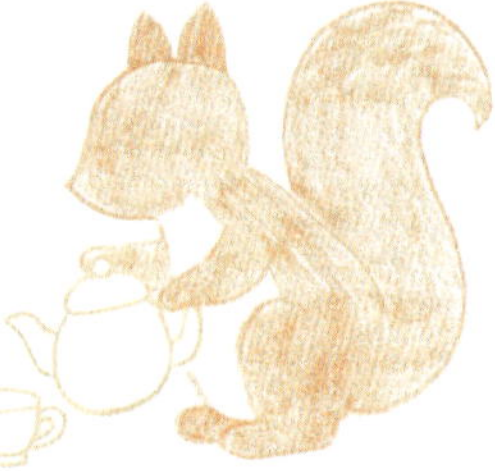

5.

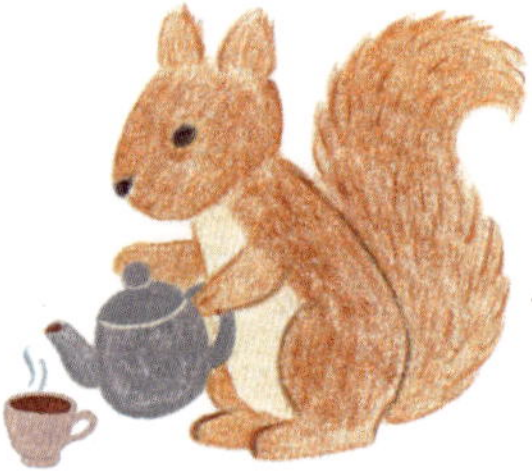

6.

USING SHORT STROKES BRINGS OUT THE SOFT FUR TEXTURE.

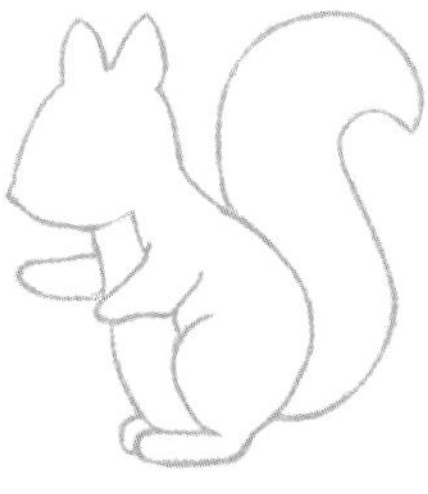

SCARECROW

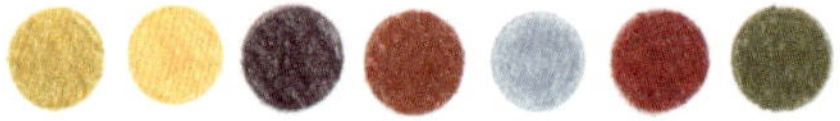

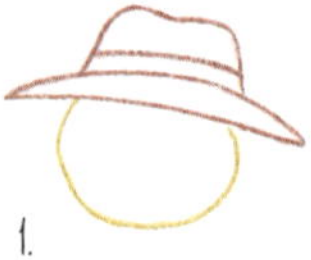

1.

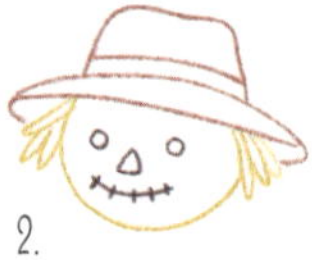

2.

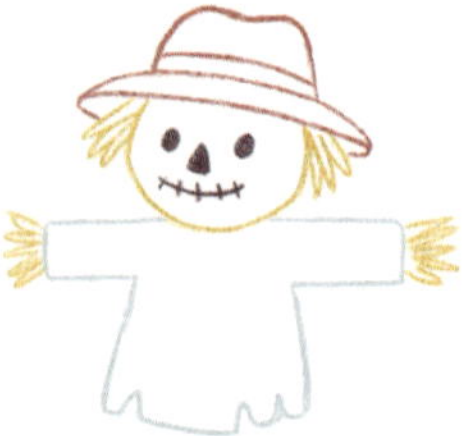

3.

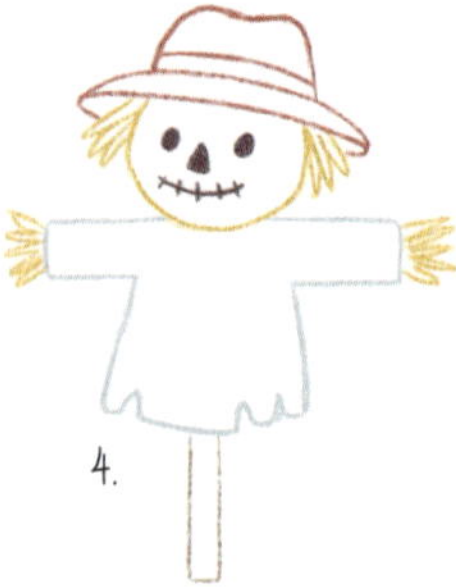

4.

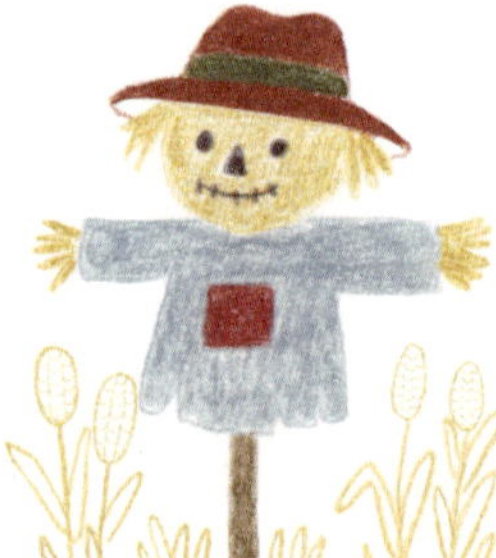

5.

USE THE RICHER GOLD FOR THE STRAW AND SMALL SHADED ACCENTS.

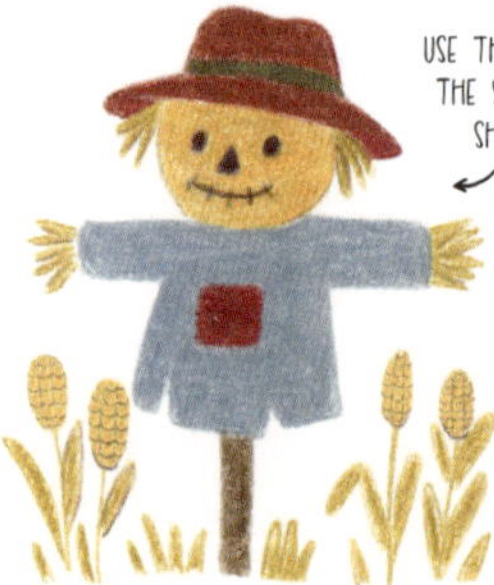

6.

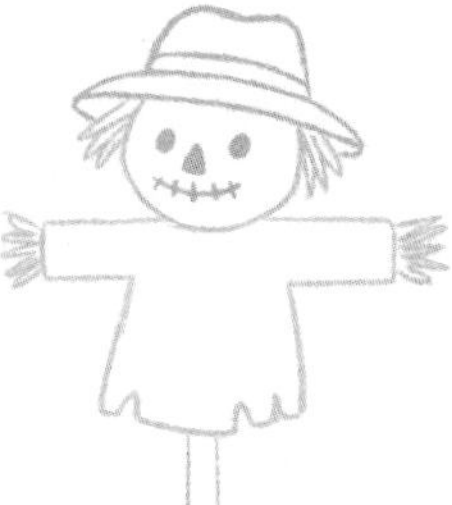

SLEEPY FOX

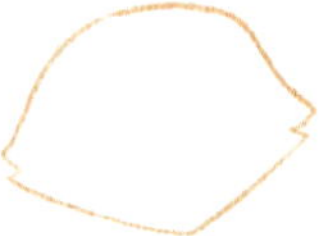

1.

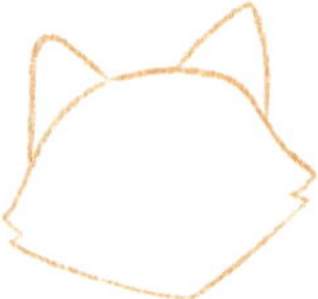

2.

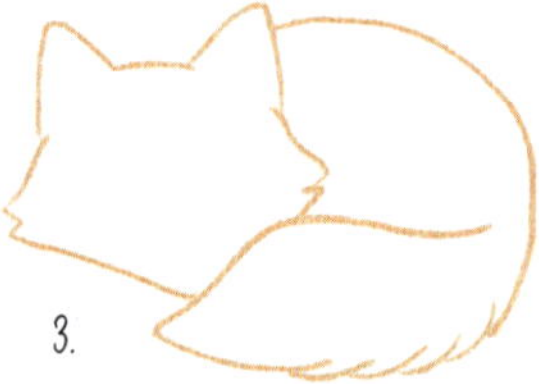

3.

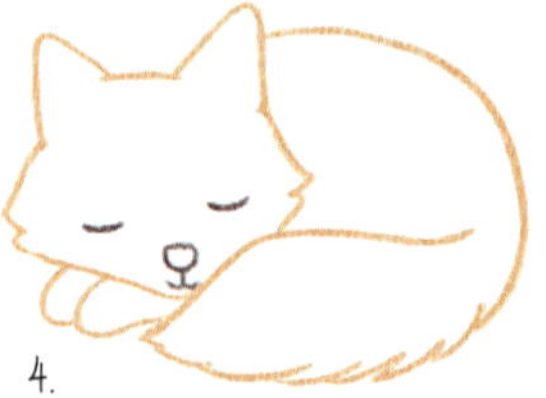

4.

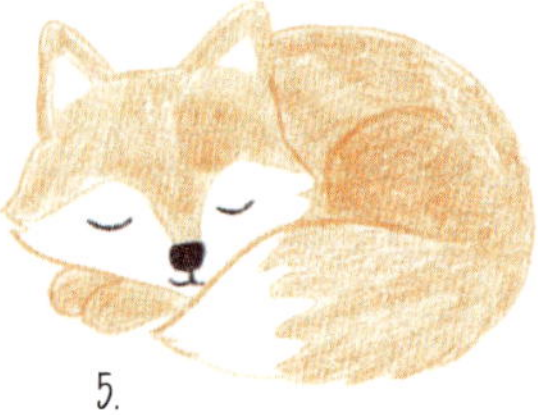

5.

USE VARIED PRESSURE TO BUILD SOFT, LAYERED FUR, ESPECIALLY AROUND THE TAIL AND FOREHEAD.

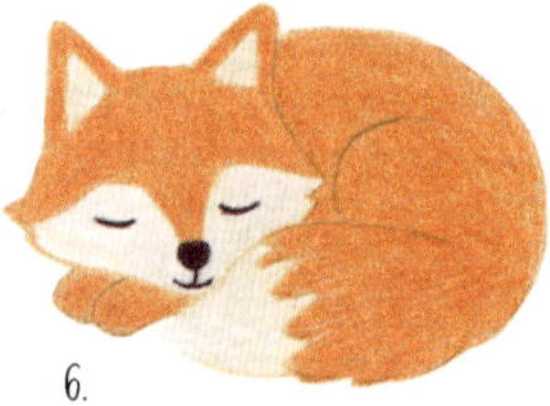

6.

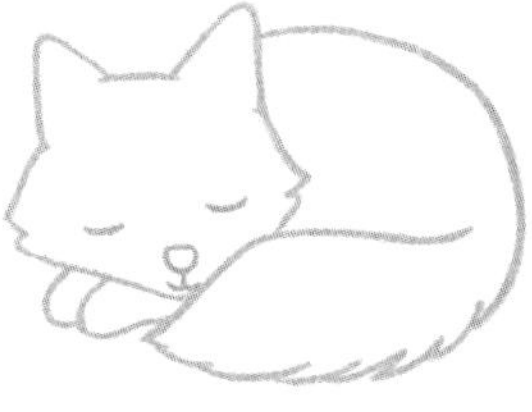

PiNECONE

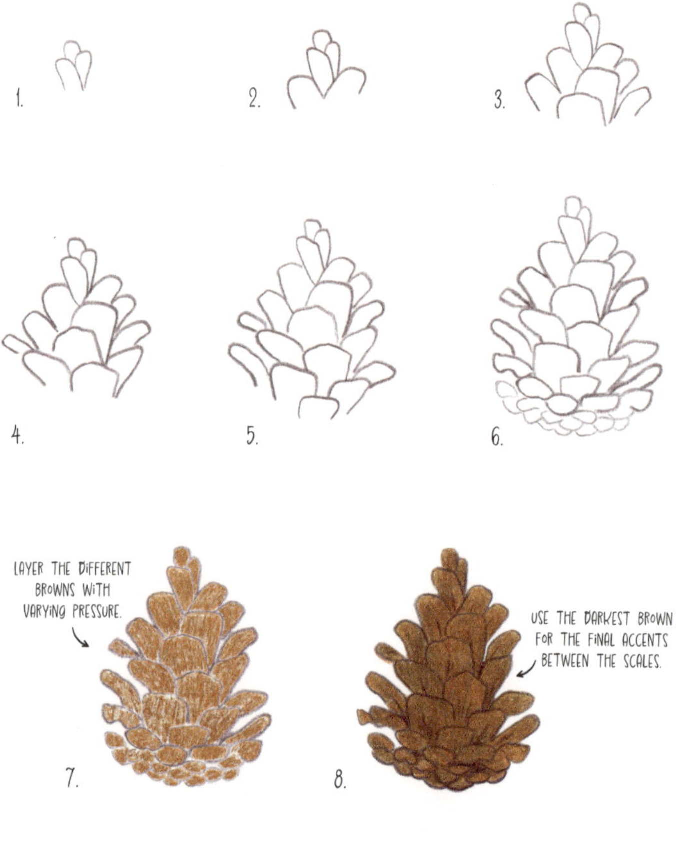

1.
2.
3.
4.
5.
6.
LAYER THE DIFFERENT BROWNS WITH VARYING PRESSURE.
7.
8.
USE THE DARKEST BROWN FOR THE FINAL ACCENTS BETWEEN THE SCALES.

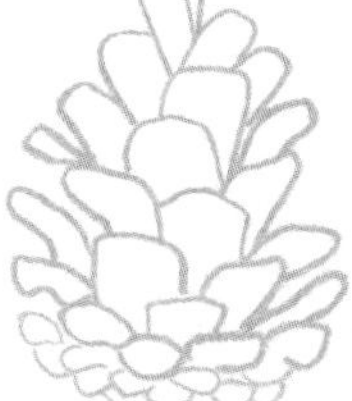

WATERING CAN

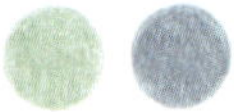

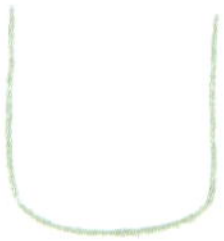
1.

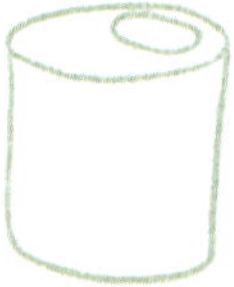
2.

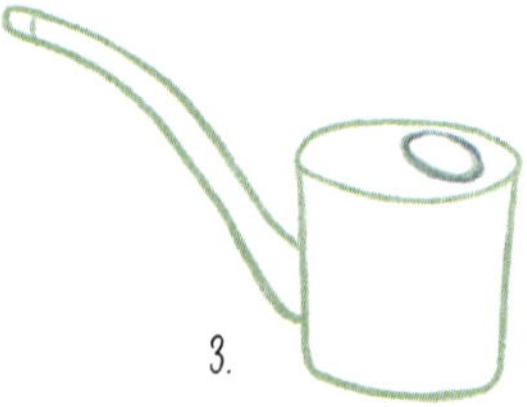
3.

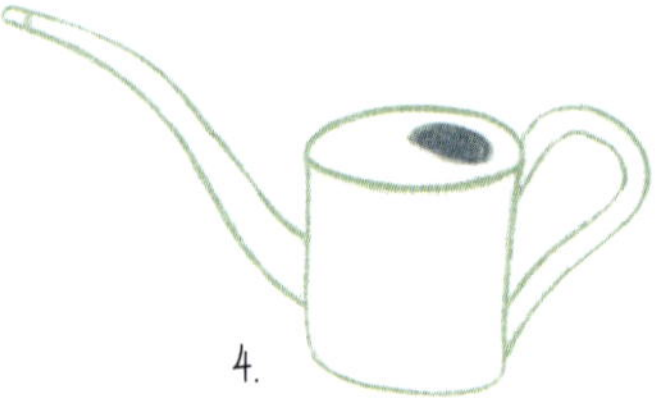
4.

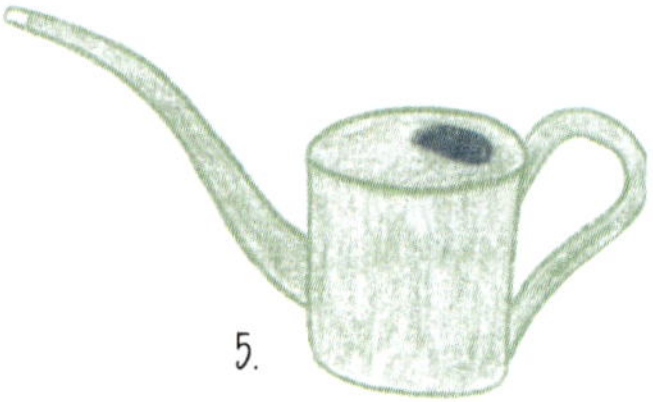
5.

USE THE DARKER BLUE TO ADD DETAILS ON THE TOP AND SPOUT.

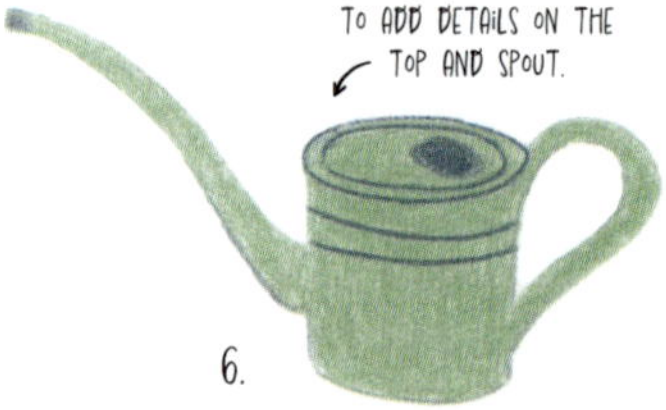
6.

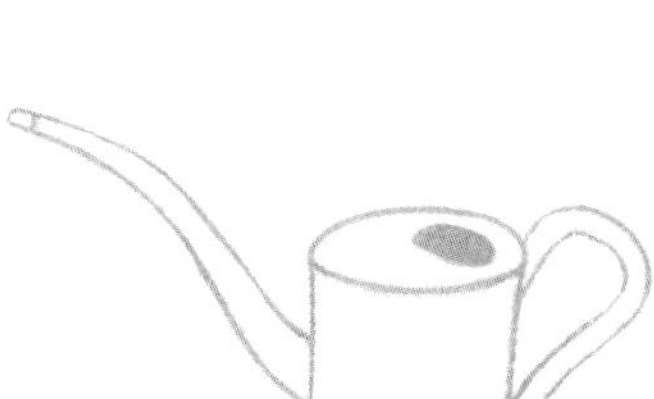

FERN LEAF

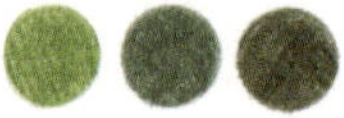

1.

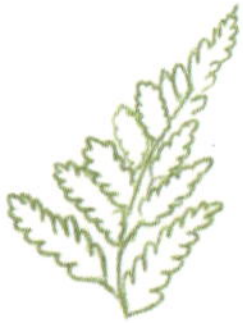

2.

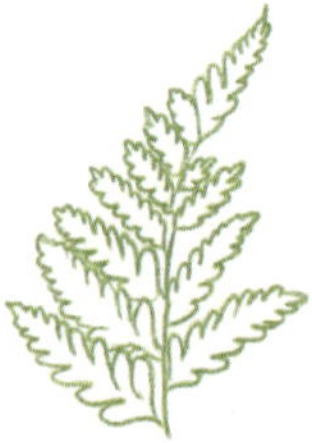

3.

START THE OUTLINE WITH THE LIGHT GREEN, THEN REINFORCE IT WITH THE DARKER GREEN.

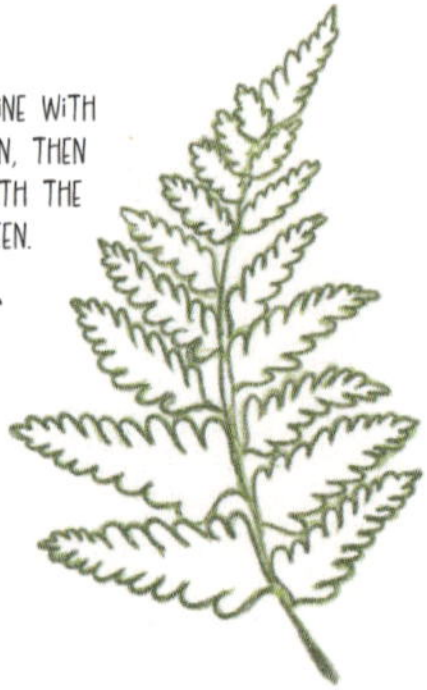

4.

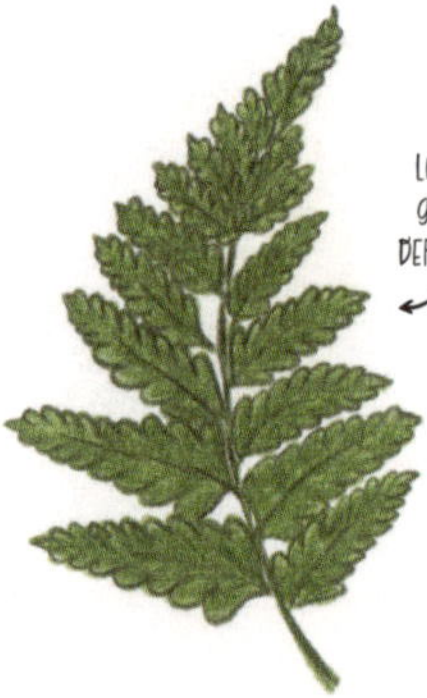

5.

LAYER ALL THREE GREENS TO BUILD DEPTH IN THE LEAF.

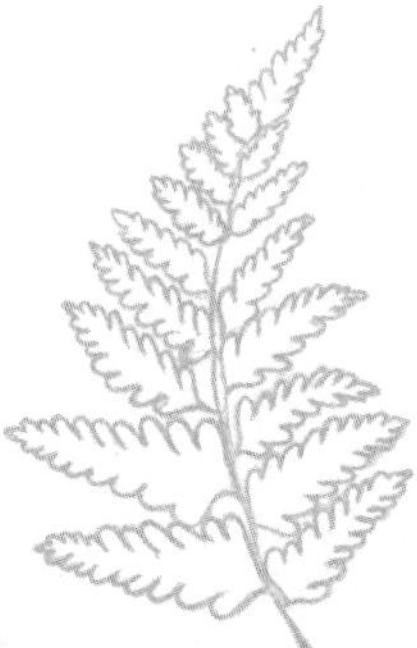

MARIGOLD

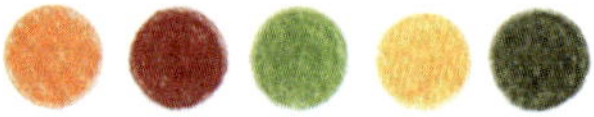

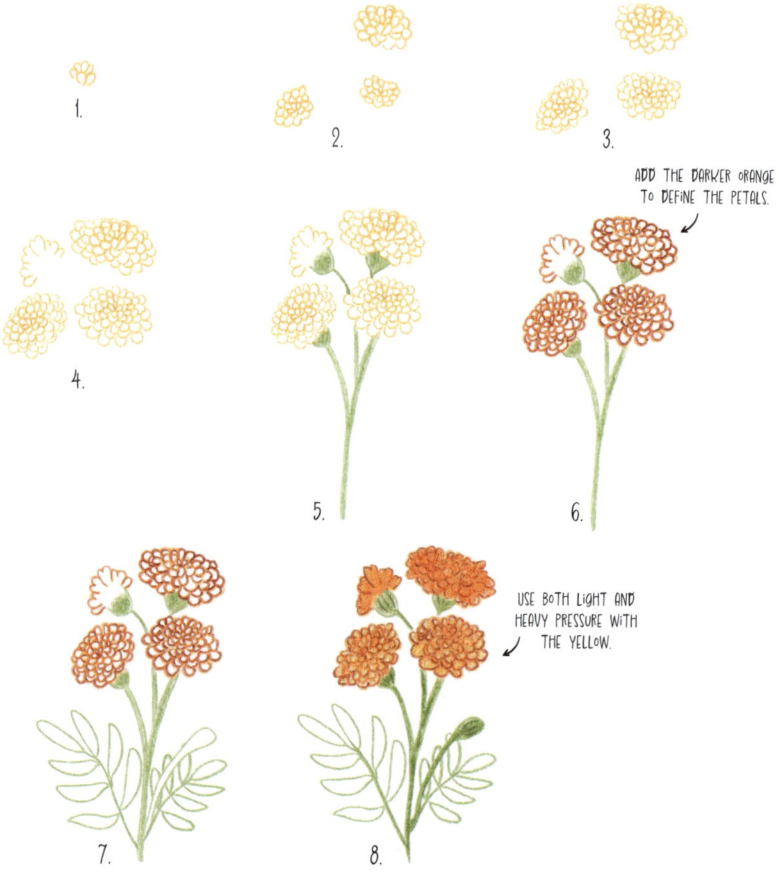
1.
2.
3.
ADD THE DARKER ORANGE TO DEFINE THE PETALS.
4.
5.
6.
USE BOTH LIGHT AND HEAVY PRESSURE WITH THE YELLOW.
7.
8.

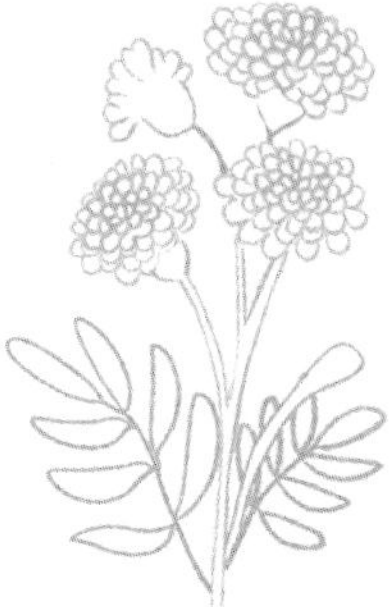

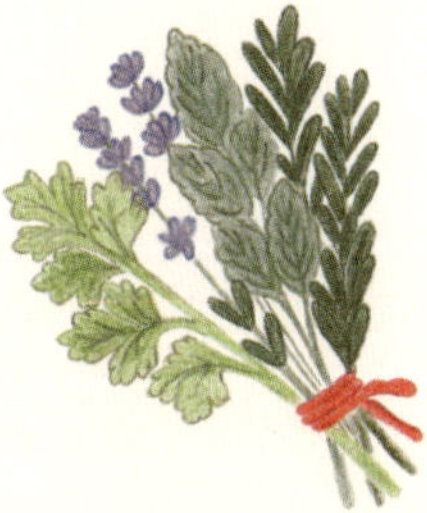

SLOW LIVING

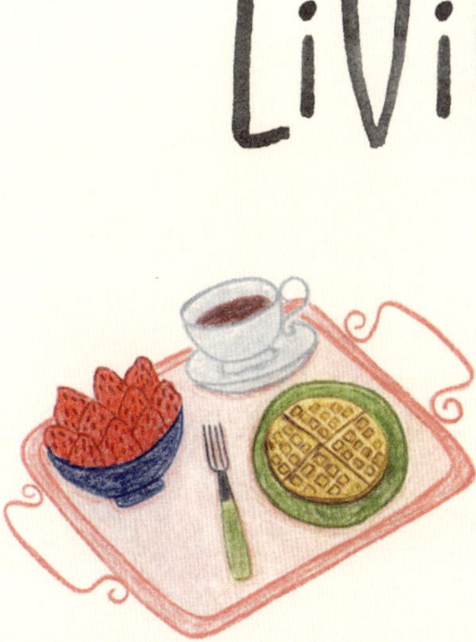

FRESHLY BAKED BREAD

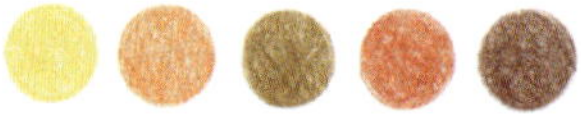

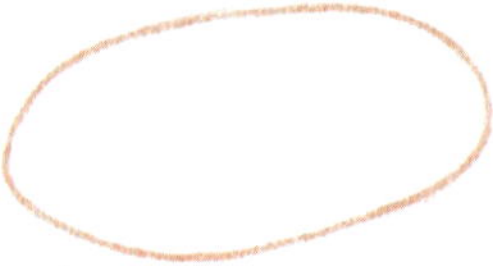

1.

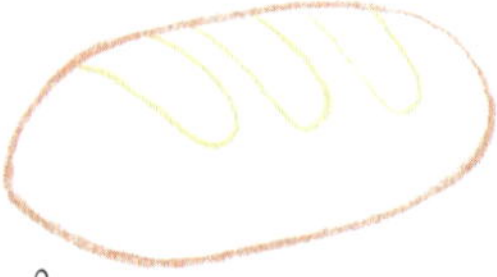

2.

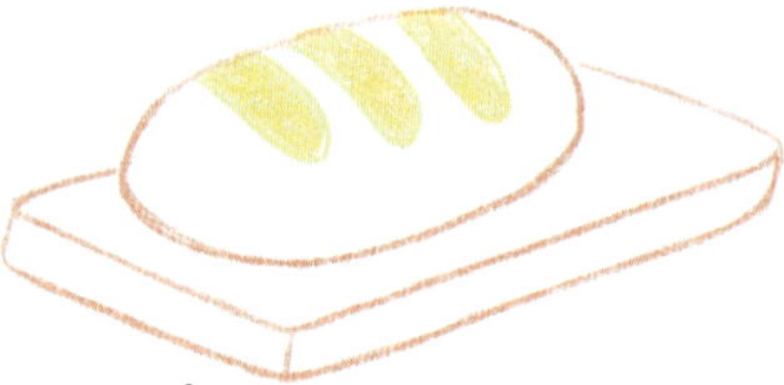

3.

BLEND THE BROWNS WITH VARIED PRESSURE TO CREATE THE TEXTURE.

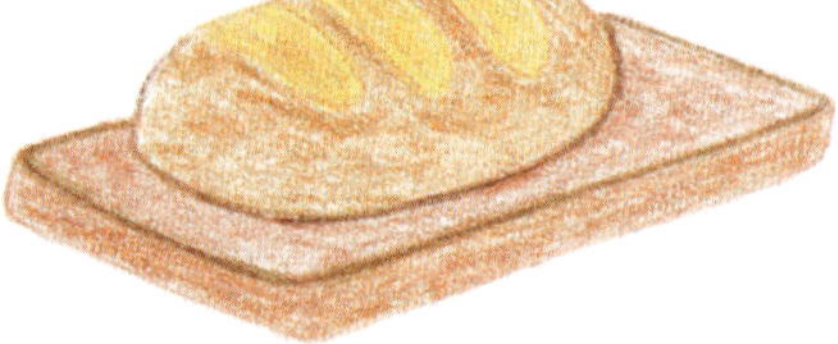

4.

ADD THE DARKEST BROWN LAST FOR THE BAKED COLOUR AND THE BOARD.

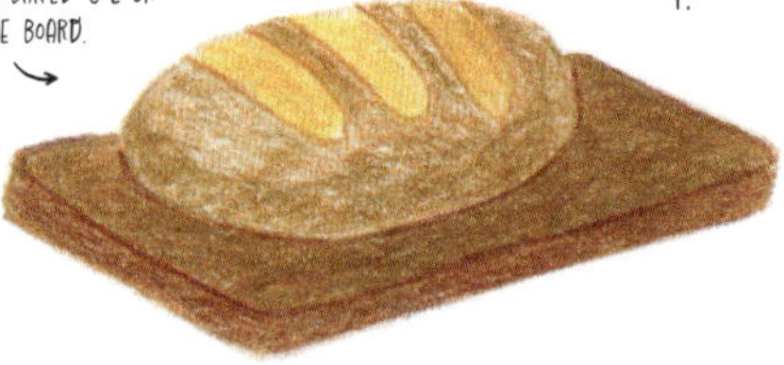

5.

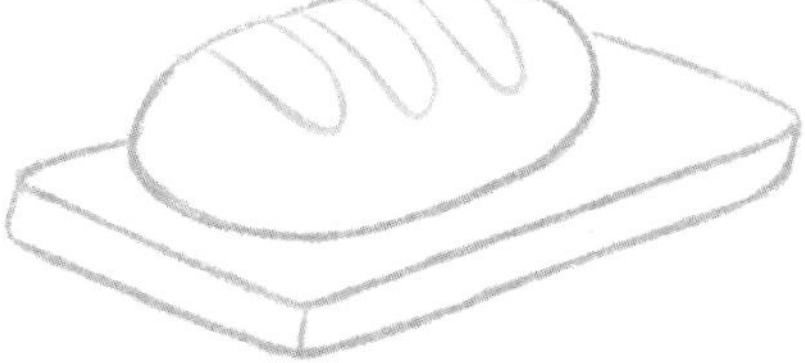

CROCHETED BASKET

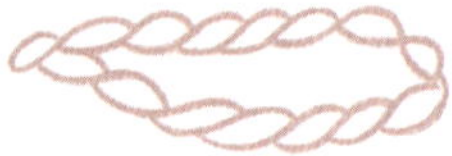

1.

THE TOP EDGE IS DRAWN BY JOINING A SERIES OF WAVY LINES.

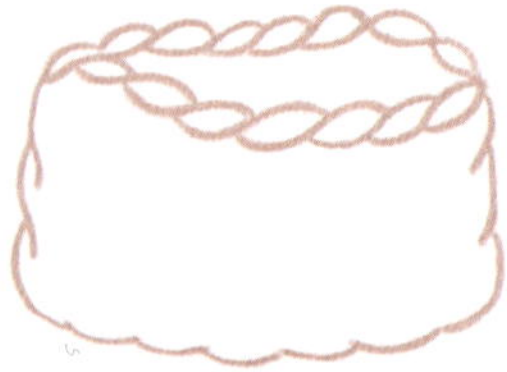

2.

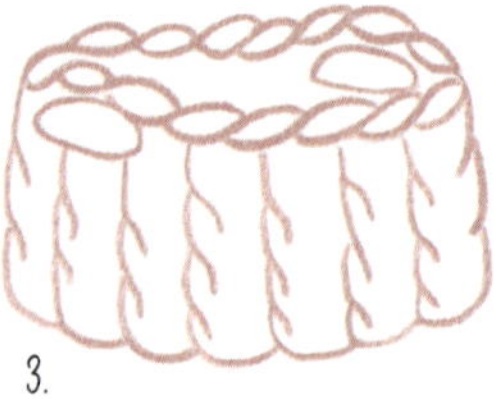

3.

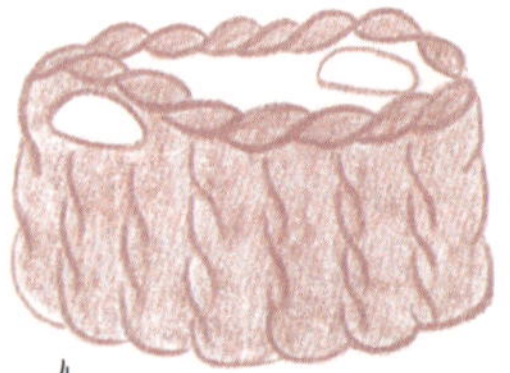

4.

LAYER THE COLOURS WITH DIFFERENT PRESSURE TO BRING THE WOVEN TEXTURE TO LIFE.

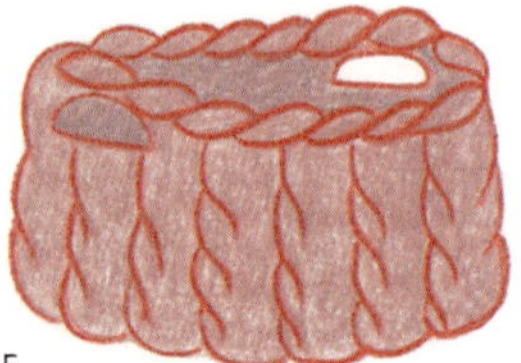

5.

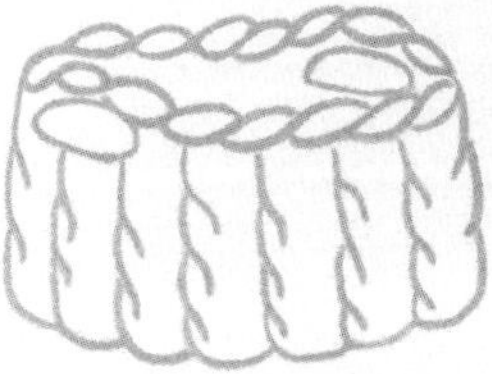

LETTER AND ENVELOPE

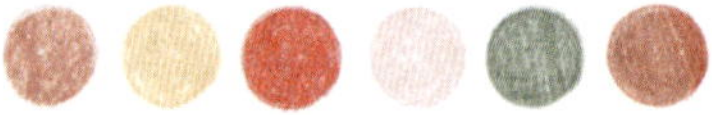

1.

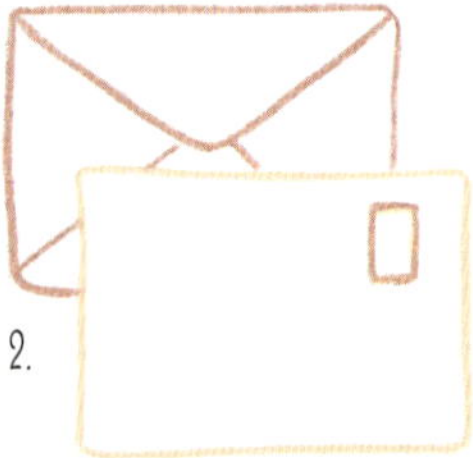

2.

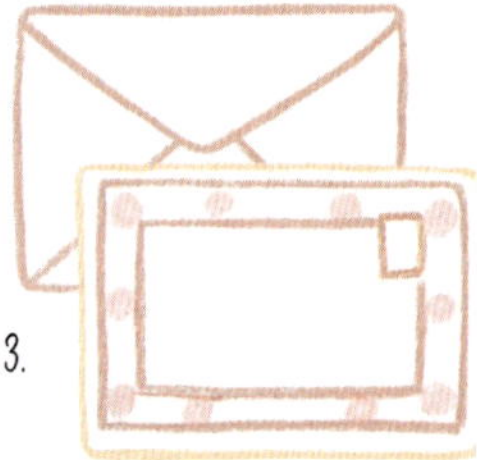

3.

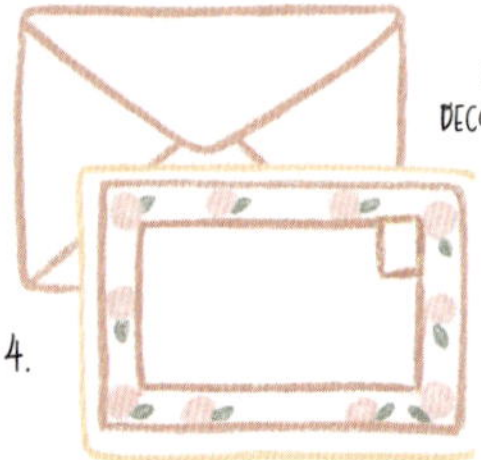

4.

SKETCH THE DECORATIONS SOFTLY.

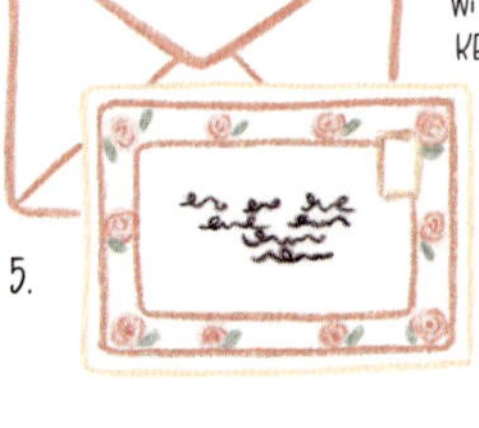

5.

REINFORCE THE OUTLINES WITH FIRMER STROKES TO KEEP THE DETAILS CRISP.

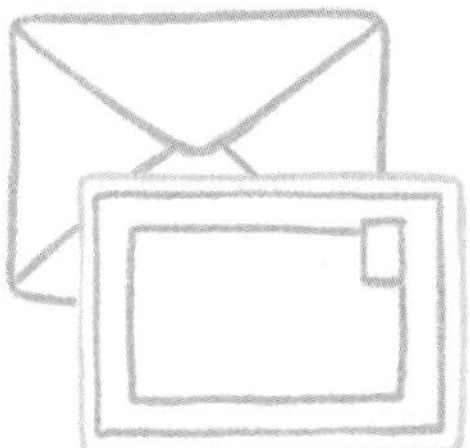

KETTLE

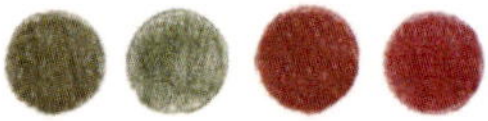

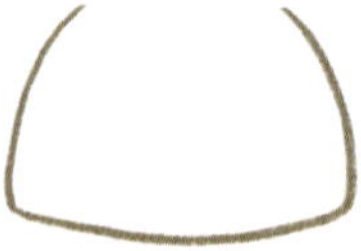

1.

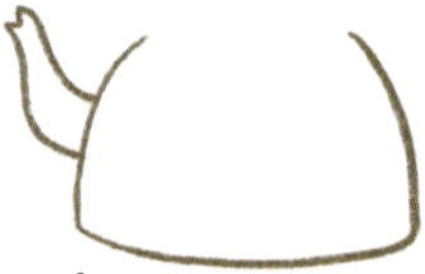

2.

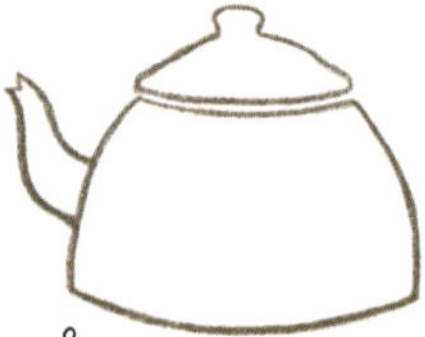

3.

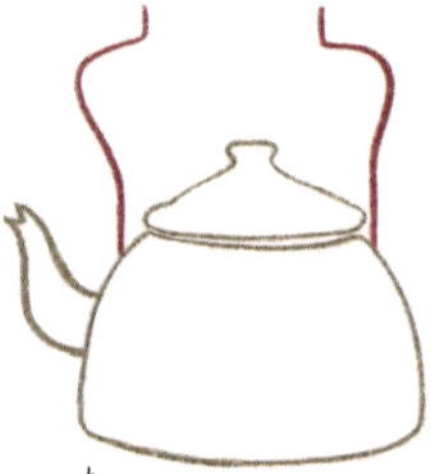

4.

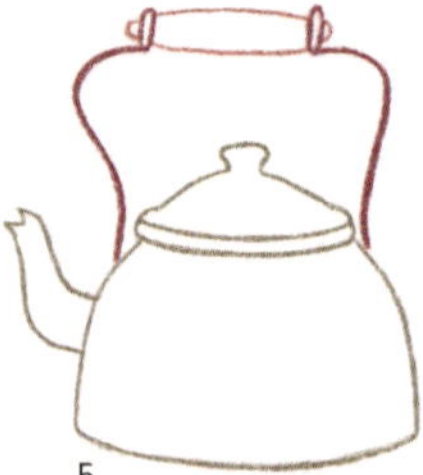

5.

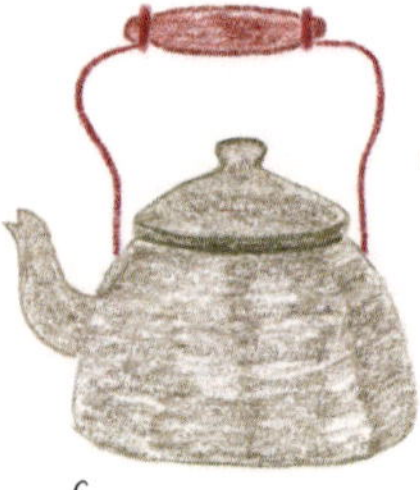

BUILD UP THE OLIVE GREEN GRADUALLY IN SMALL CIRCULAR STROKES TO GIVE A SOFT, METAL TEXTURE WITHOUT HARSH LINES.

6.

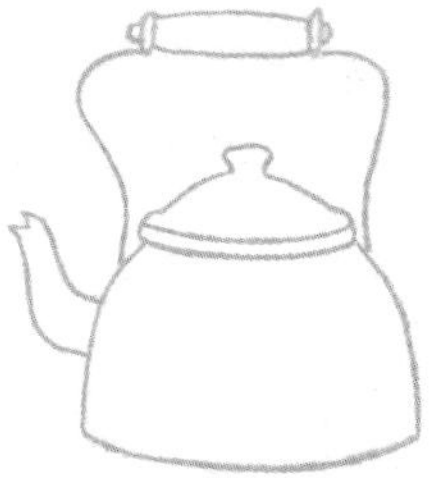

TEAPOT AND SCONES

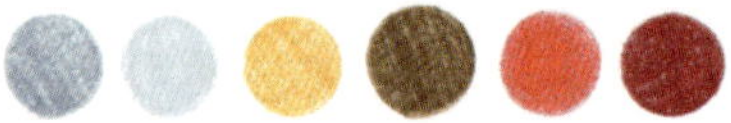

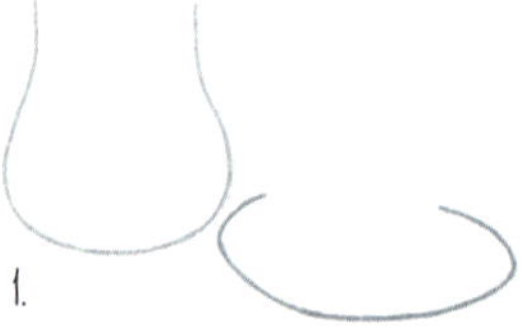

1.

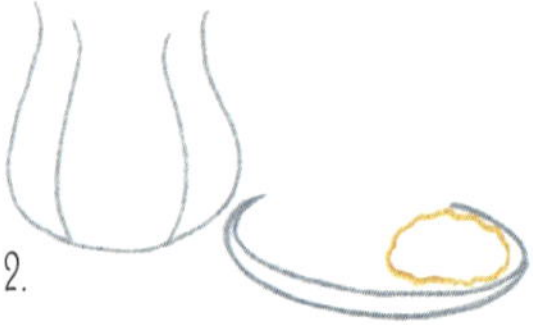

2.

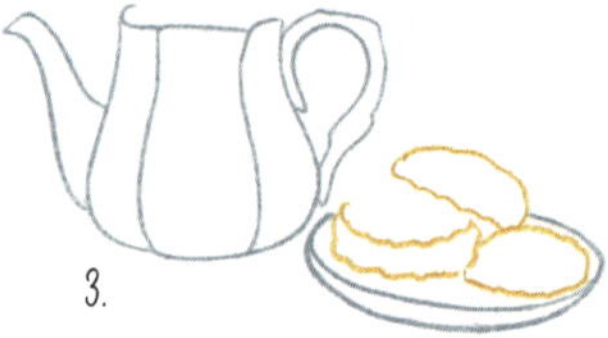

3.

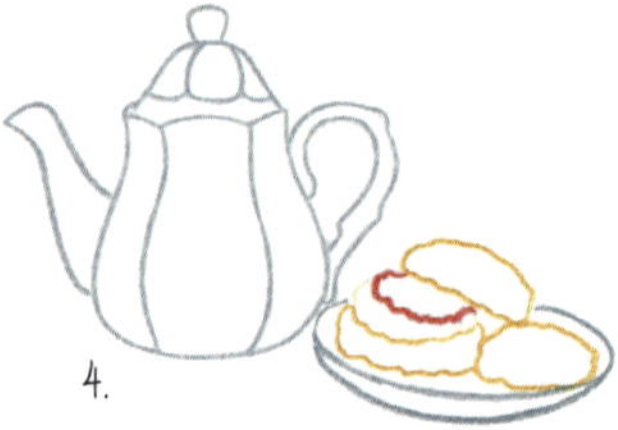

4.

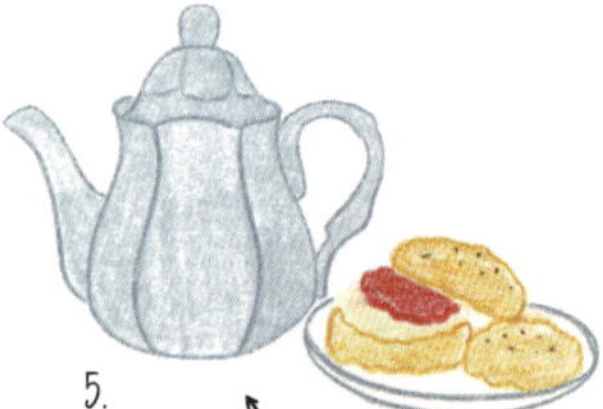

5.

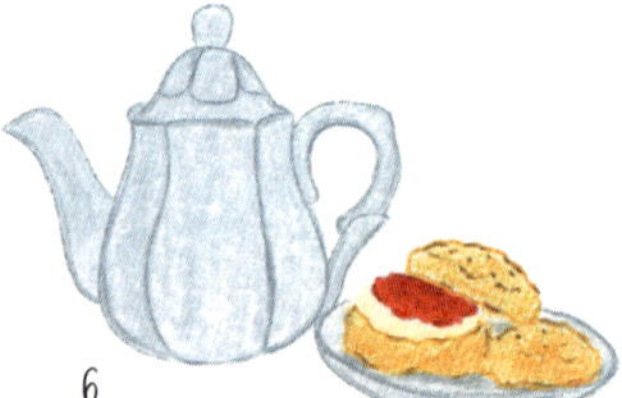

6.

SHADE ALONG THE LENGTH OF EACH PANEL TO CREATE DIMENSION AND A ROUNDED FEEL.

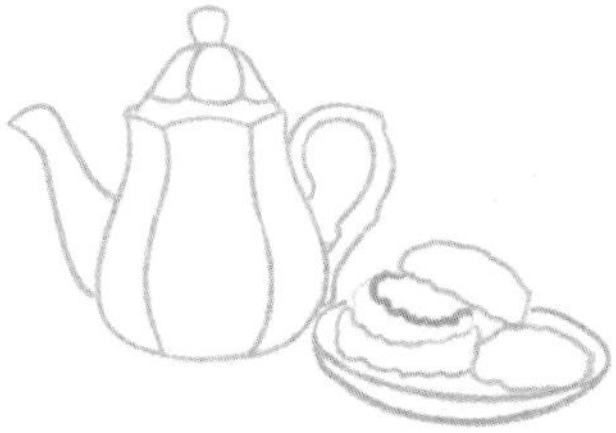

CANDLES

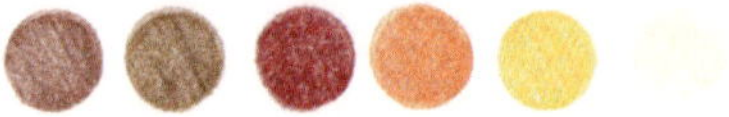

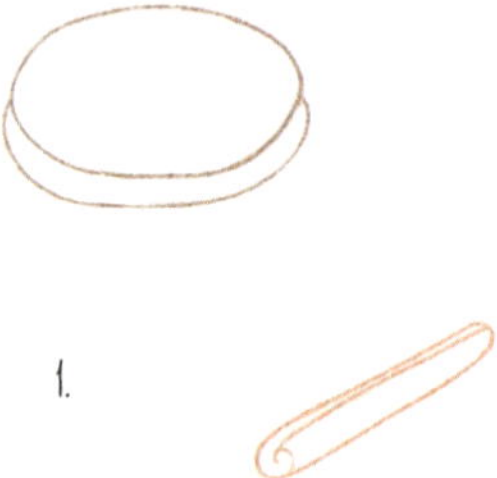

1.

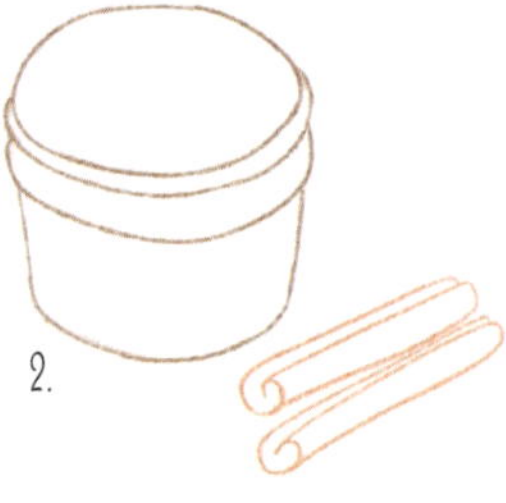

2.

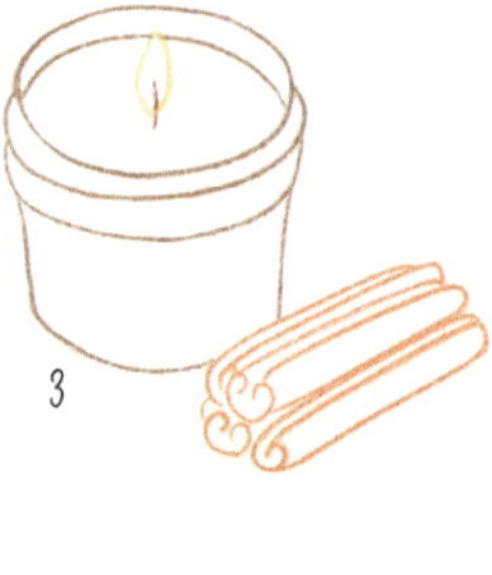

3

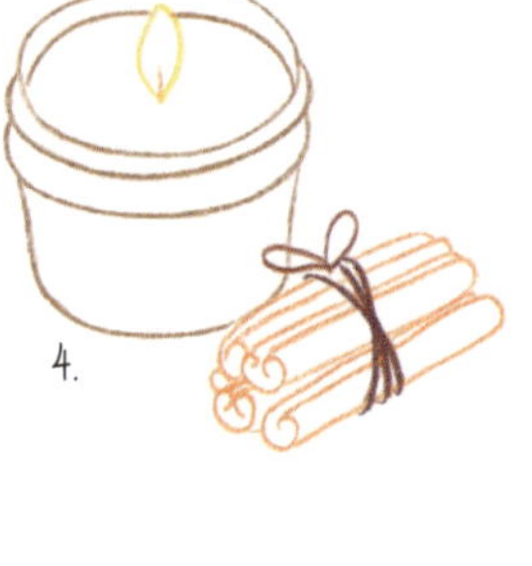

4.

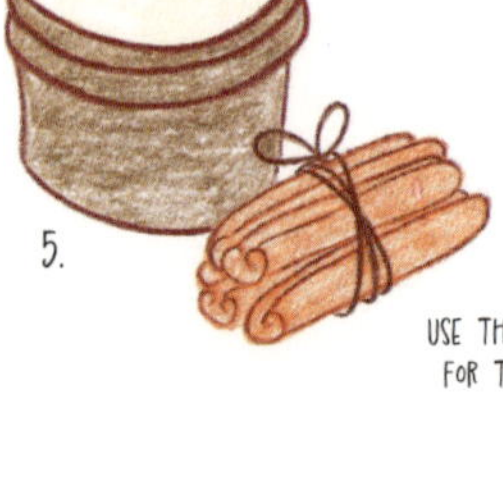

5.

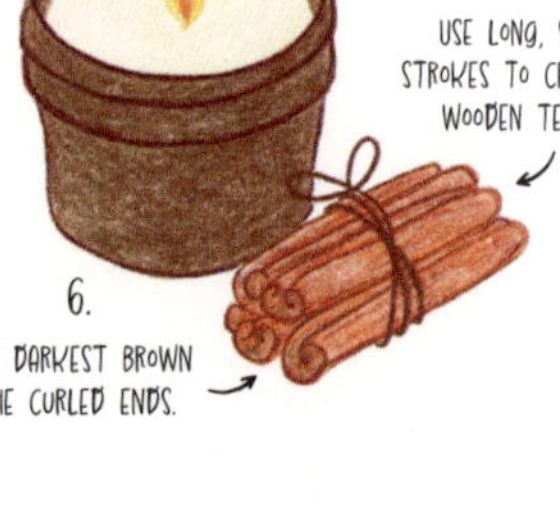

6.

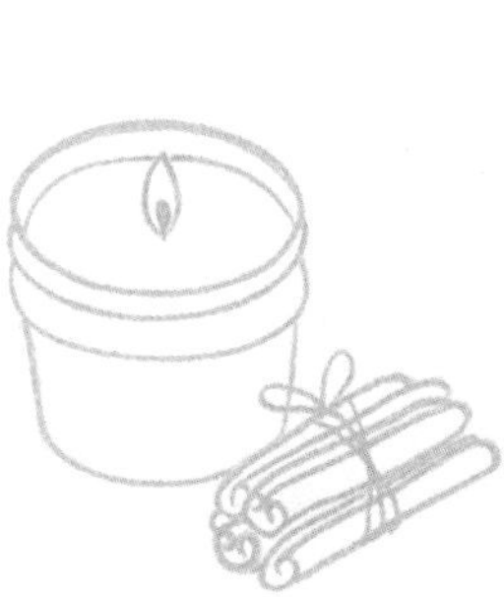

HERB BUNDLE

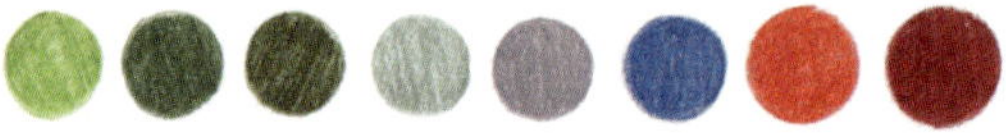

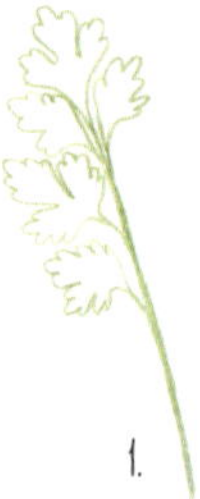

1.

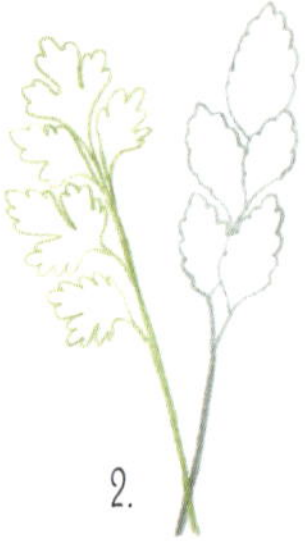

2.

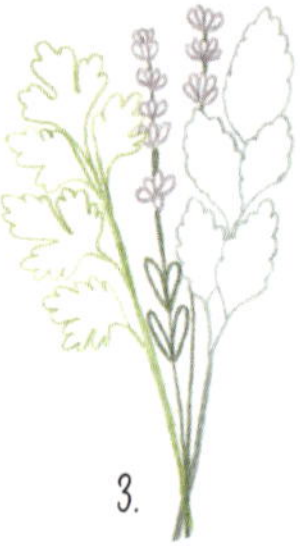

3.

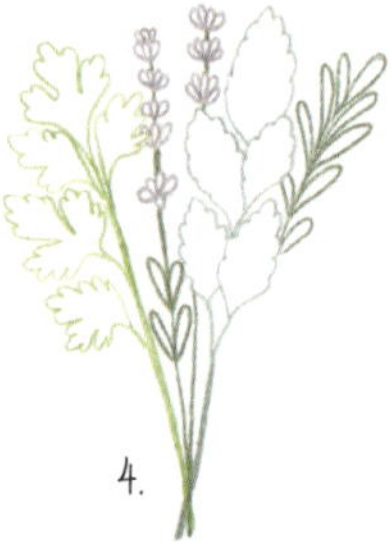

4.

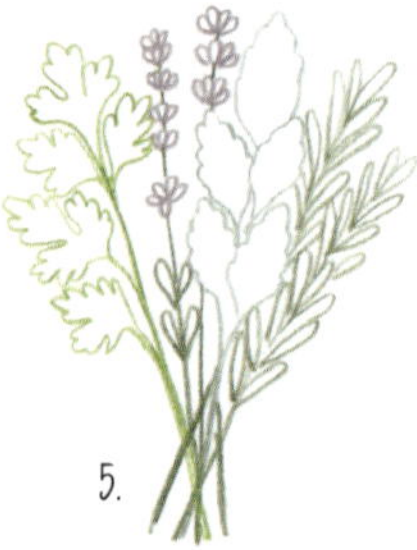

5.

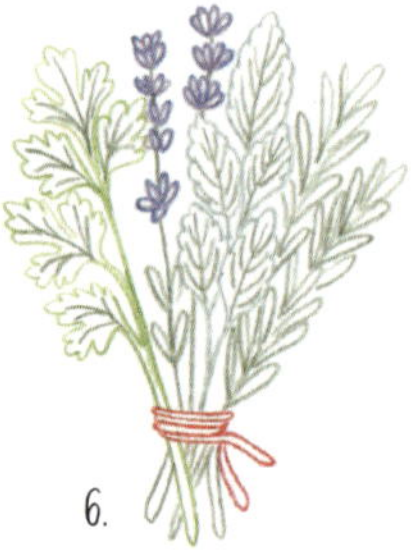

6.

BUILD EACH HERB WITH SOFT BASE LAYERS.

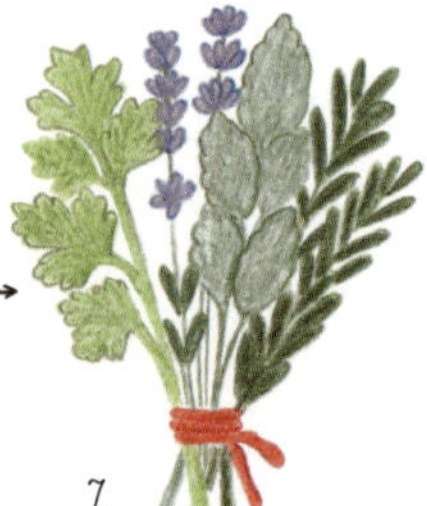

7.

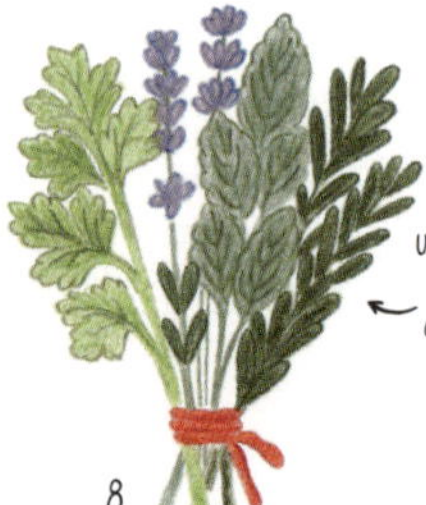

8.

USE FIRMER STROKES IN THE DARKER GREENS TO BRING OUT THE LEAF SHAPES AND NATURAL VARIETY.

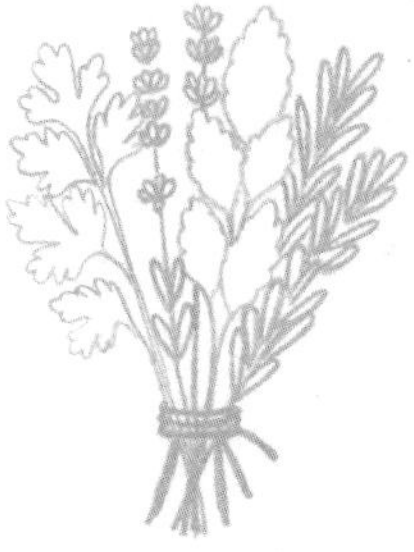

VINTAGE POSTCARD

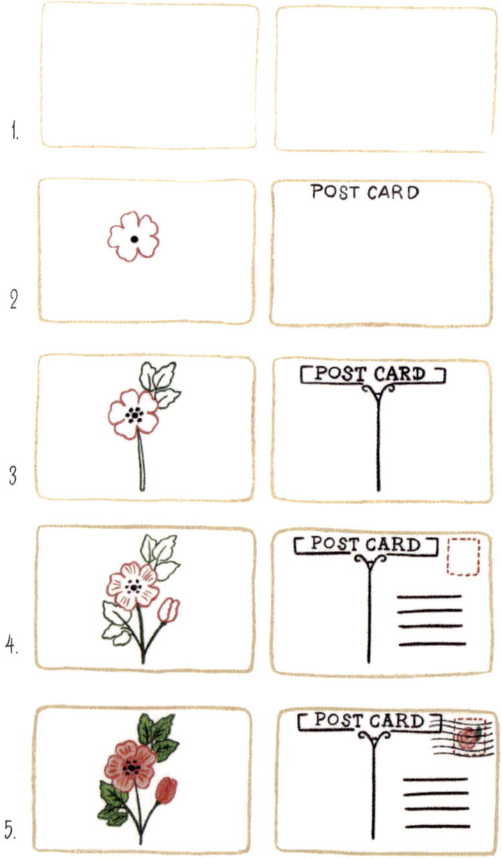

USE SLIGHTLY DARKER STROKES ON THE LETTERING, STAMP AND FLOWER DETAILS.

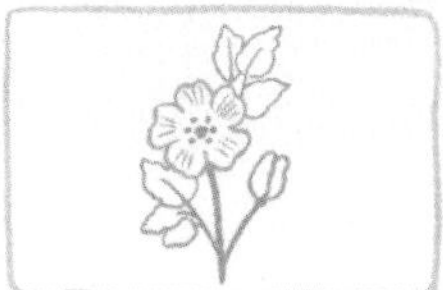

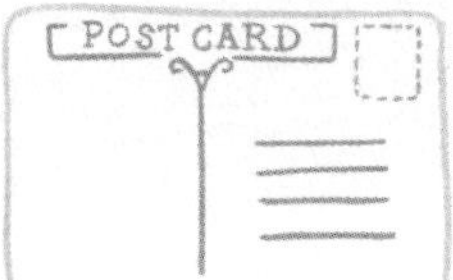
POST CARD

TYPEWRITER

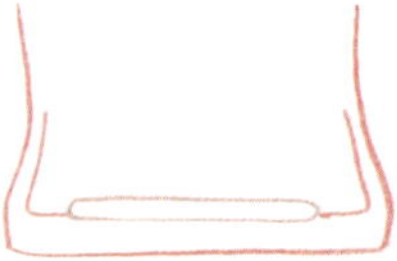

1.

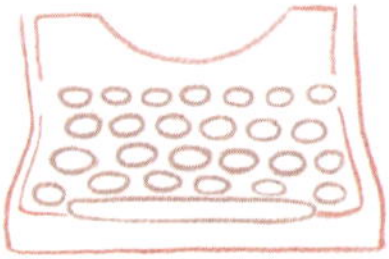

2.

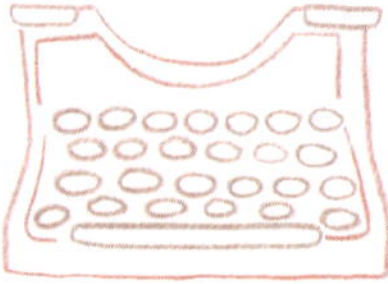

3.

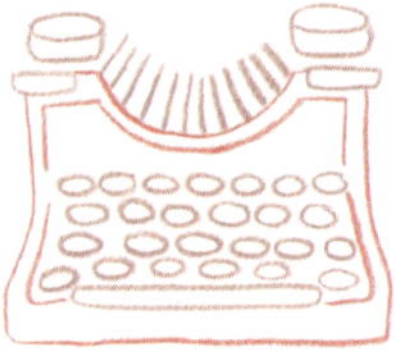

4.

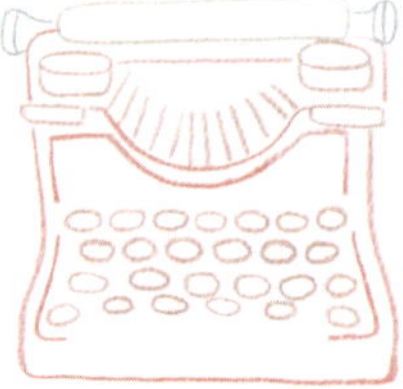

5.

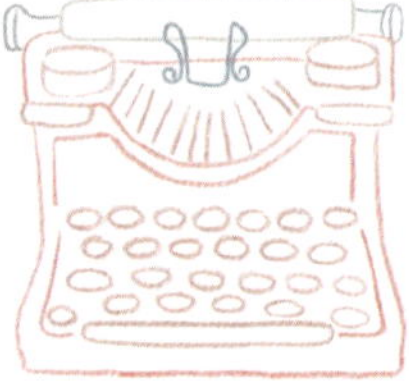

6.

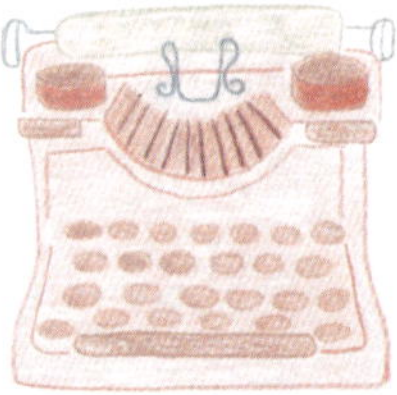

7.

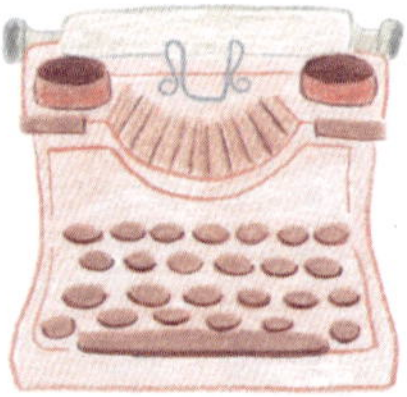

8.

USE THE DARKER PINK TONES WITH SLIGHTLY HEAVIER PRESSURE TO BRING DEPTH TO THE KEYS AND THE CURVED FRONT PANEL.

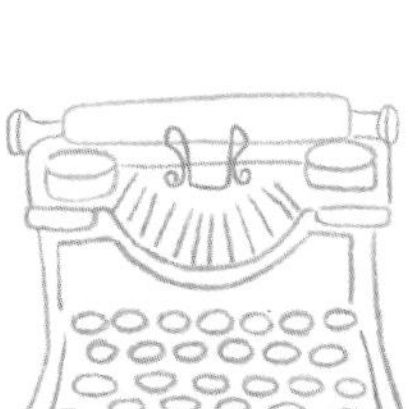

RECORD PLAYER

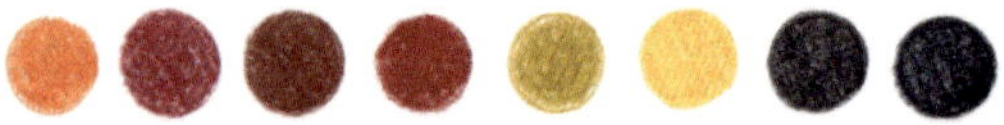

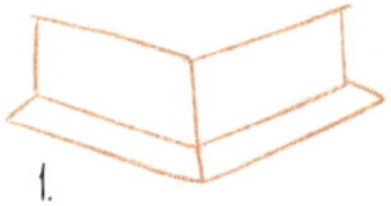

1.

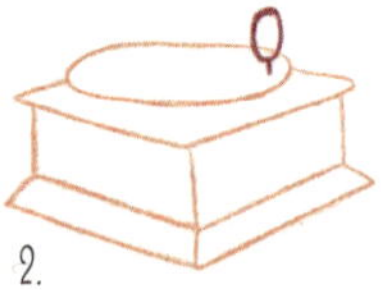

2.

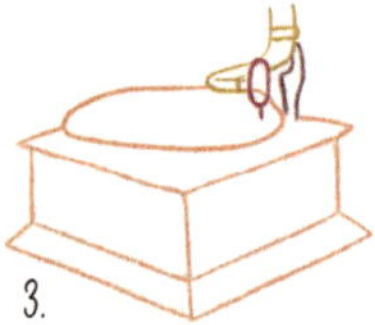

3.

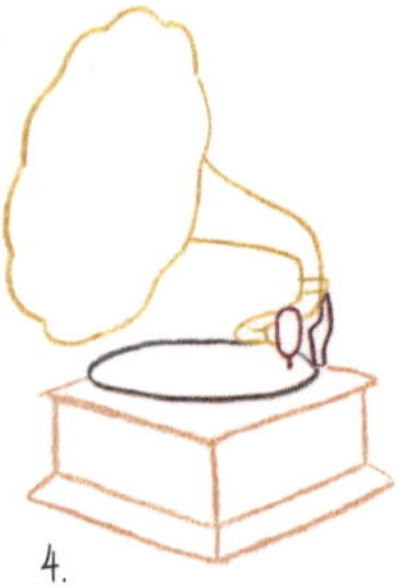

4.

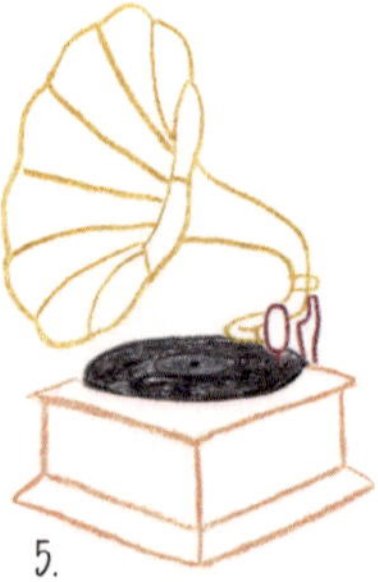

5.

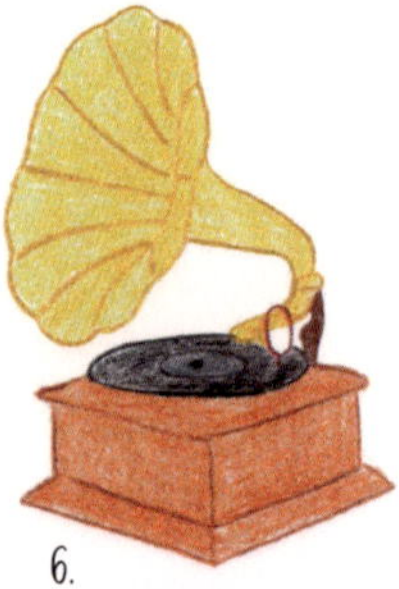

6.

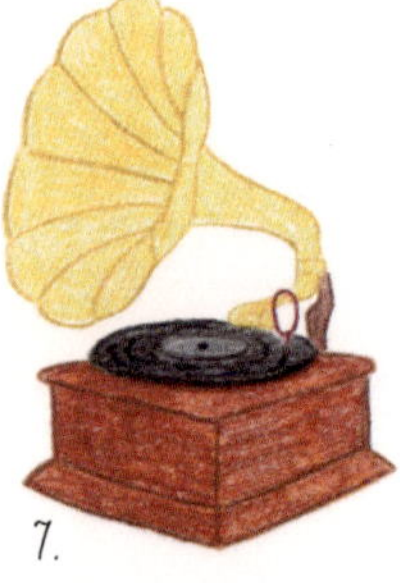

7.

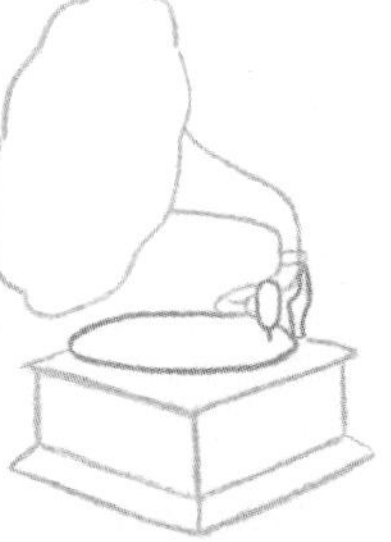

TRAVEL SUITCASE

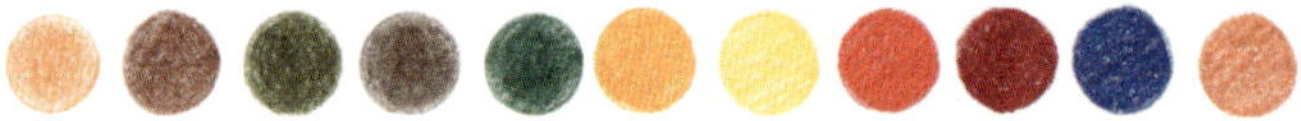

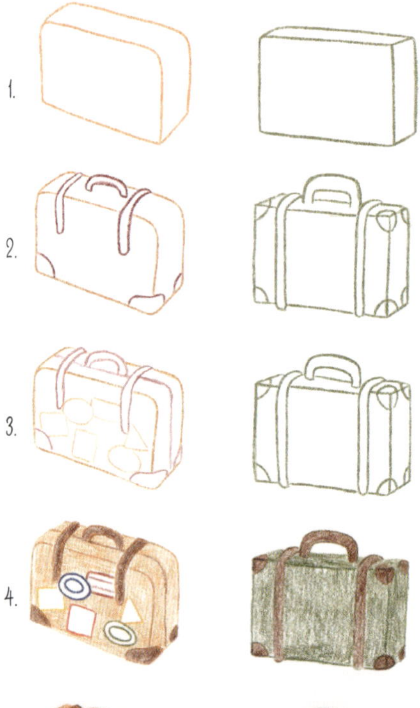

APPLY THE COLOUR IN LAYERS IN THE SHAPE OF EACH SUITCASE TO CREATE THE LEATHER TEXTURE.

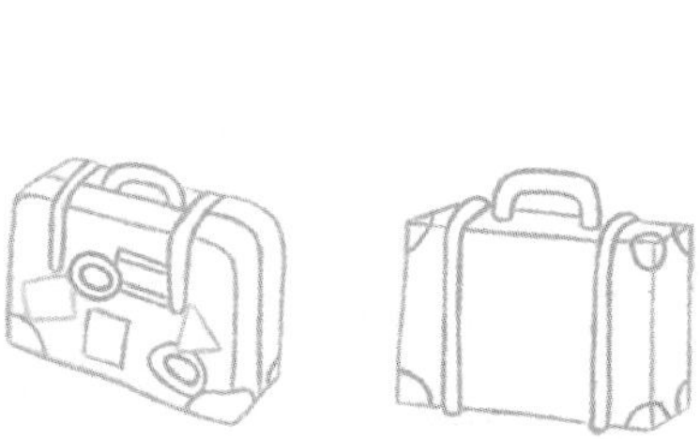

CROCHET SQUARES

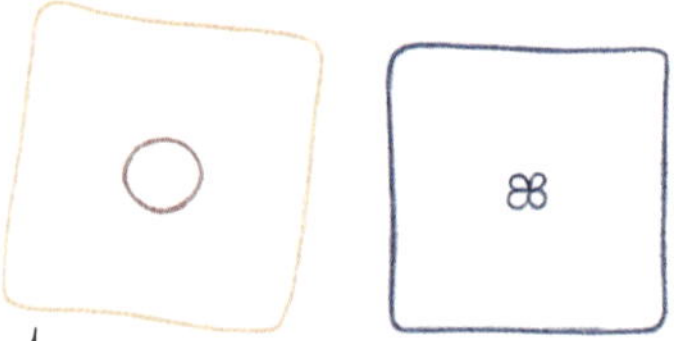

1.

2.

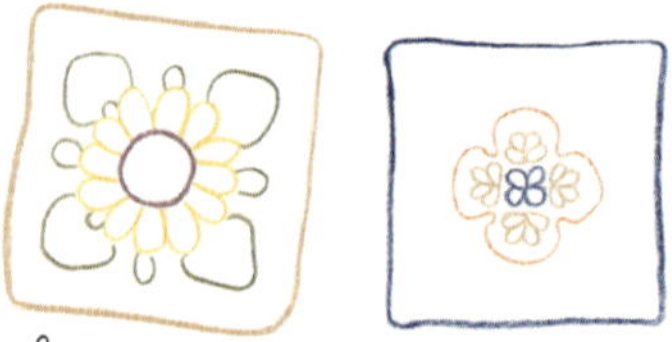

3.

4.

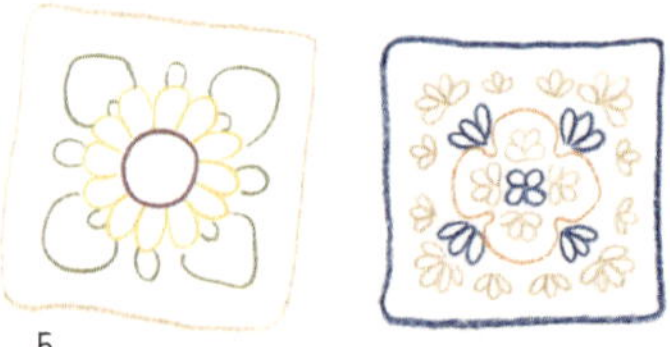

5.

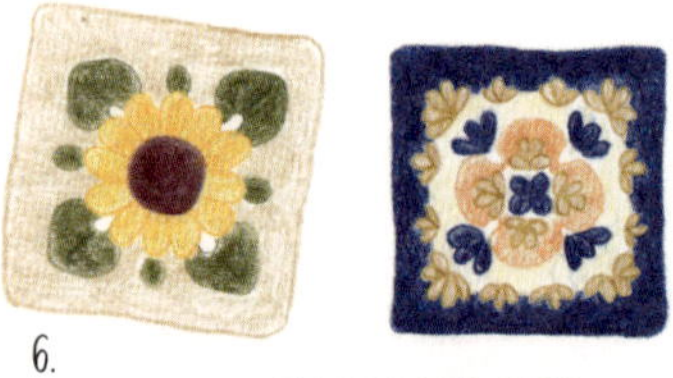

6.

ADD SLIGHT BORDER SHADING AND SMALL LAYERED STROKES INSIDE THE MOTIFS TO GIVE A STITCHED, FABRIC FEEL.

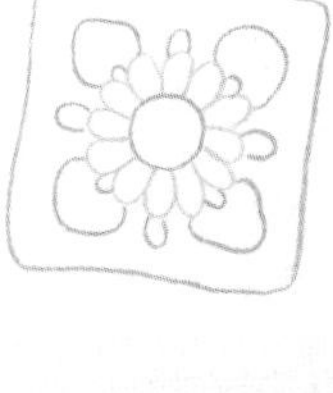

SOUP BOWL

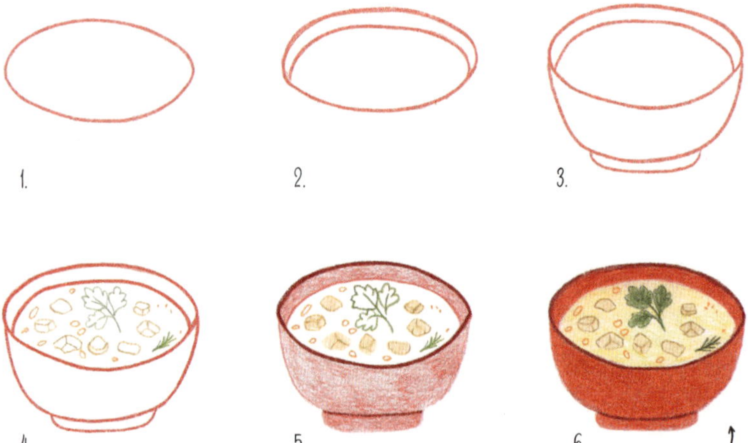

ADD GENTLE CIRCULAR SHADING ON THE SURFACE TO GIVE IT WARMTH AND A SUBTLE SIMMERING LOOK.

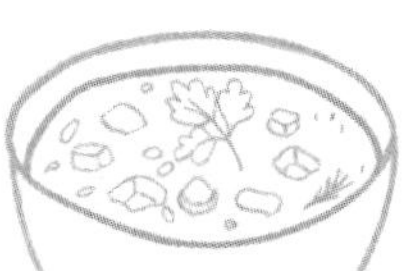

COOKIE TRAY

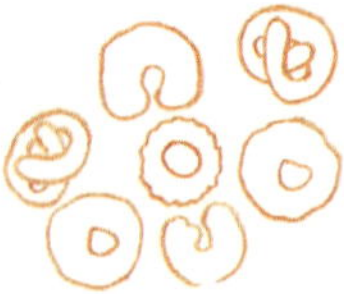

1.

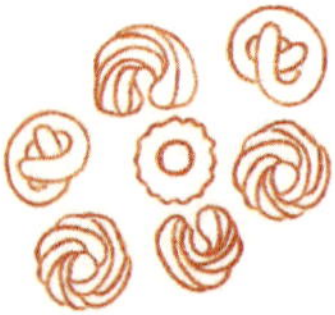

2.

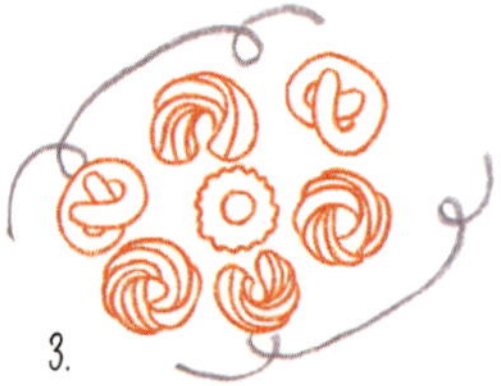

3.

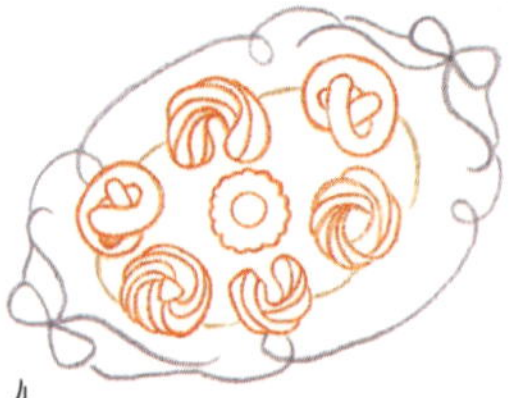

4.

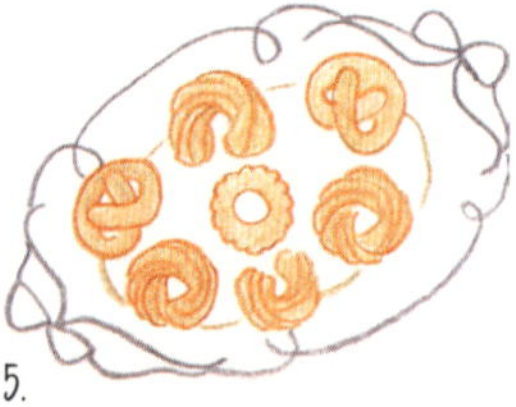

5.

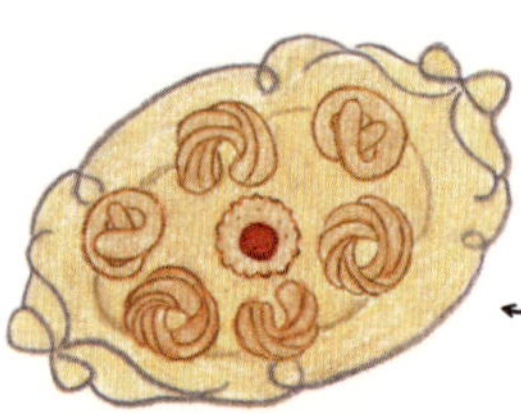

6.

USE THE WARMER GOLD TONES WITH FIRMER, CURVED STROKES TO ACCENT THE PASTRY FOLDS AND MAKE THE COOKIES LOOK MORE LAYERED.

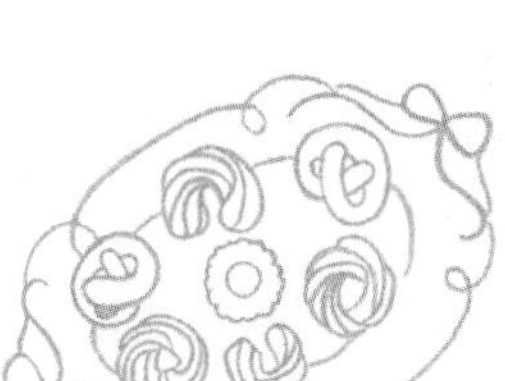

SIMMERING STEW POT

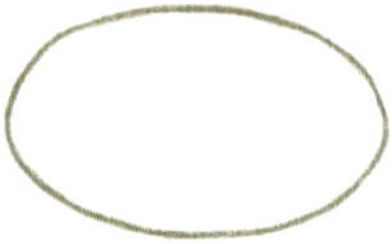

1.

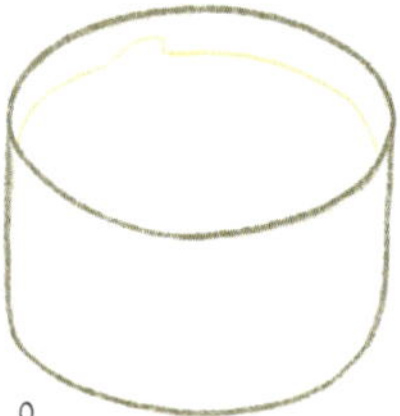

2.

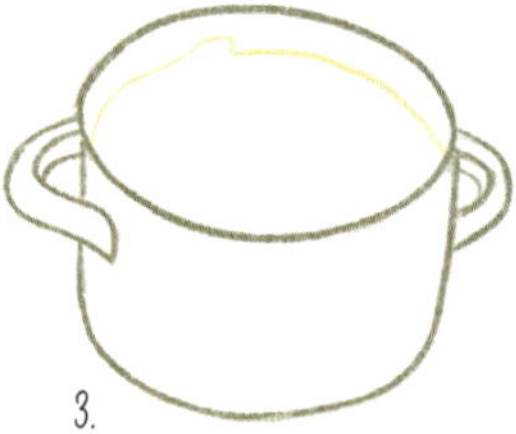

3.

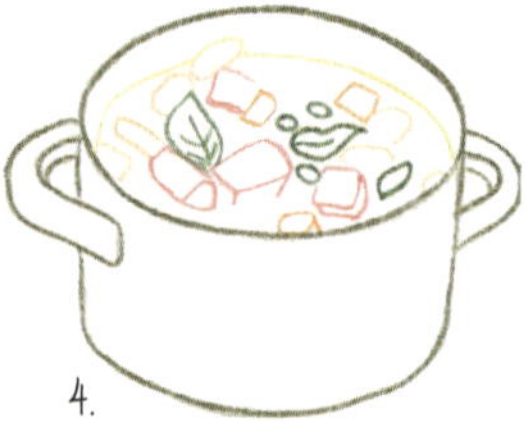

4.

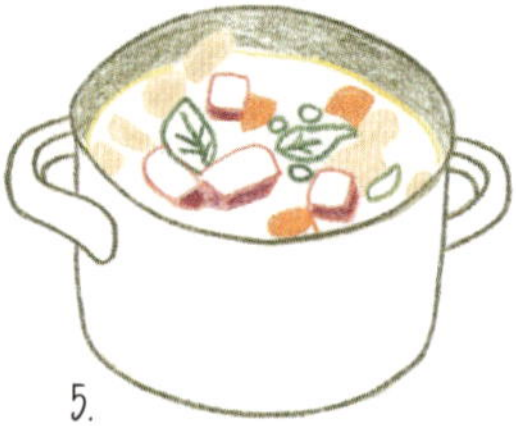

5.

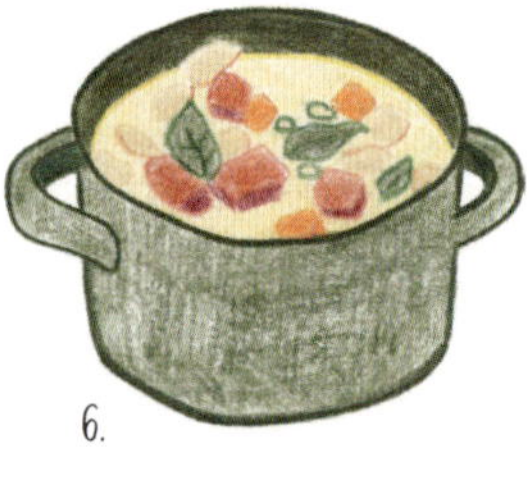

6.

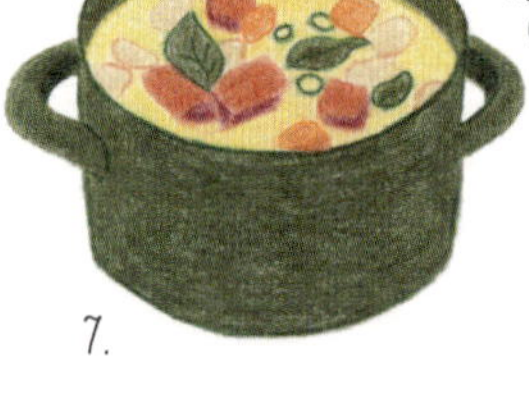

7.

ADD FIRMER, LAYERED SHADING ON THE INGREDIENTS SO THEY FEEL CHUNKY AND SETTLED INTO THE STEW.

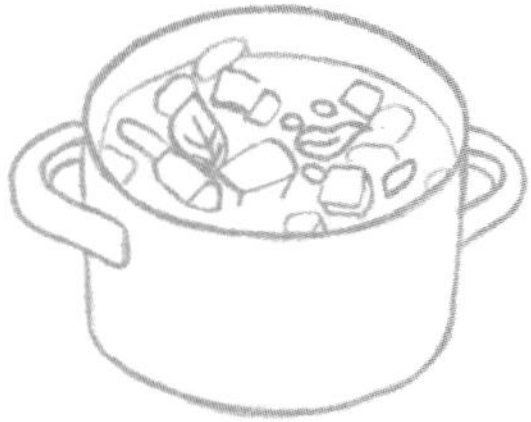

EMBROIDERY RINGS

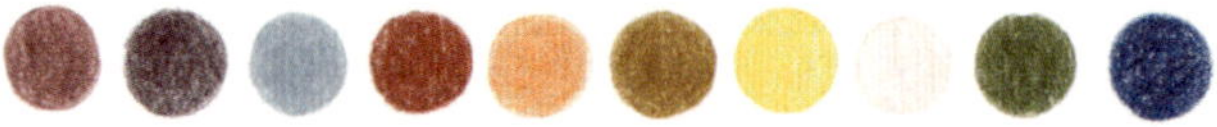

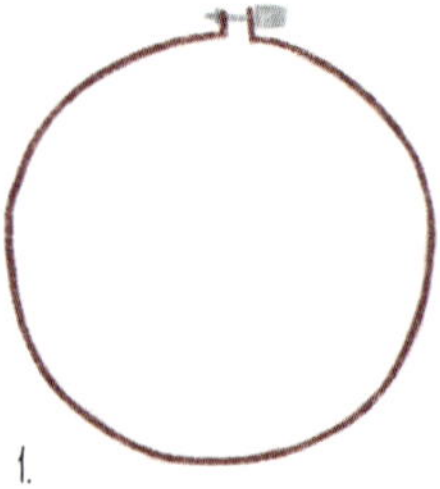

1.

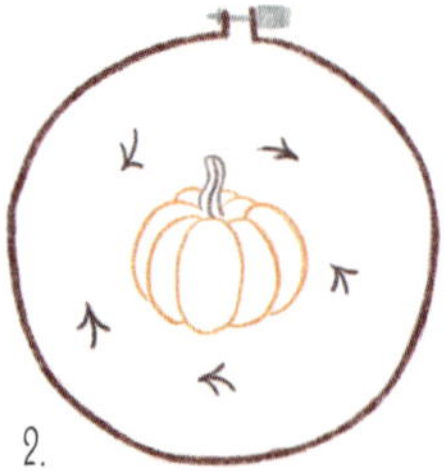

2.

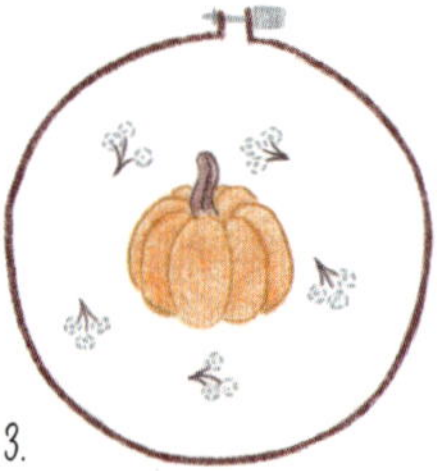

3.

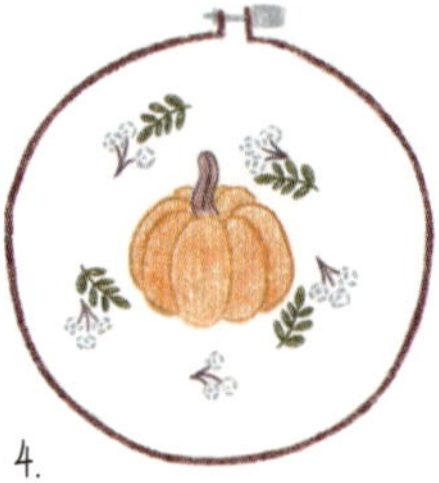

4.

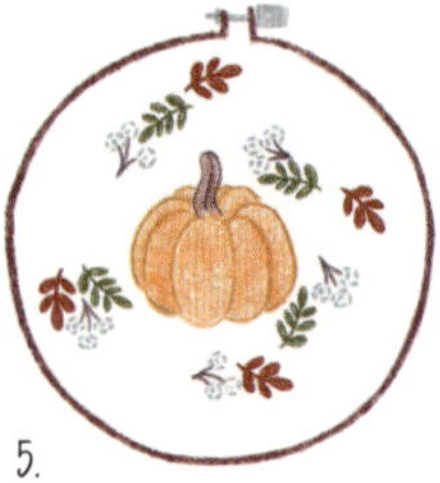

5.

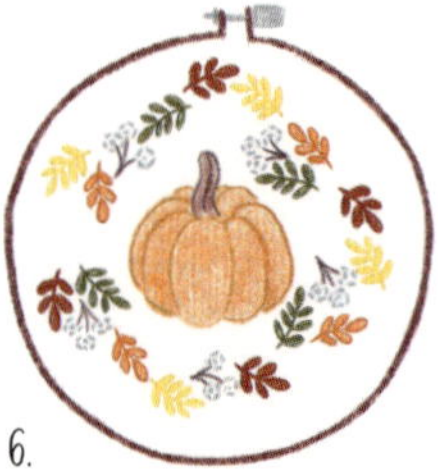

6.

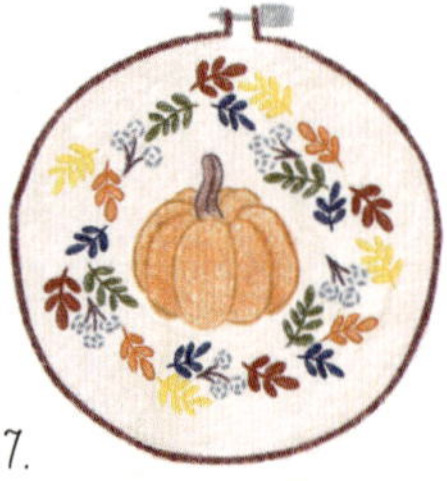

7.

LIGHT CROSS-CUT SHADING ACROSS THE BACKGROUND GIVES THE CANVAS A SUBTLE WOVEN FABRIC FEEL.

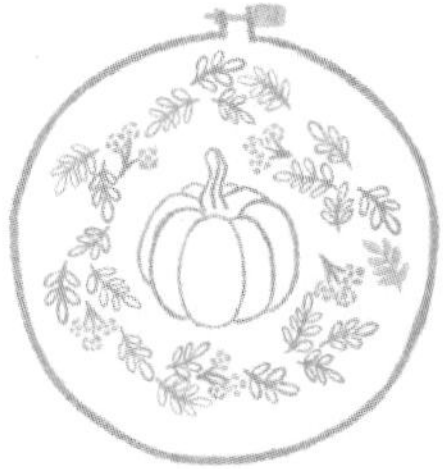

FLUFFY ROBE

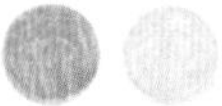

USE SHORT, UNEVEN STROKES TO BUILD UP THE SOFT, FLUFFY TEXTURE. OR, LIGHTLY SKETCH THE SHAPE FIRST AND ADD THE SHORT STROKES AFTERWARDS.

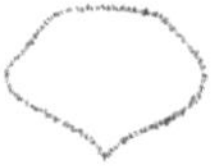

1.

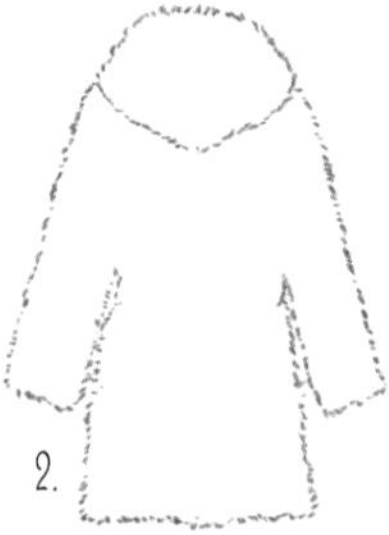

2.

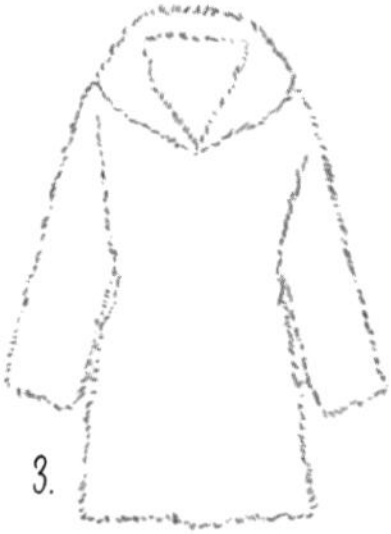

3.

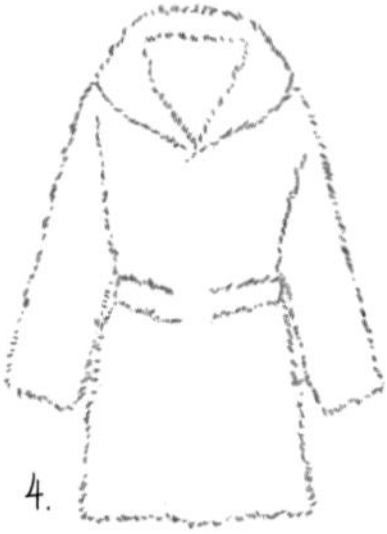

4.

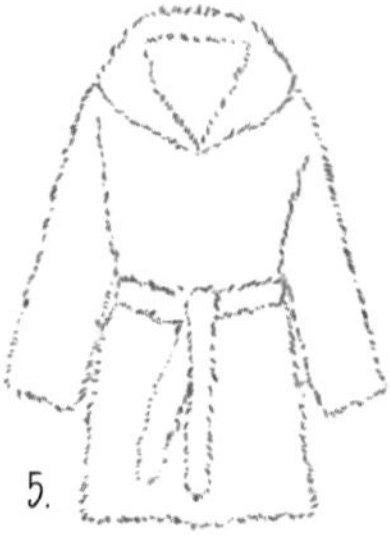

5.

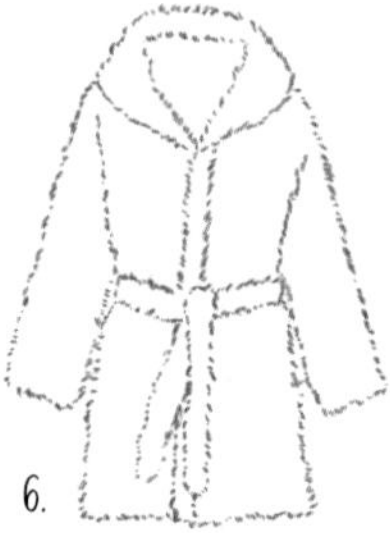

6.

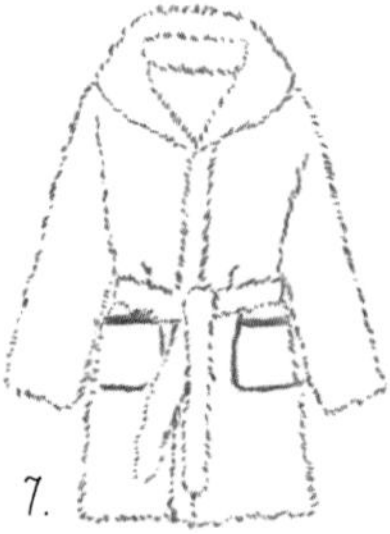

7.

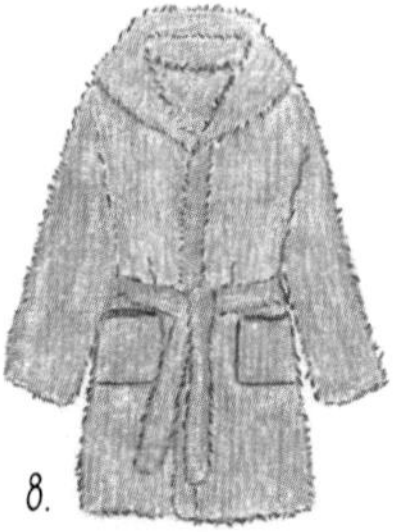

8.

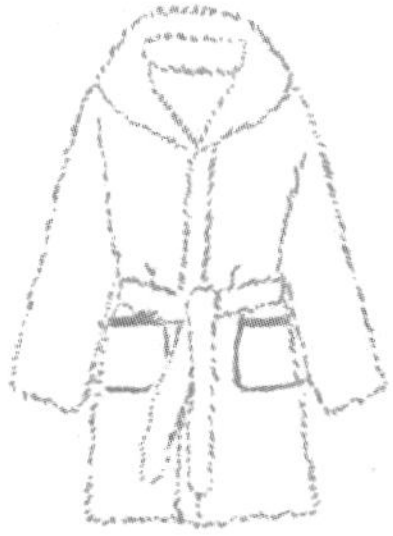

BREAKFAST TRAY

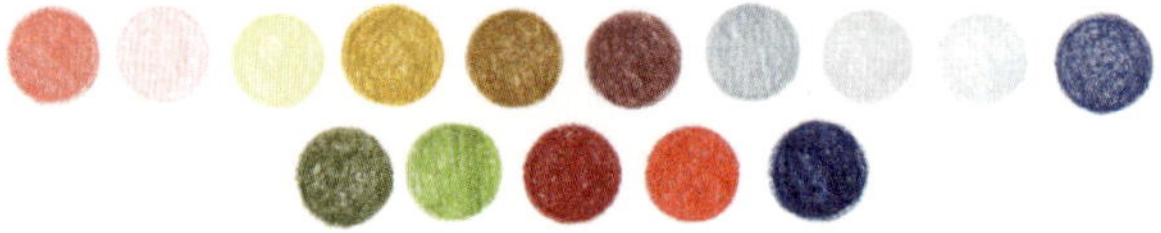

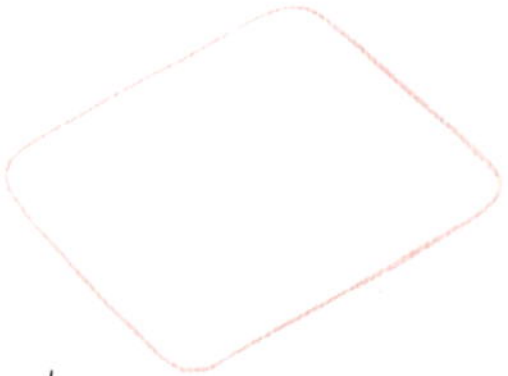

1.

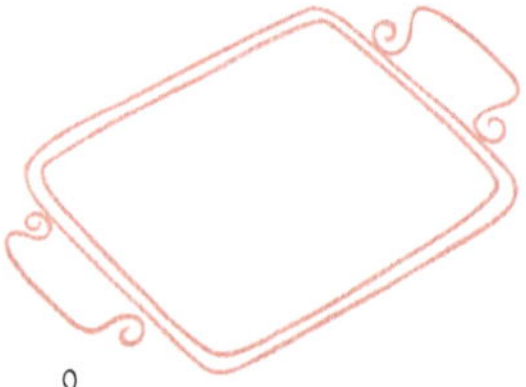

2.

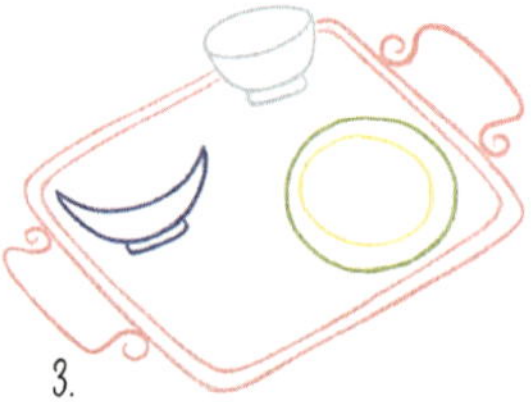

3.

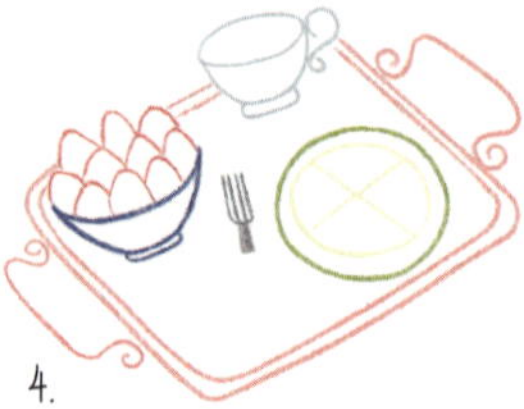

4.

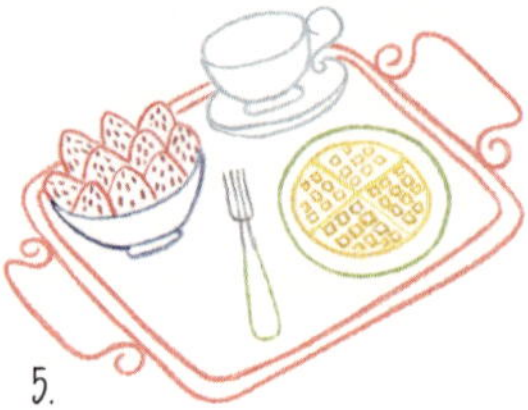

5.

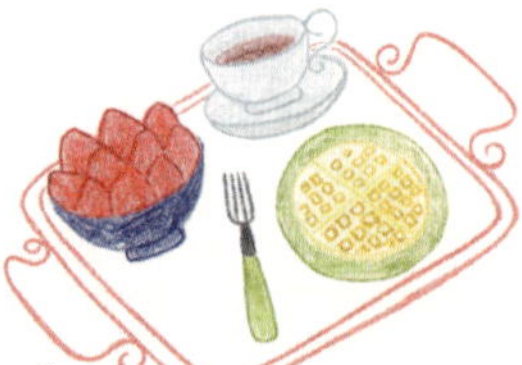

6.

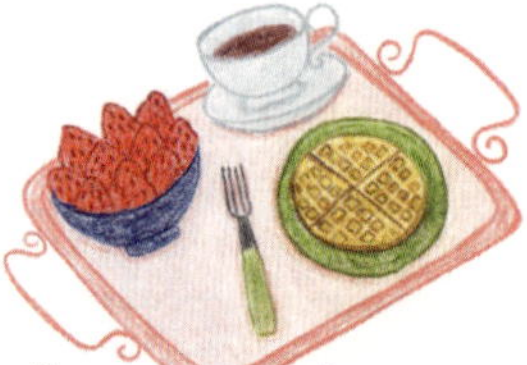

7.

ADD SOFT SHADING BENEATH EACH ITEM SO THEY FEEL GROUNDED ON THE TRAY AND NOT FLOATING.

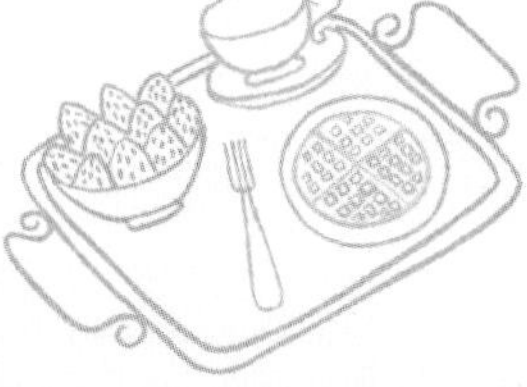

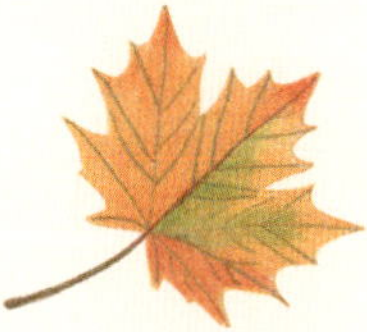

SEASONAL COMFORTS

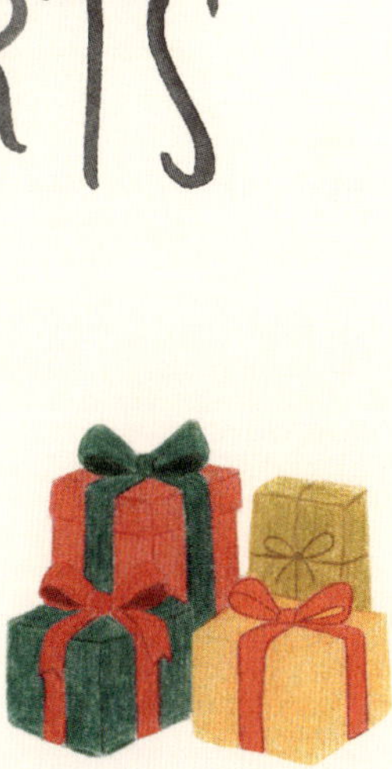

PUMPKIN

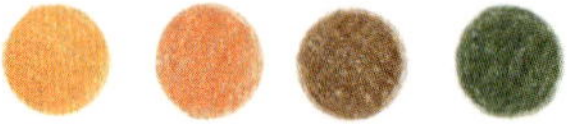

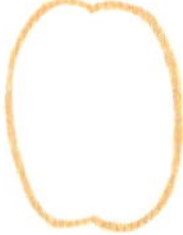

1.

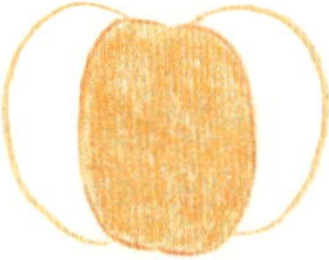

2.

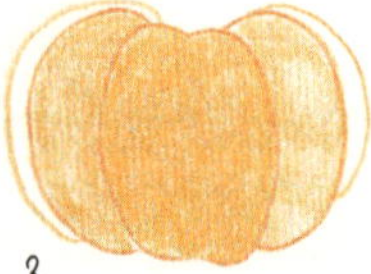

3.

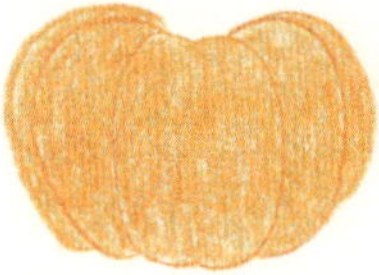

4.

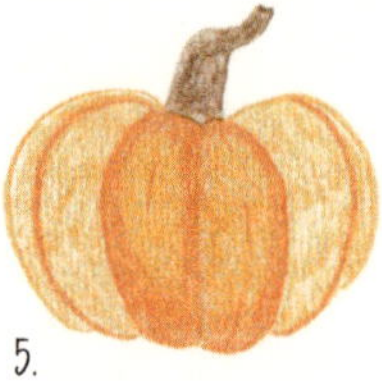

5.

USE FIRM, ROUNDED STROKES TO BUILD EACH SECTION.

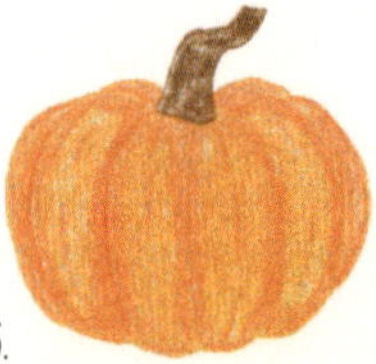

6.

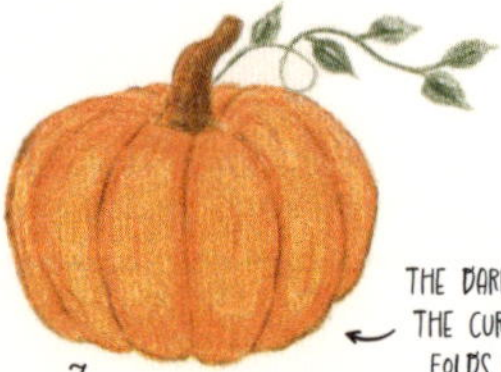

7.

THE DARKER ORANGE INSIDE THE CURVES DEEPENS THE FOLDS AND KEEPS THE SHAPE PLUMP.

WINTER MITTENS

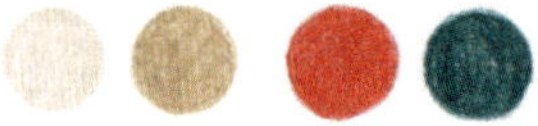

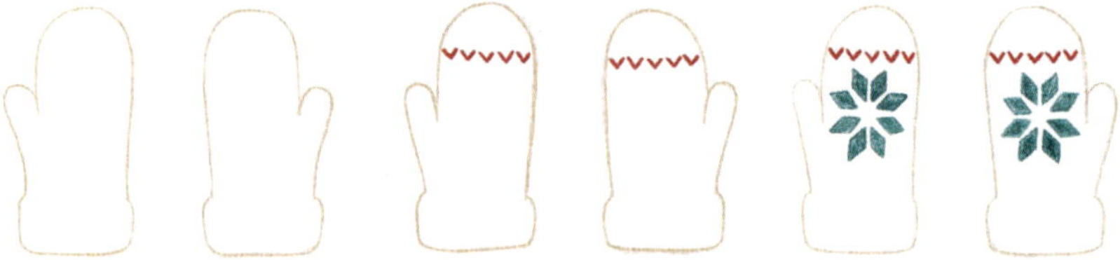

1. 2. 3.

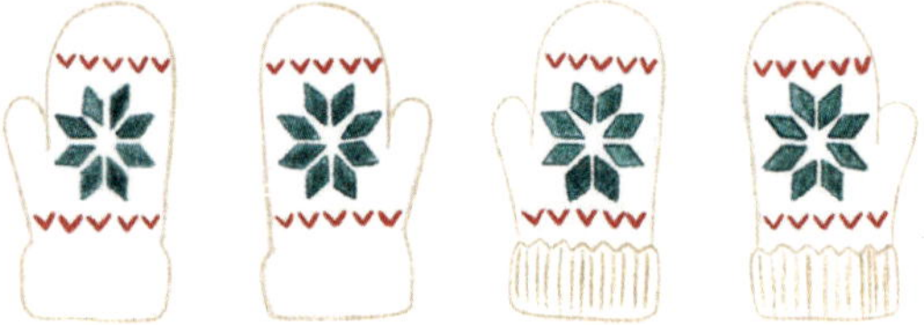

4. 5.

LAYER SOFT STROKES IN DIFFERENT DIRECTIONS TO GIVE THE MITTENS A COZY KNITTED TEXTURE.

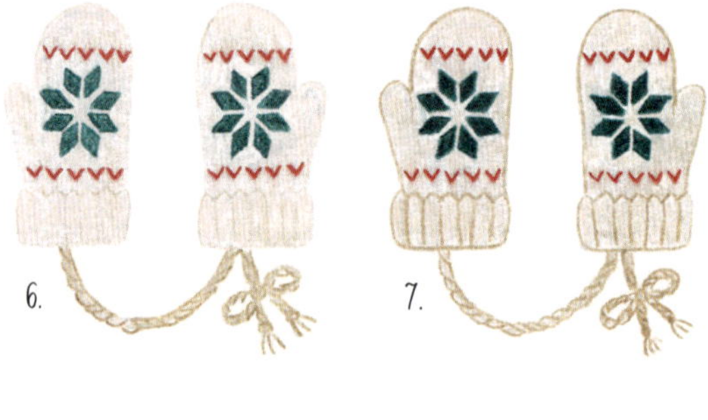

6. 7.

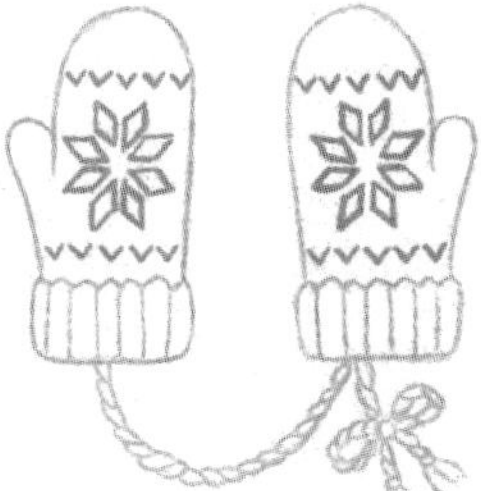

SEASONAL WREATH

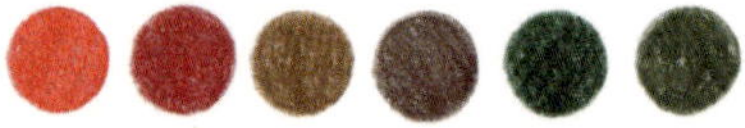

1.

2.

3.

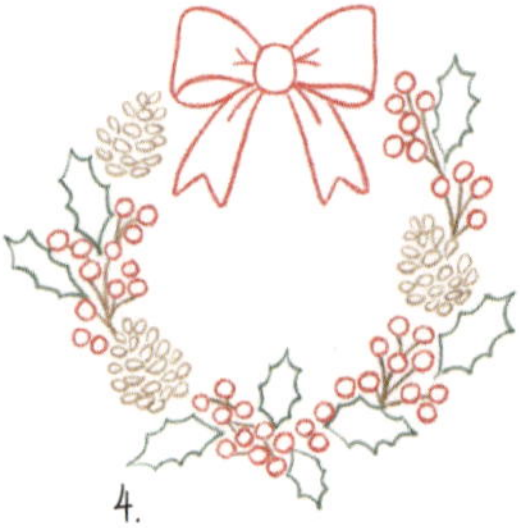

4.

5.

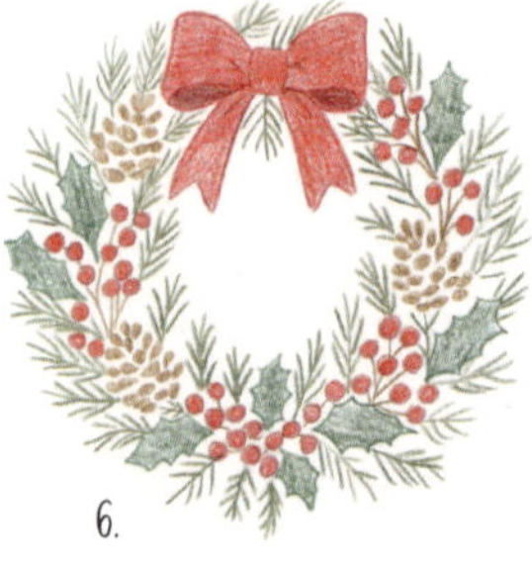

6.

7.

INCREASE PRESSURE ON THE FINAL LAYER TO CREATE RICHER COLOUR AND DEPTH.

GARLAND OF LEAVES

1.

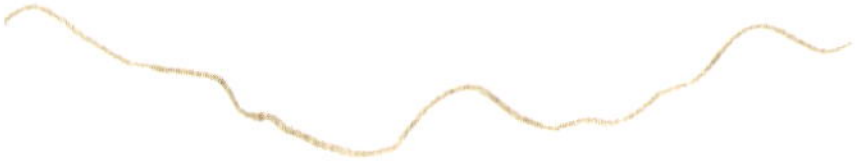

2.

3.

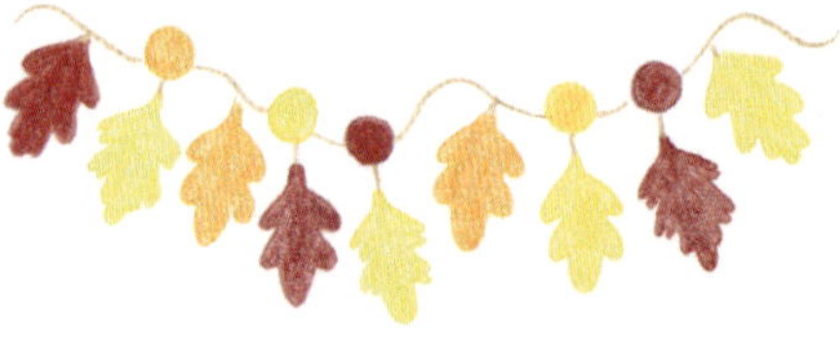

VARY YOUR PENCIL PRESSURE ON EACH LEAF TO KEEP THE GARLAND LIVELY AND TEXTURED.

4.

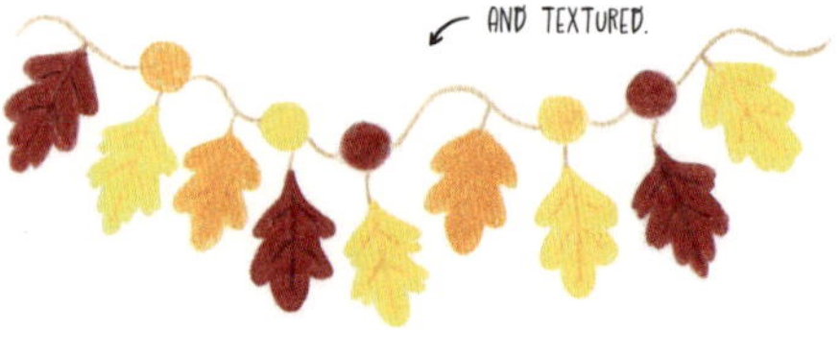

SNOW GLOBE

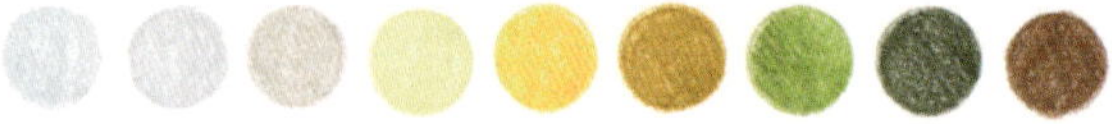

1.

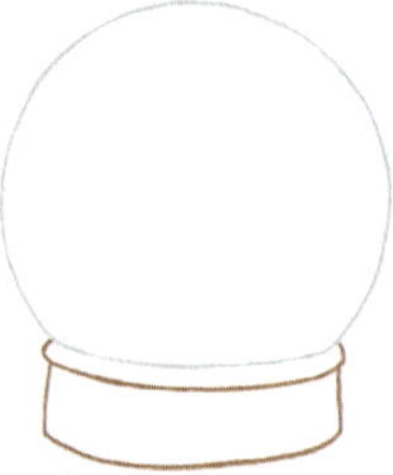

2.

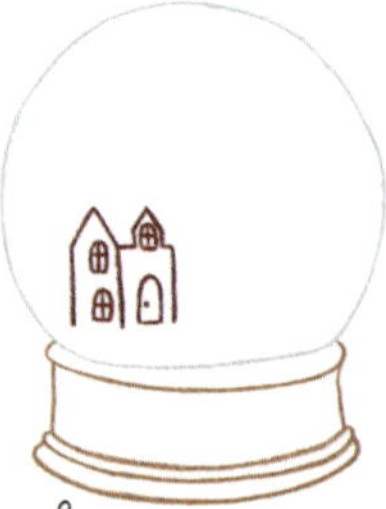

3.

4.

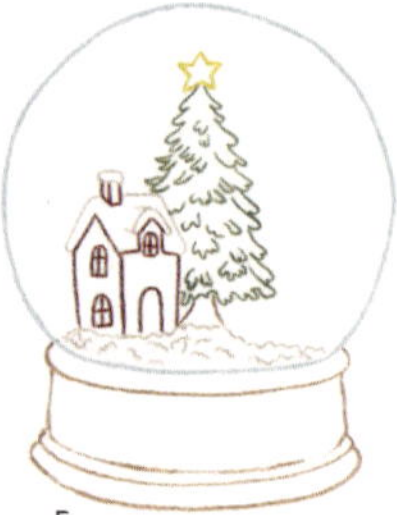

5.

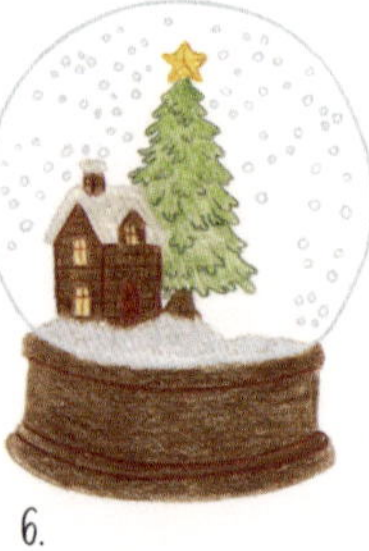

ROUNDED SHADING STROKES ON THE BASE ECHO THE CURVE OF THE GLOBE.

6.

MAPLE LEAF

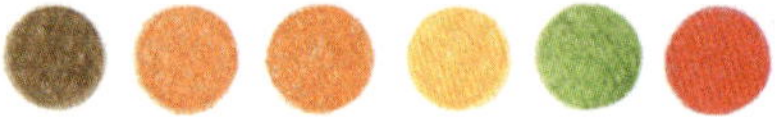

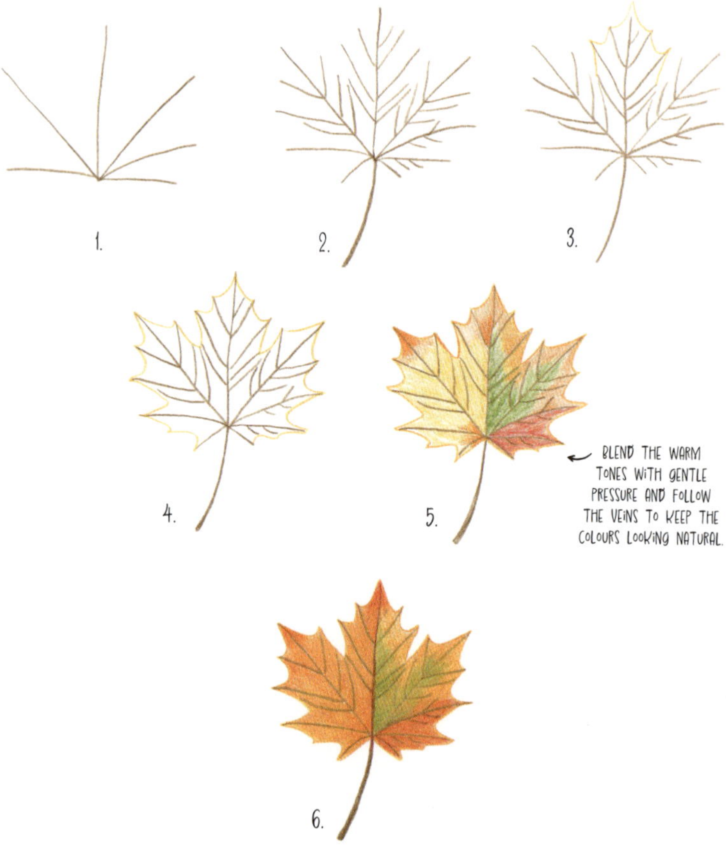
1.
2.
3.
4.
5.
BLEND THE WARM TONES WITH GENTLE PRESSURE AND FOLLOW THE VEINS TO KEEP THE COLOURS LOOKING NATURAL.
6.

WOOLLEN BEANIE

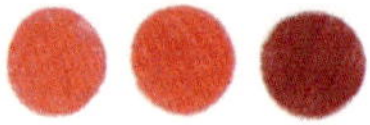

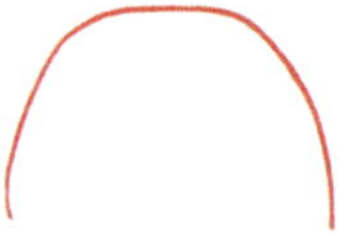

1.

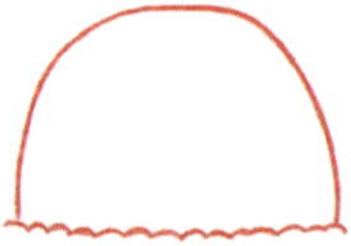

2.

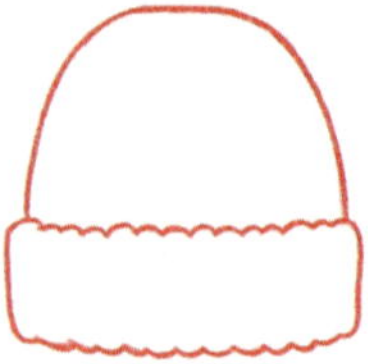

3.

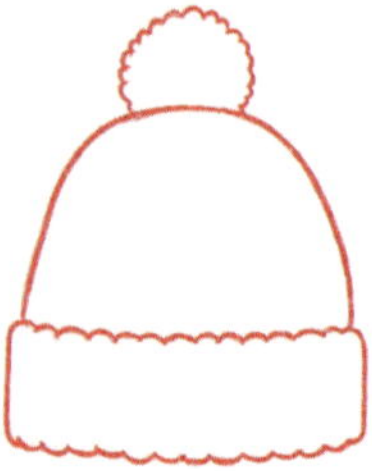

4.

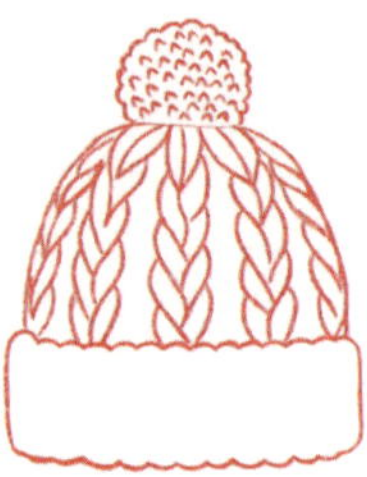

5.

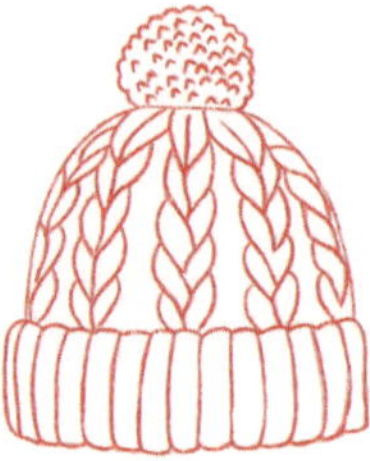

6.

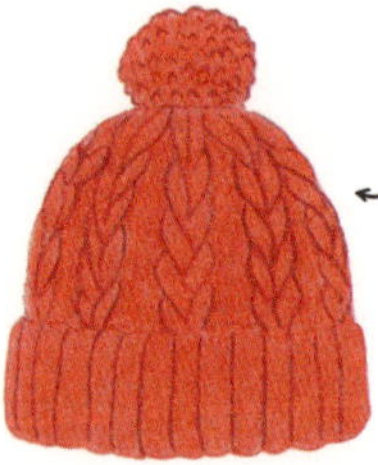

7.

USE FIRMER SHADING ALONG THE EDGES OF THE CABLES TO ACCENTUATE THE KNITTED TEXTURE.

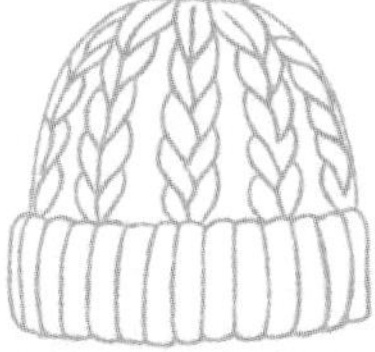

CANDY CANE

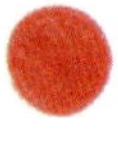

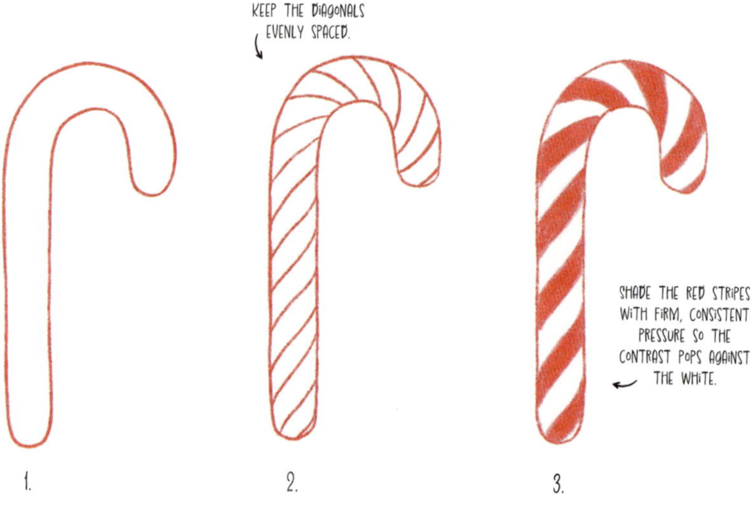
KEEP THE DIAGONALS EVENLY SPACED.
SHADE THE RED STRIPES WITH FIRM, CONSISTENT PRESSURE SO THE CONTRAST POPS AGAINST THE WHITE.
1.
2.
3.

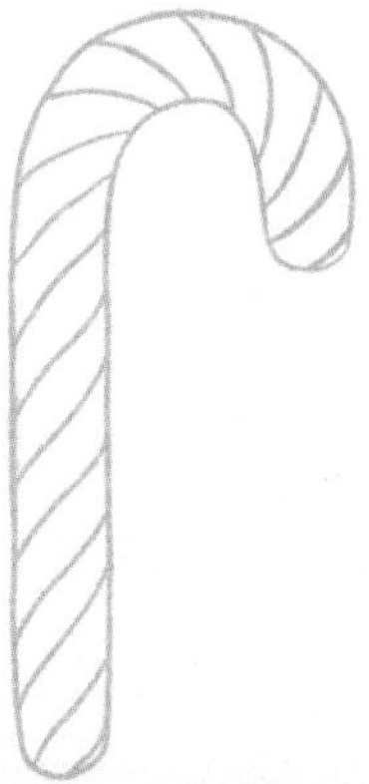

CINNAMON STICK

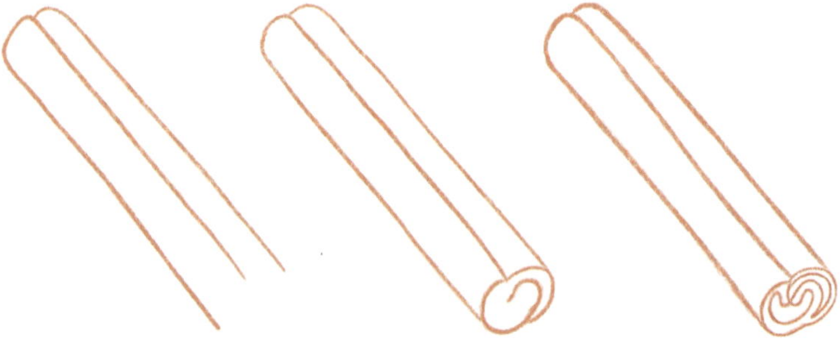

1. 2. 3.

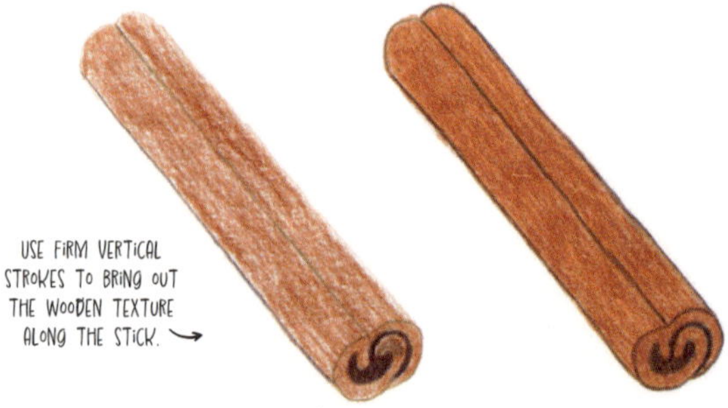

4. 5.

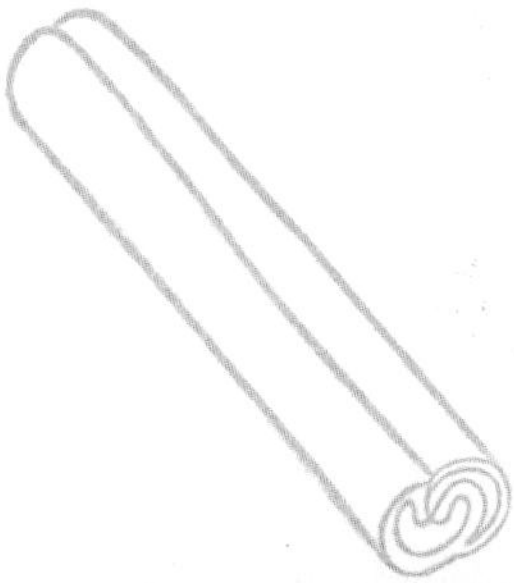

HOLLY BRANCH

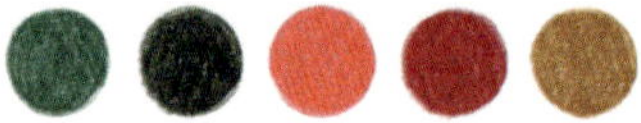

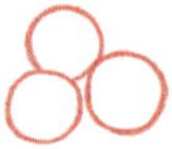

1.

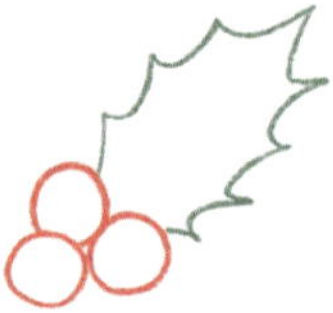

2.

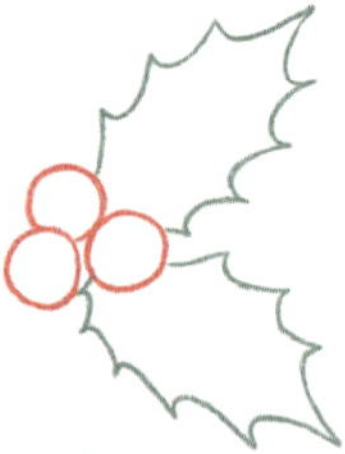

3.

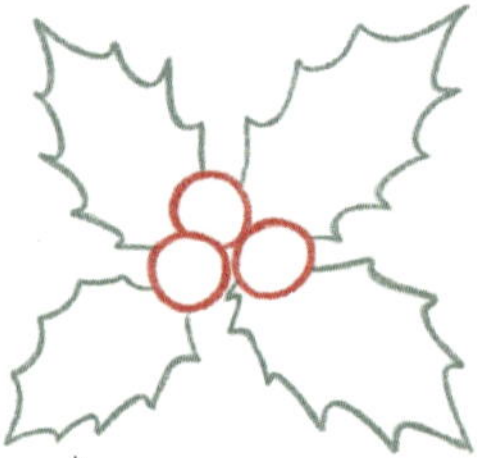

4.

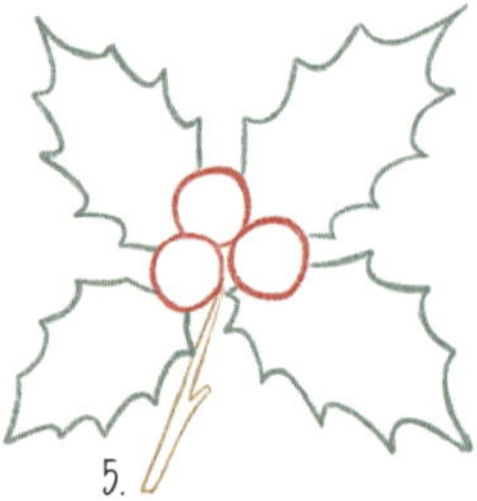

5.

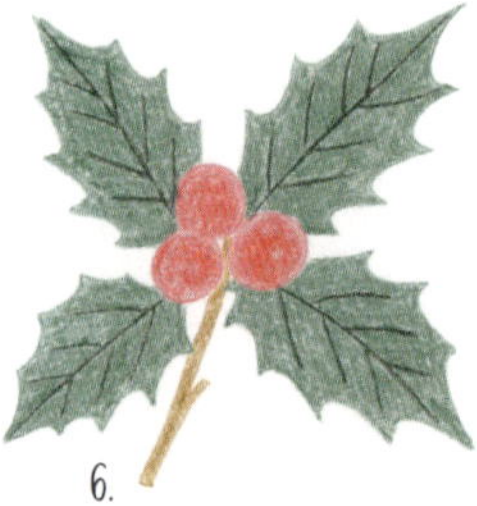

6.

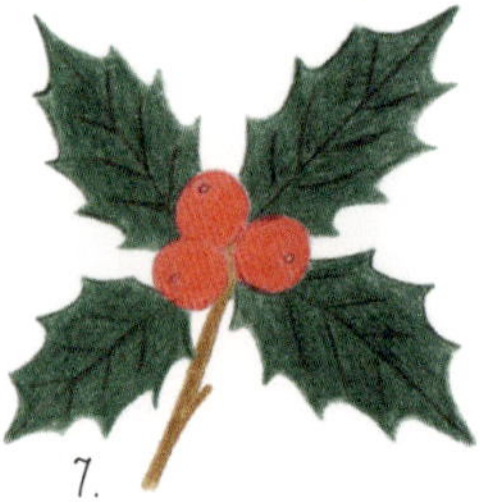

7.

STRENGTHEN THE FINAL LAYER OVER THE LEAF VEINS TO BRING OUT THE SHARP HOLLY TEXTURE.

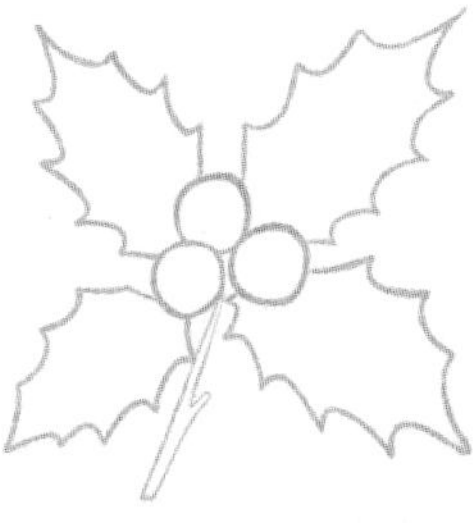

CINNAMON ROLL

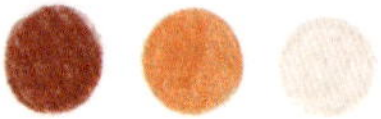

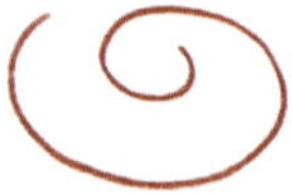

1.

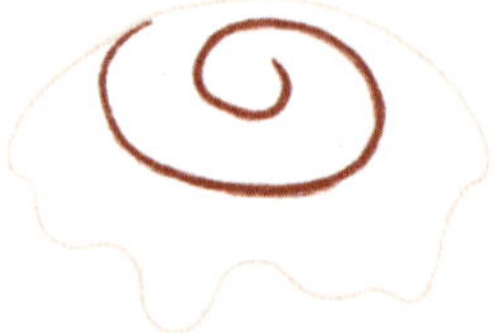

2.

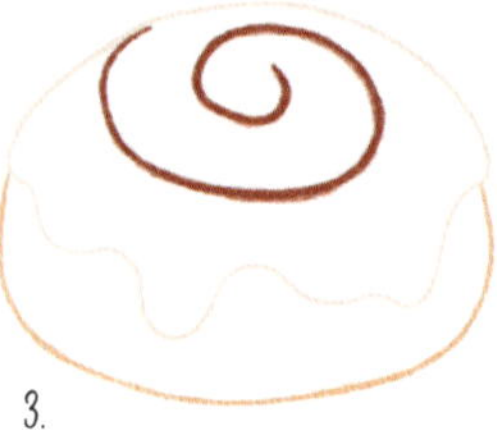

3.

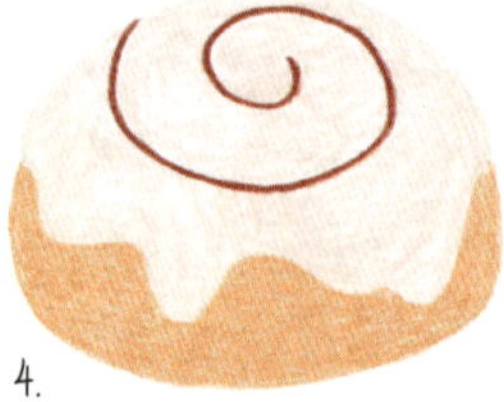

4.

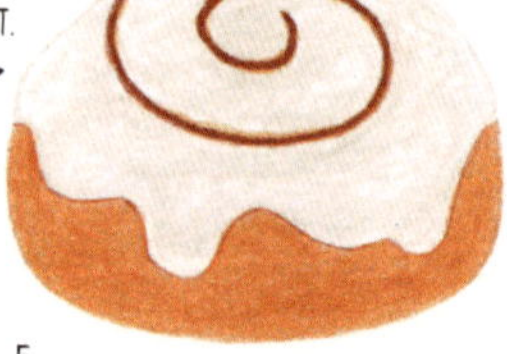

5.

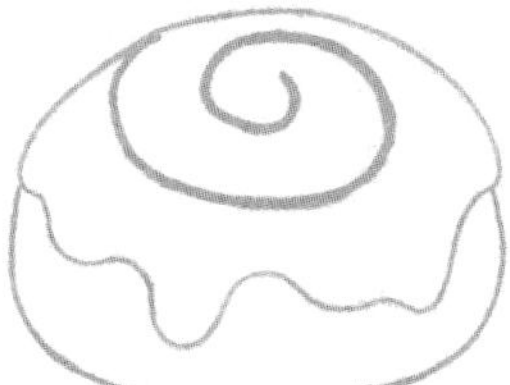

GINGERBREAD HOUSE

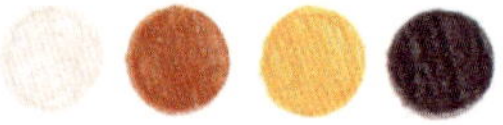

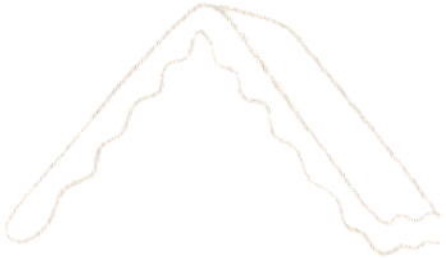

1.

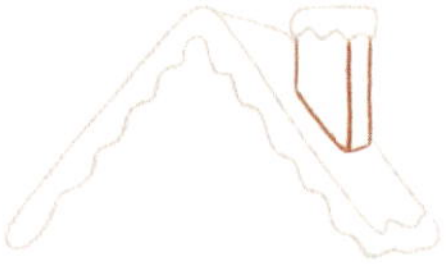

2.

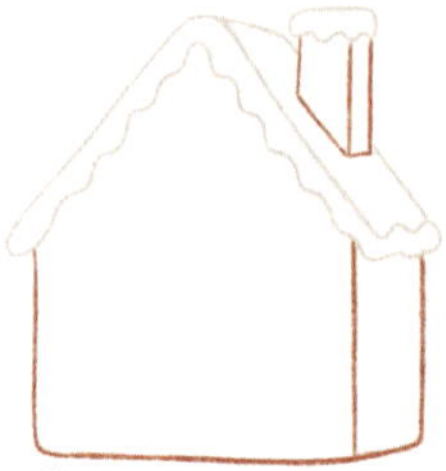

3.

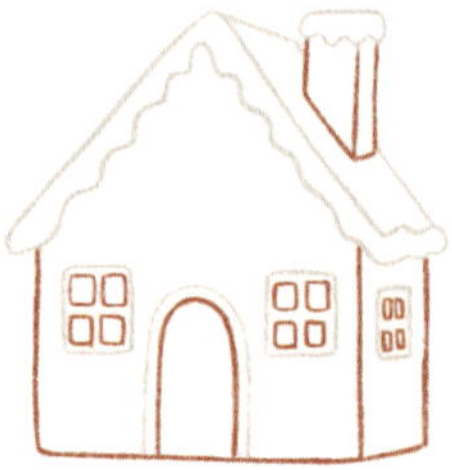

4.

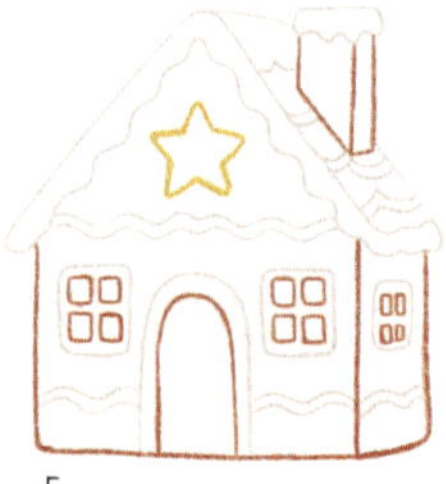

5.

6.

7.

DARK-BROWN LINES ADD DIMENSION.

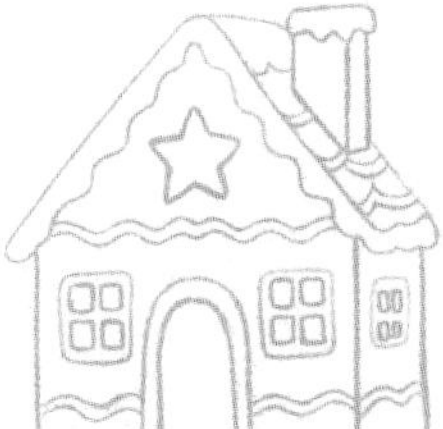

WRAPPED PRESENTS

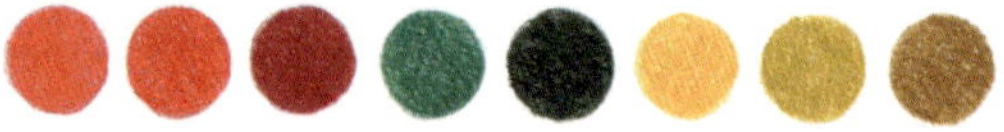

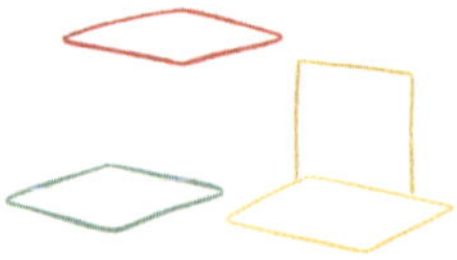

1.

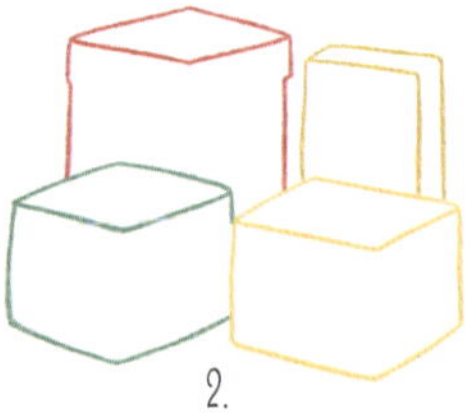

2.

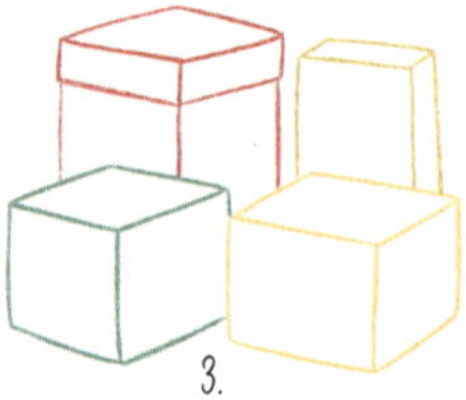

3.

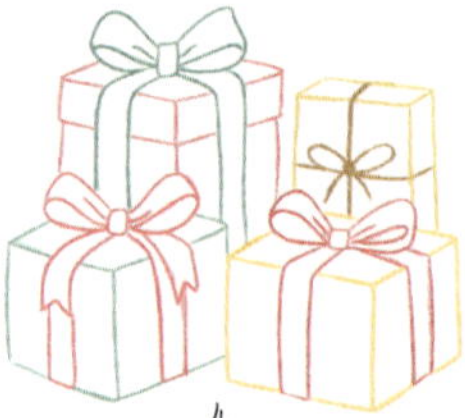

4.

ADD VERTICAL OR ANGLED SHADING TO EACH SIDE OF THE BOXES, FOLLOWING THE SHAPE, TO MAKE THE PRESENTS APPEAR MORE THREE-DIMENSIONAL.

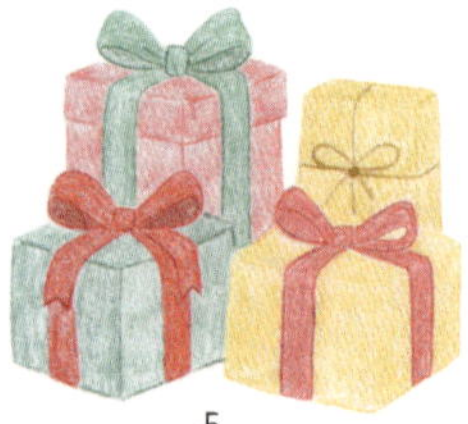

5.

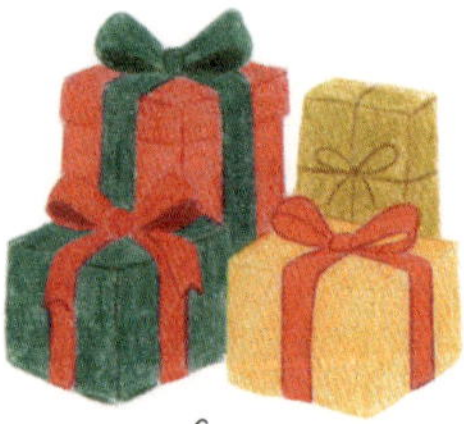

6.

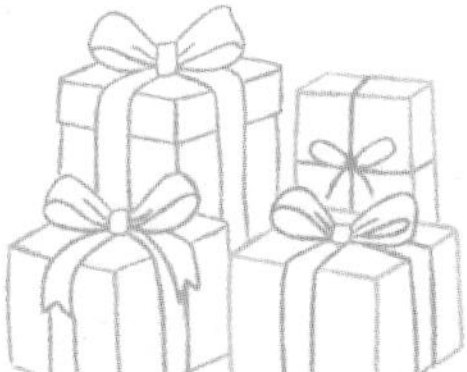

DECORATED TREE

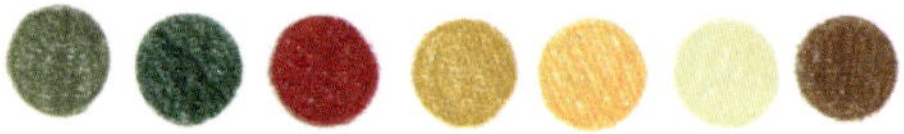

1.

2.

3.

4.

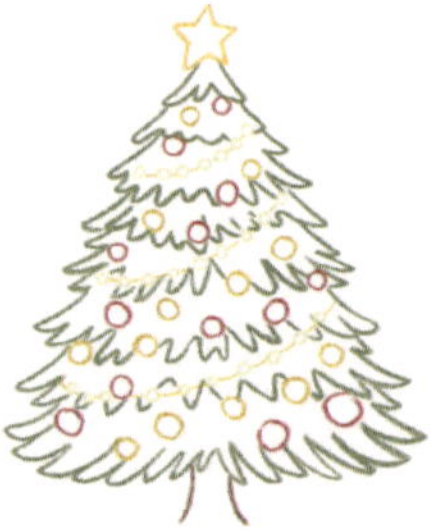

5.

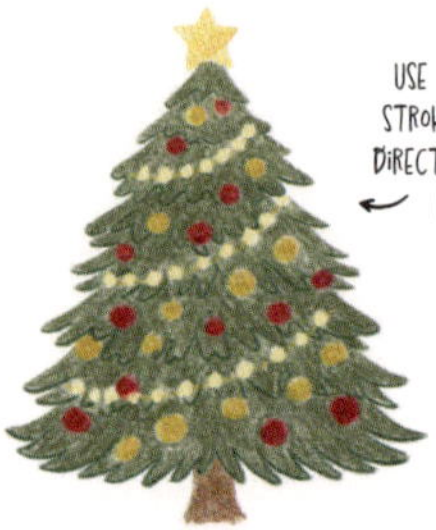

6.

USE SHORT, LAYERED STROKES IN DIFFERENT DIRECTIONS TO FILL OUT EACH LAYER.

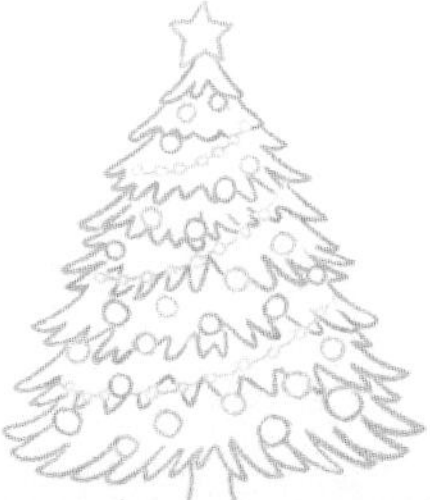

VINTAGE LANTERN

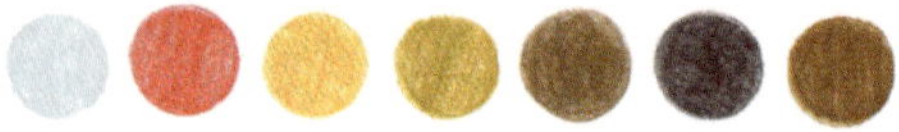

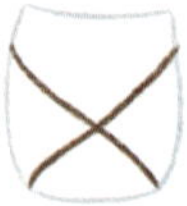

1.

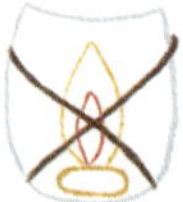

2.

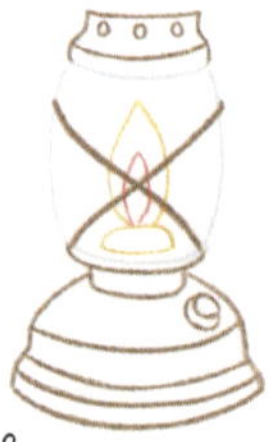

3.

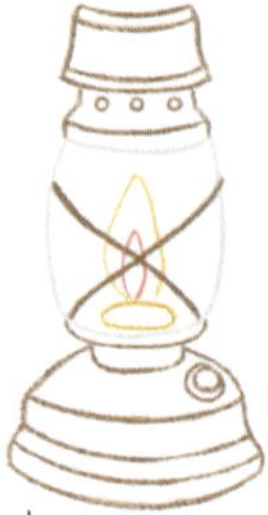

4.

5.

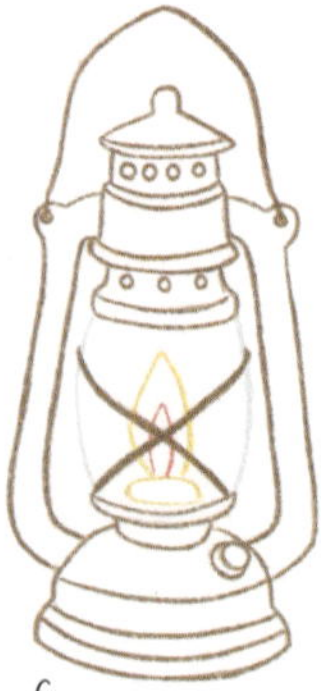

6.

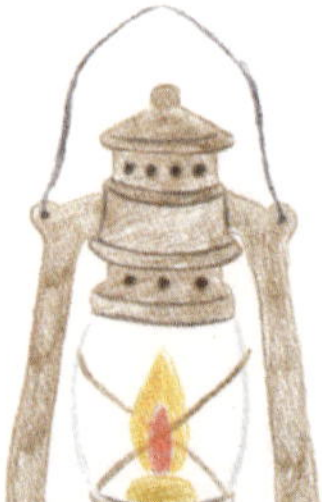

7.

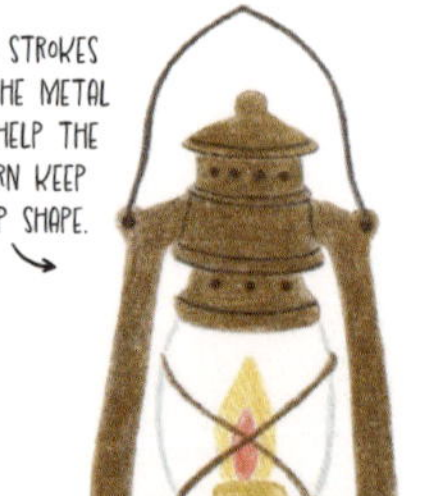

8.

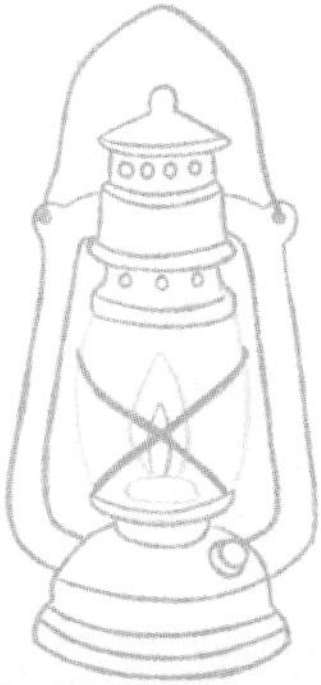

PYJAMAS

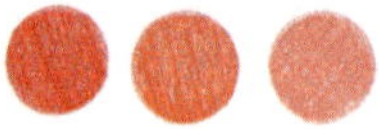

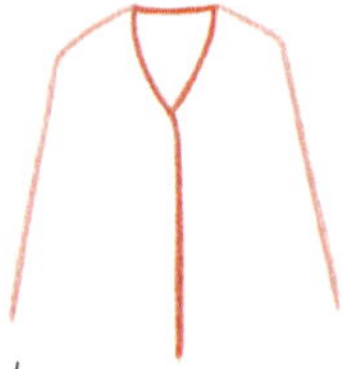

1.

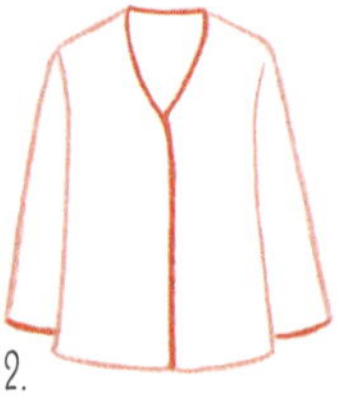

2.

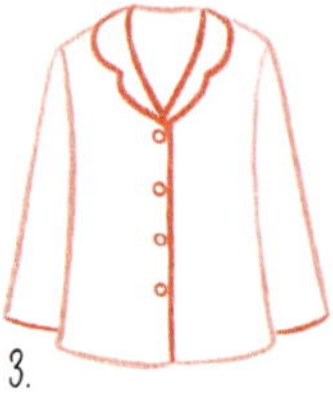

3.

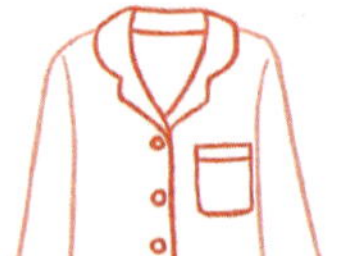

4.

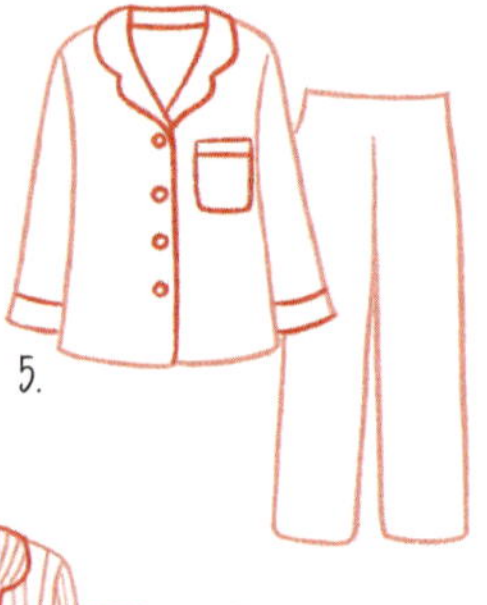

5.

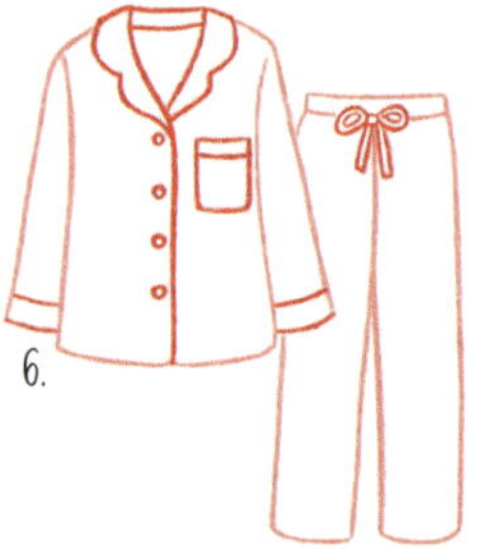

6.

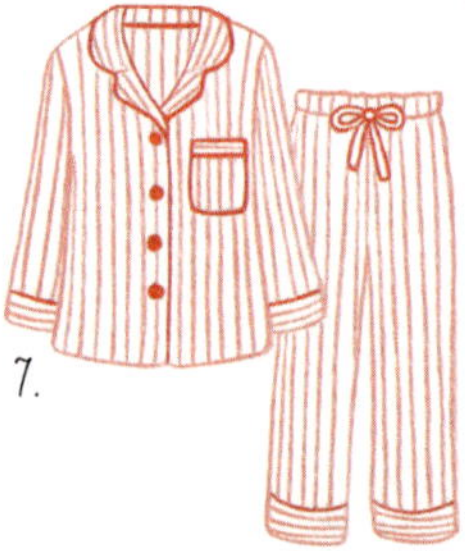

7.

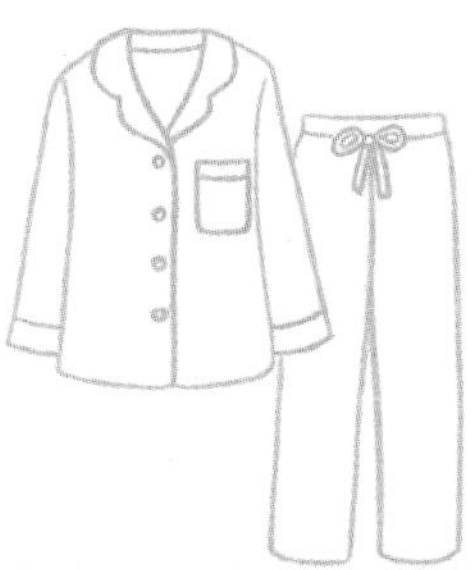

STACK OF SWEATERS

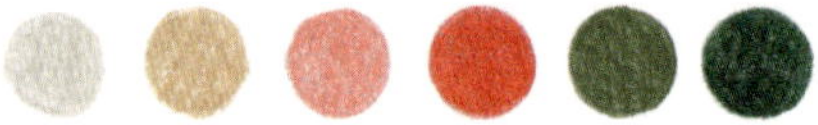

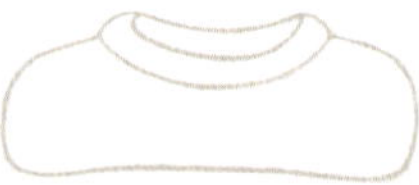

1.

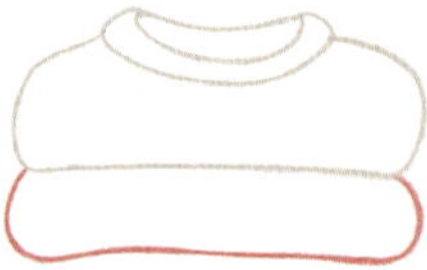

2.

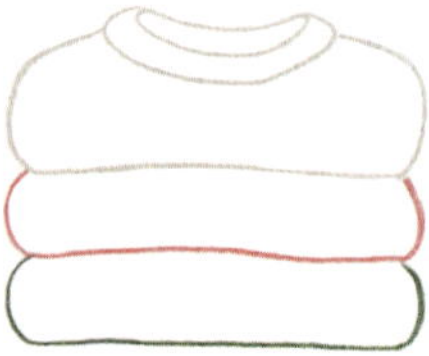

3.

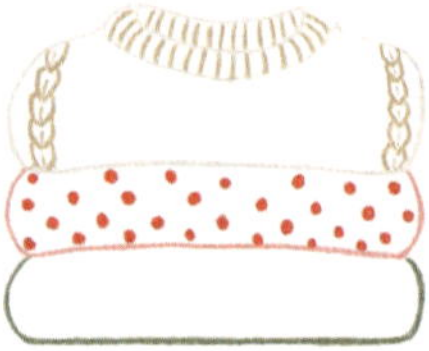

4.

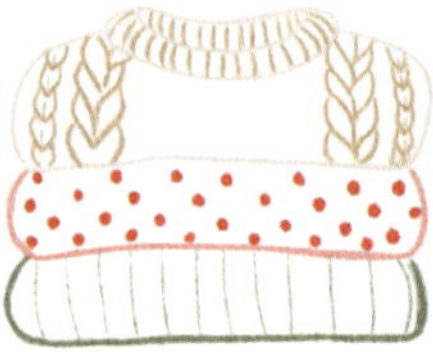

5.

ADD TINY IRREGULARITIES TO THE KNIT TEXTURE, THOSE IMPERFECT STITCHES MAKE THE STACK LOOK COZY AND HANDMADE.

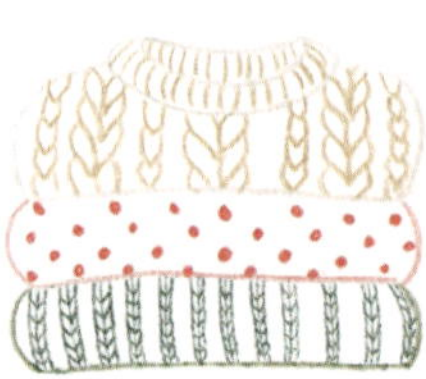

6.

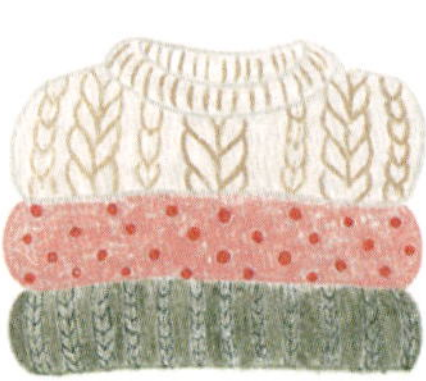

7.

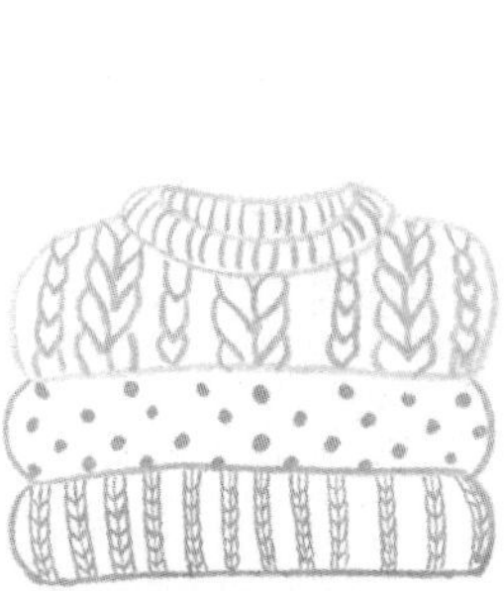

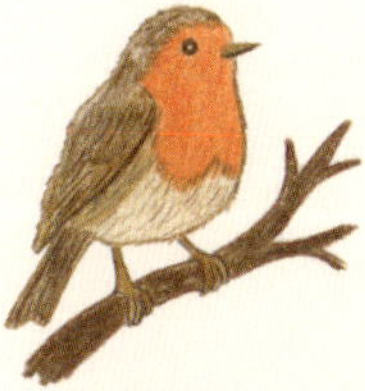

COZY SCENES

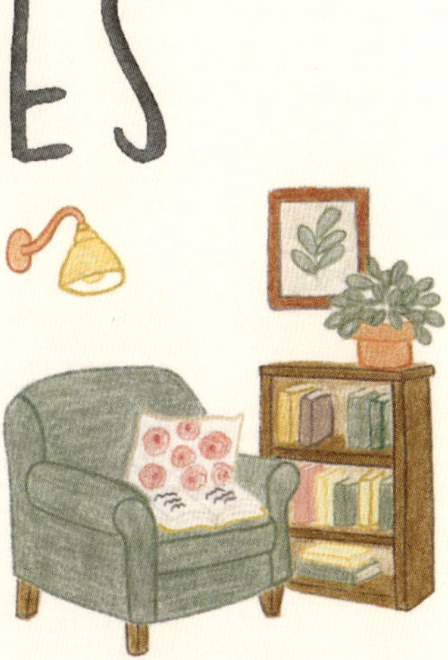

READING NOOK

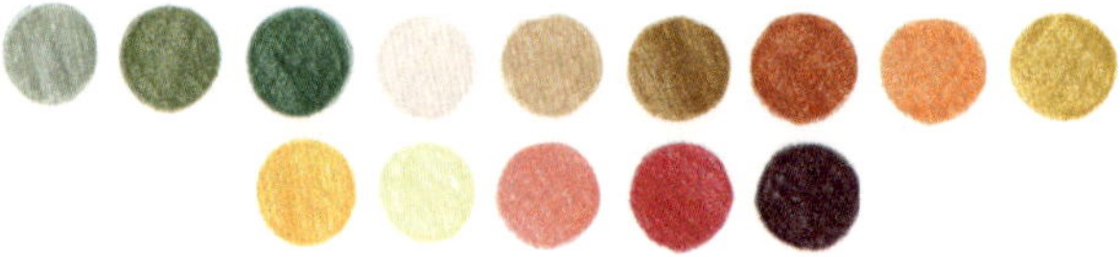

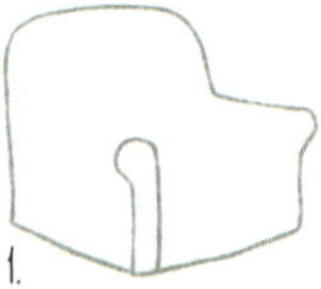

1.

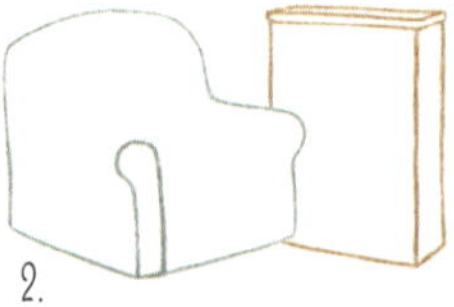

2.

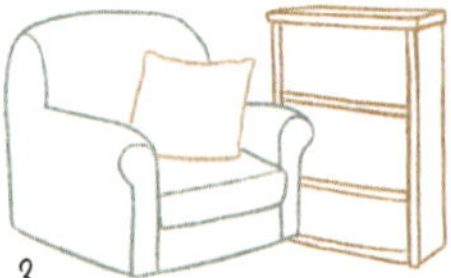

3.

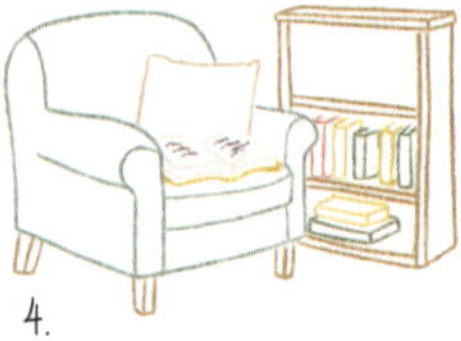

4.

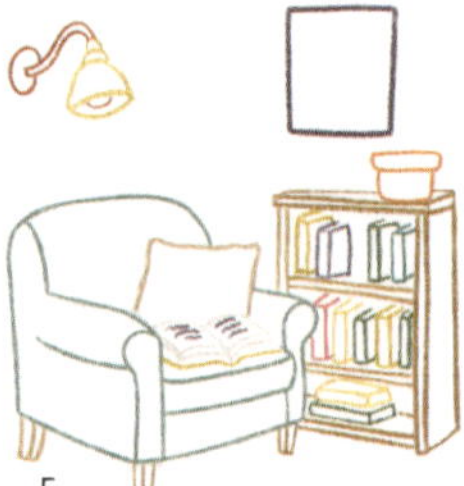

5.

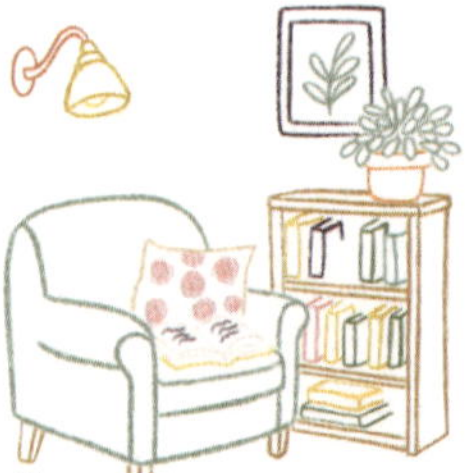

6.

7.

LAYER THE SHADING FOLLOWING THE CURVES OF THE ARMCHAIR AND THE VERTICAL LINES OF THE BOOKSHELF TO ADD SUBTLE DIMENSION.

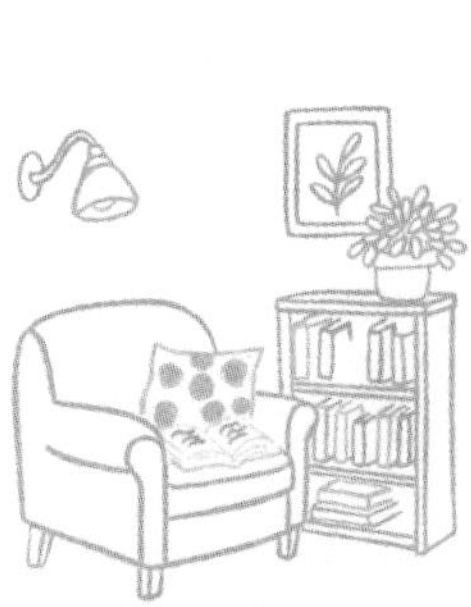

KiTCHEN SHELF

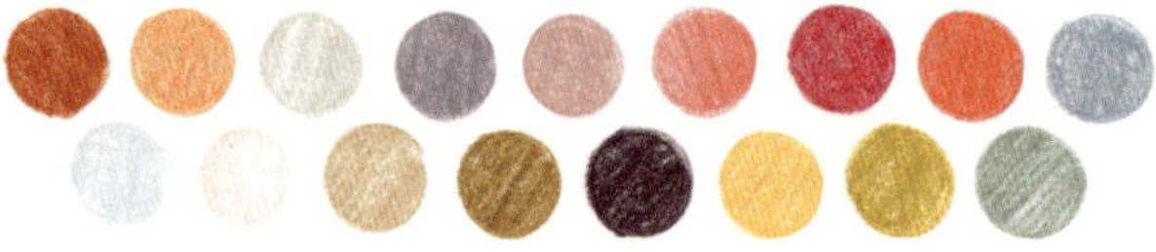

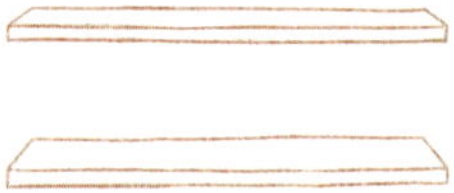

1.

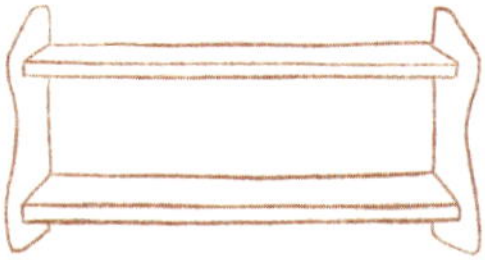

2.

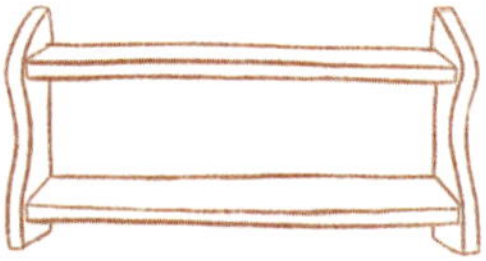

3.

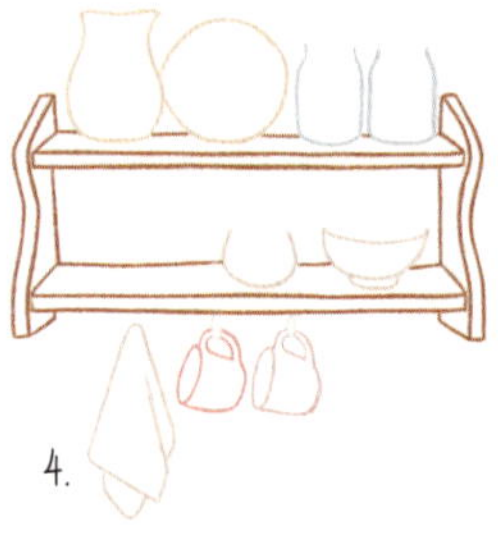

4.

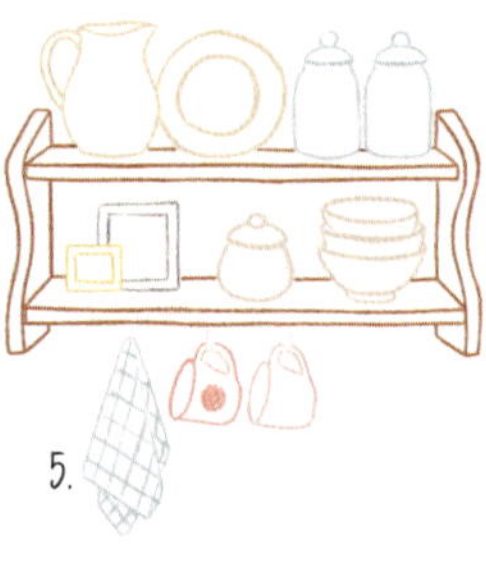

5.

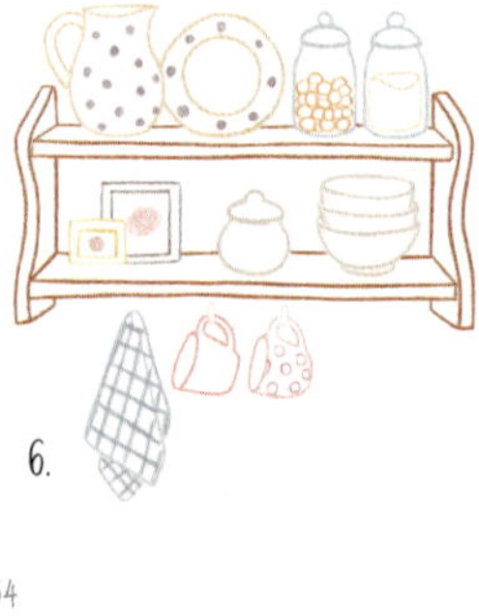

6.

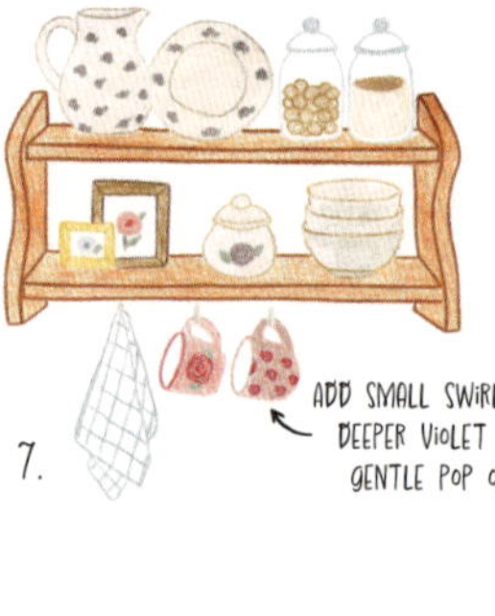

7.

ADD SMALL SWIRLS WITH THE DEEPER VIOLET TO GIVE A GENTLE POP OF DETAIL.

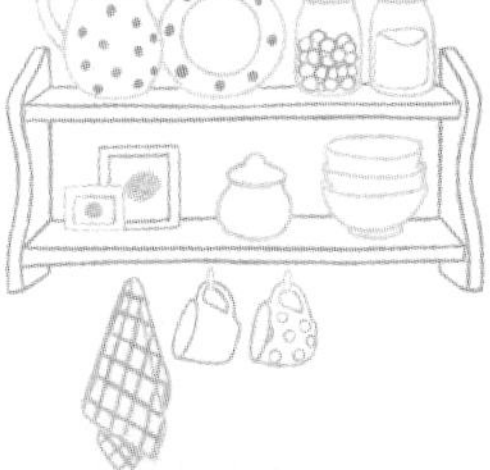

JOURNAL TIME

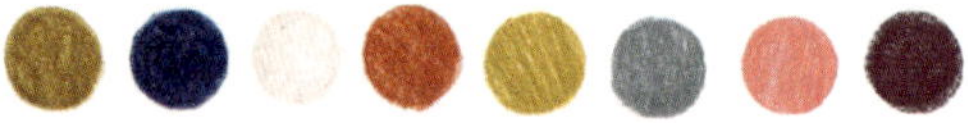

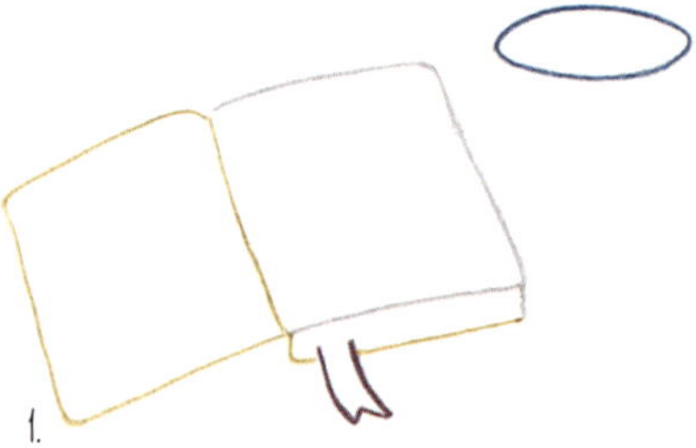

1.

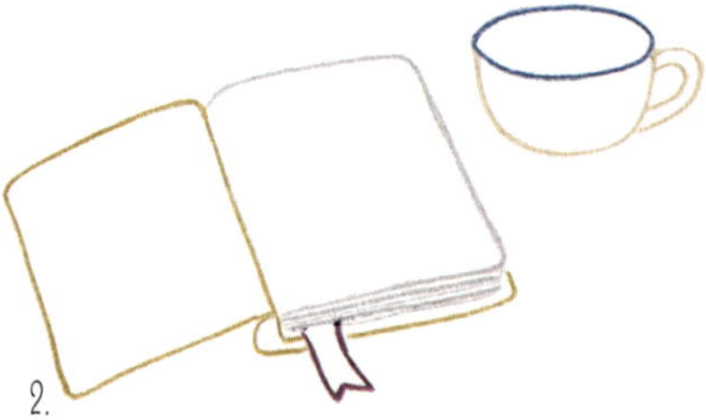

2.

3.

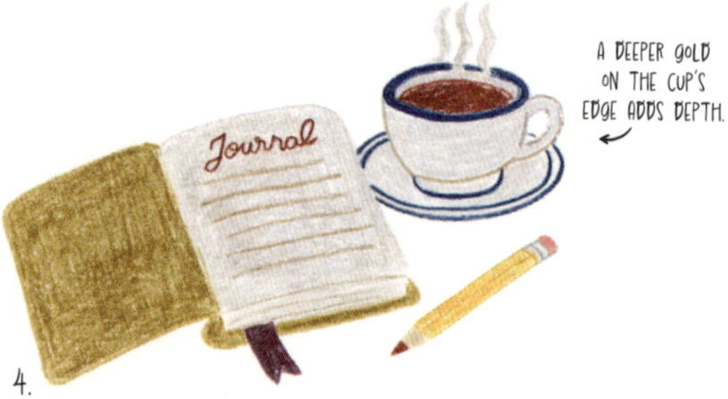

4.

Journal

BEDROOM WINDOW

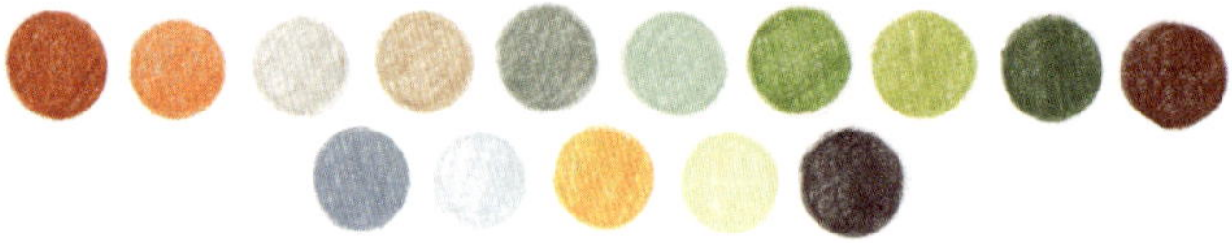

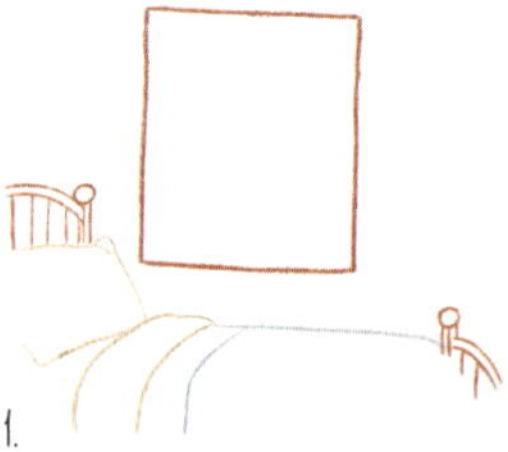

1.

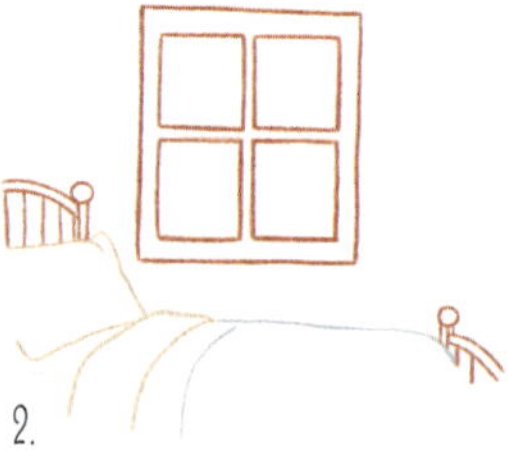

2.

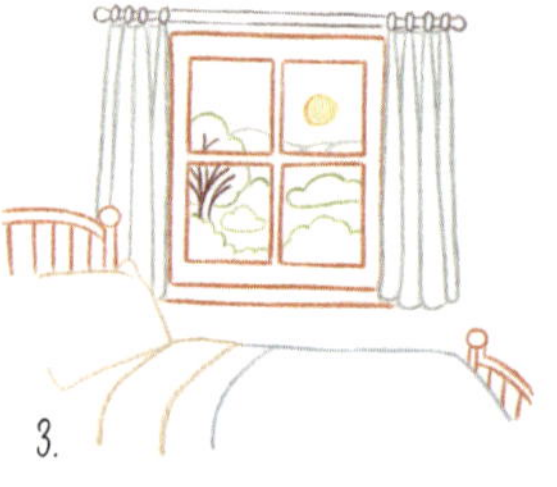

3.

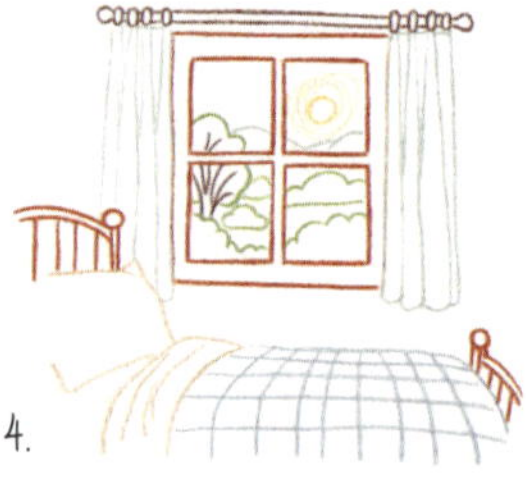

4.

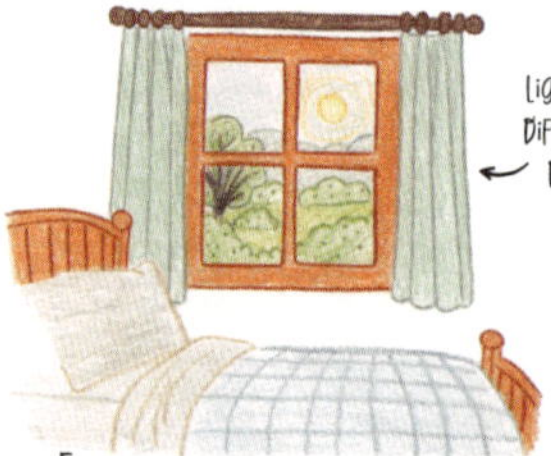

LIGHTLY LAYER THE GREENS IN DIFFERENT DIRECTIONS WITHOUT DRAWING ATTENTION AWAY FROM THE ROOM.

5.

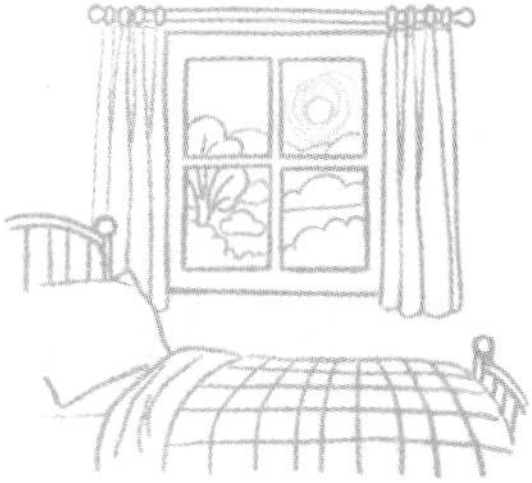

SKETCHBOOK

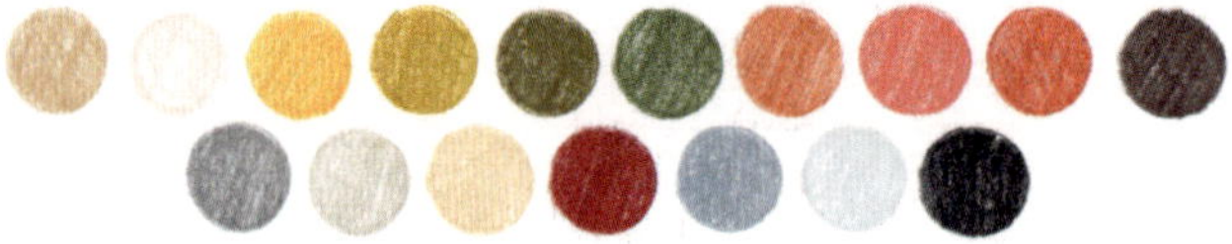

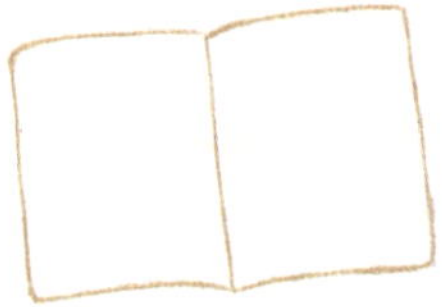

1.

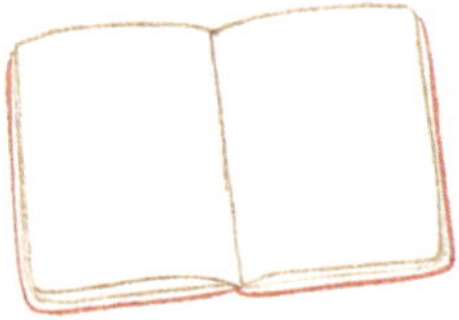

2.

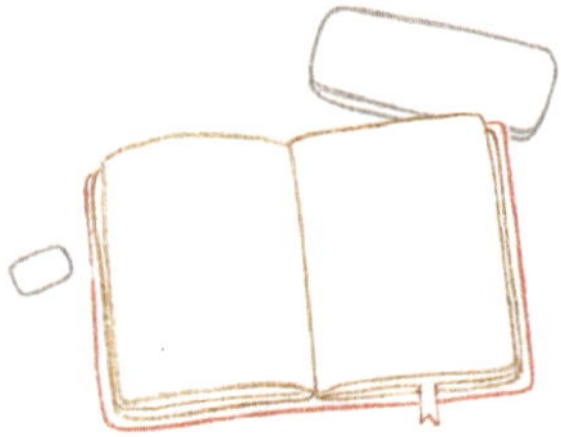

3.

4.

5.

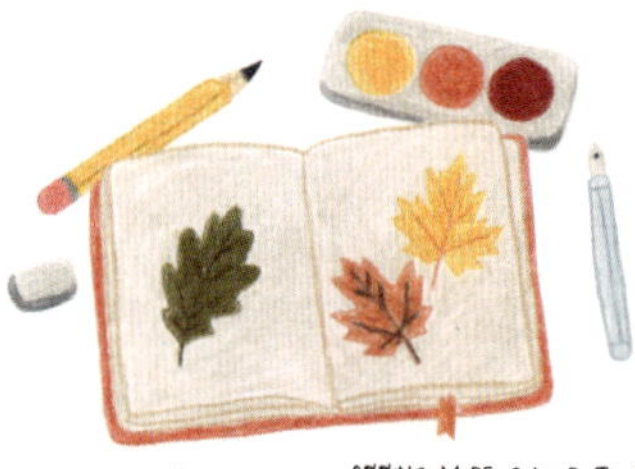

6.

ADDING MORE COLOUR TO THE LEAF EDGES MAKES THEM STAND OUT SOFTLY FROM THE PAPER.

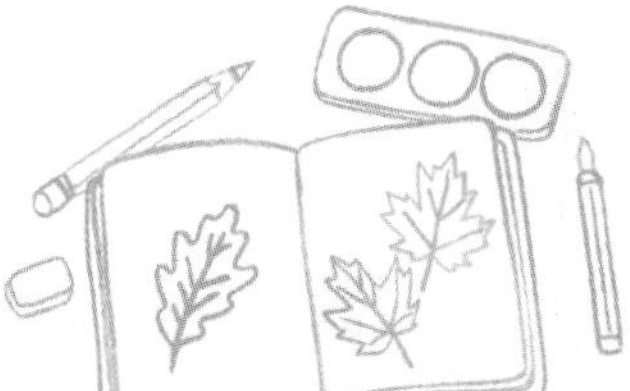

FiREPLACE

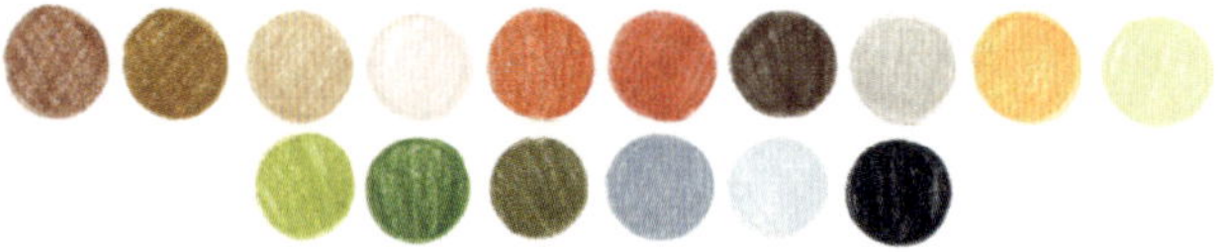

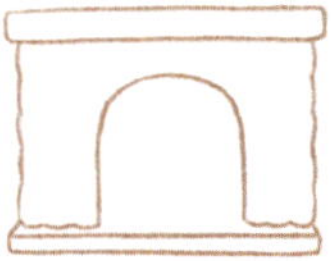

1.

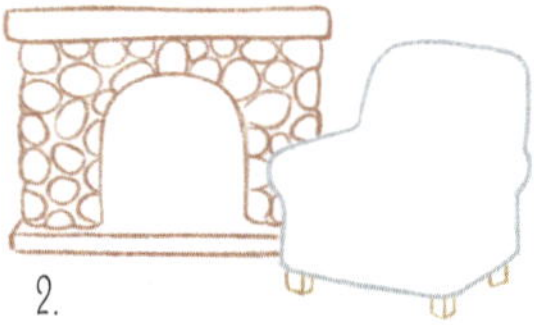

2.

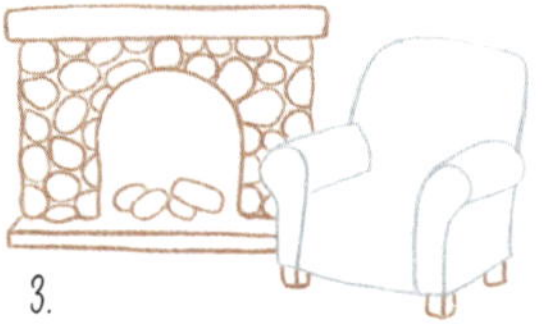

3.

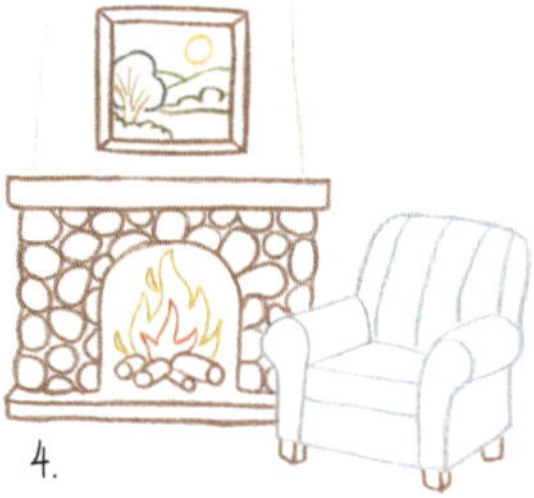

4.

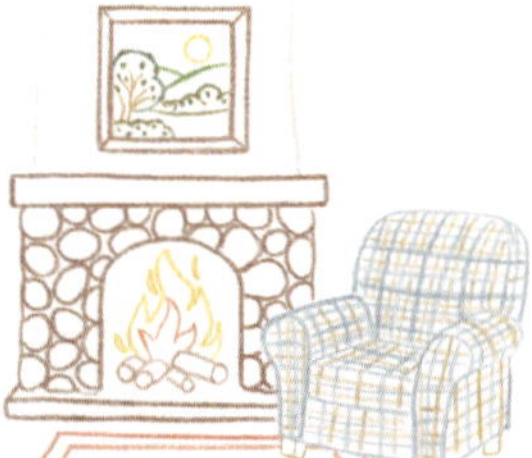

5.

DEEPEN A FEW STONES iN THE FiREPLACE WiTH AN EXTRA LAYER OF BROWN SHADiNG.

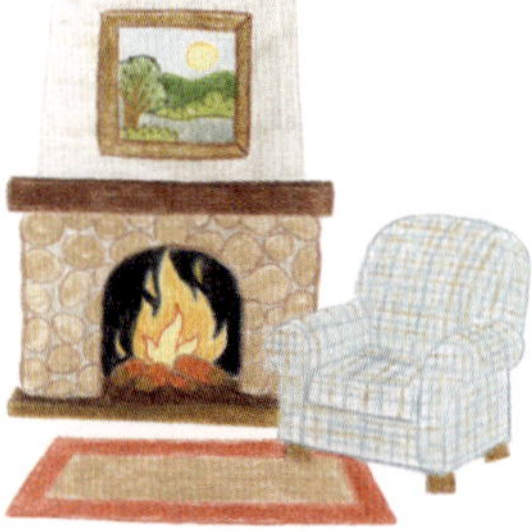

6.

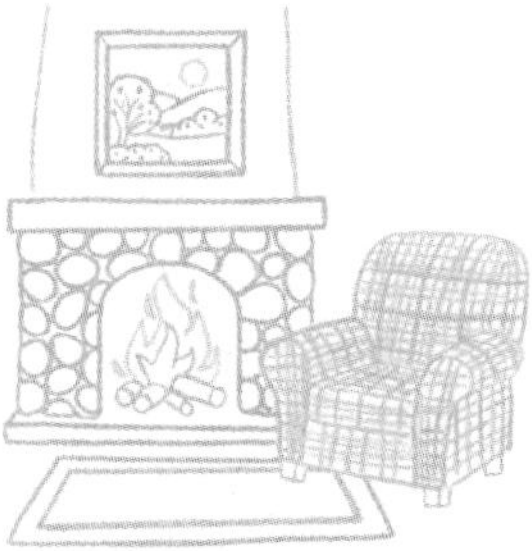

LITTLE COTTAGE

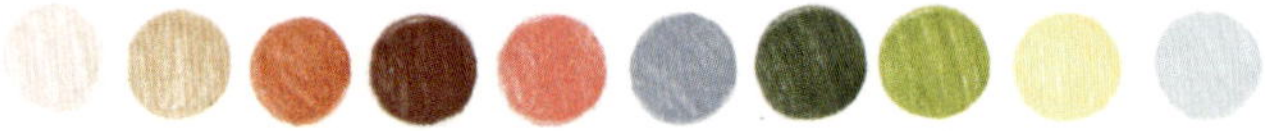

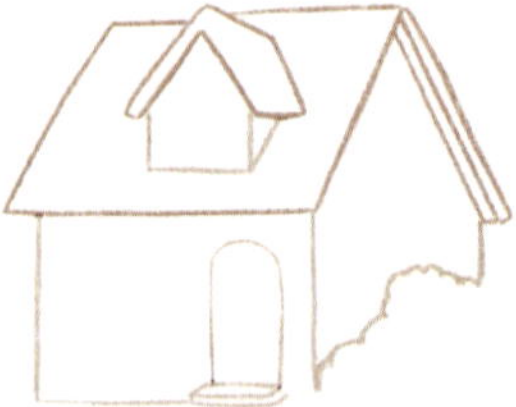

1.

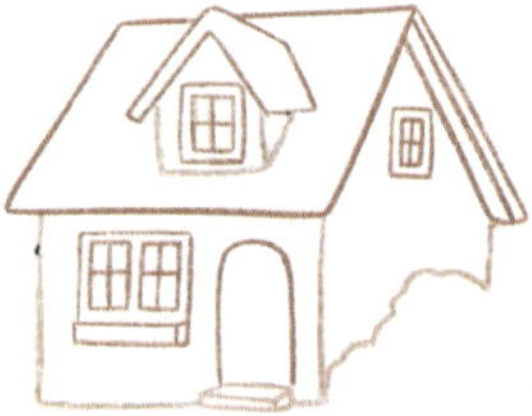

2.

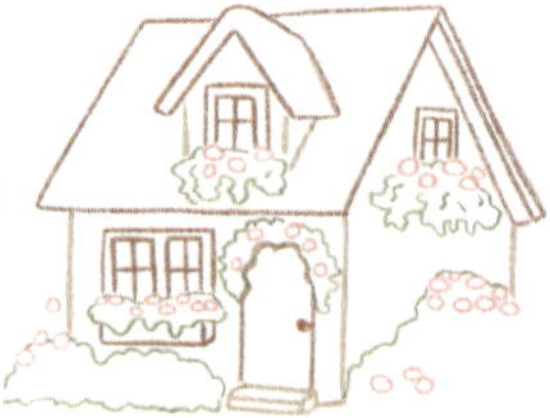

3.

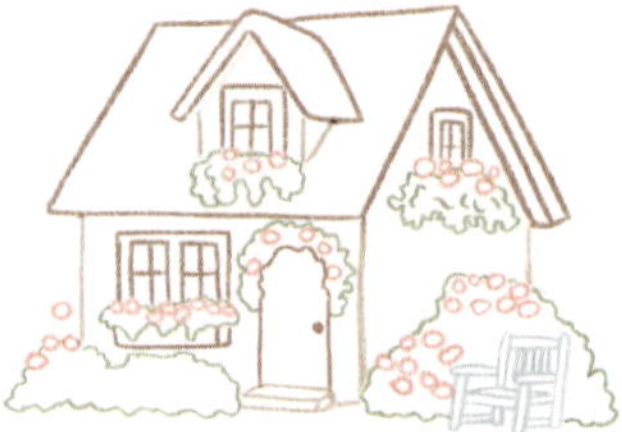

4.

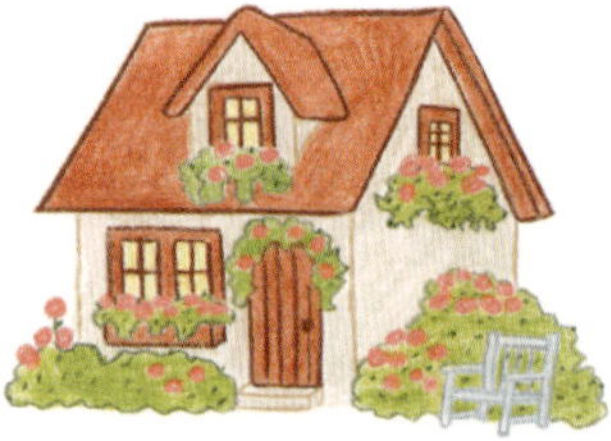

5.

LIGHT TOUCHES OF THE DARKER GREEN INSIDE THE BUSHES AND VINES SUBTLY DEEPENS THE GREENERY.

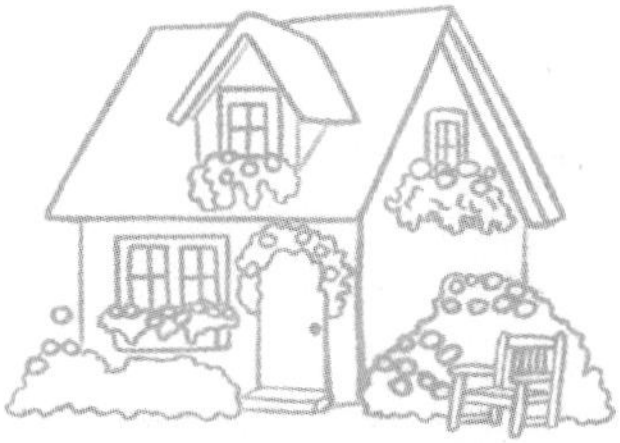

ROBIN ON A BRANCH

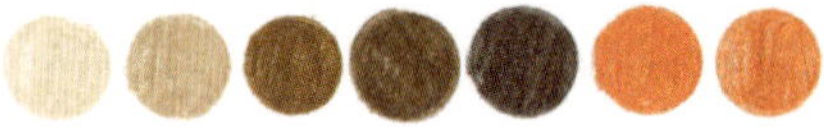

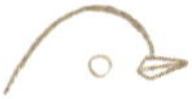

1.

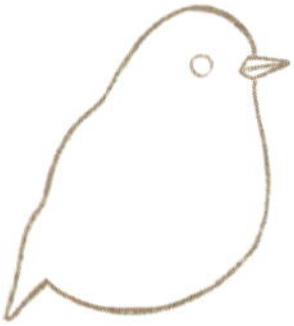

2.

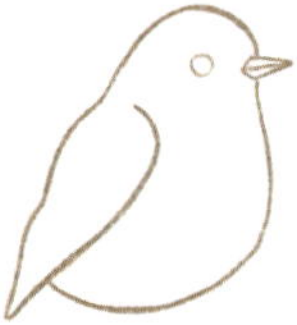

3.

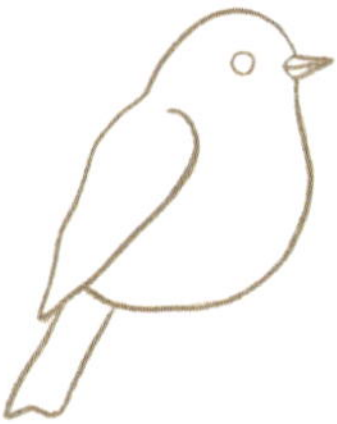

4.

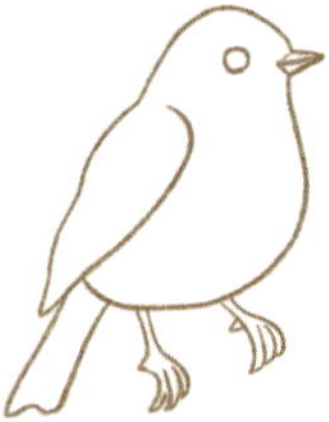

5.

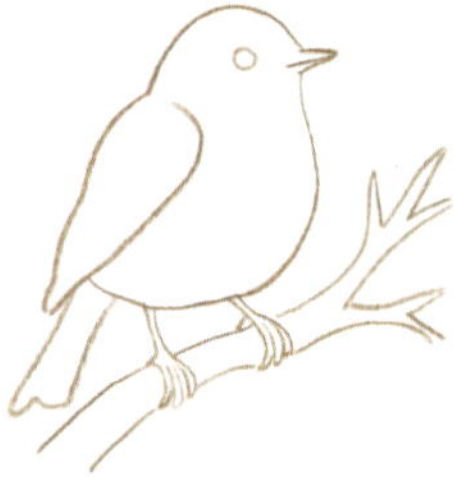

6.

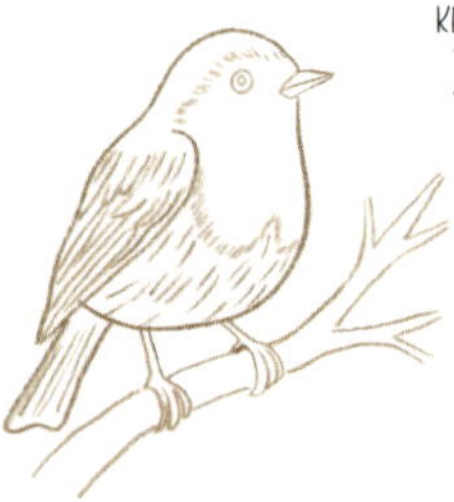

7.

KEEP THE STROKES ON THE WING POINTING TOWARDS THE TAIL.

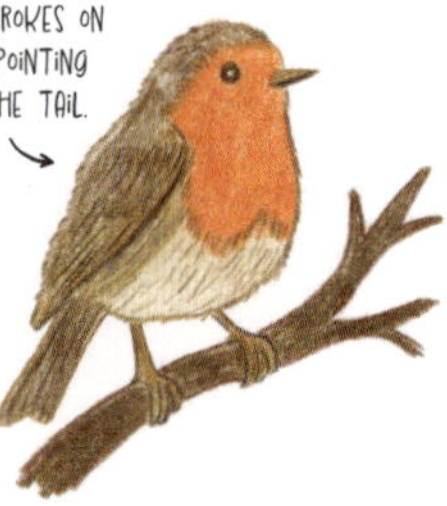

8.

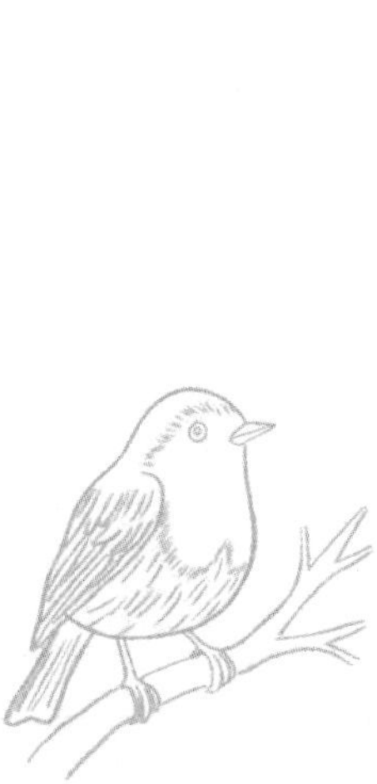

BADGER DRINKING TEA

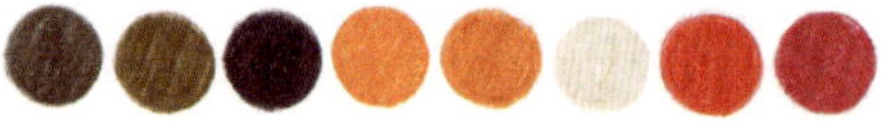

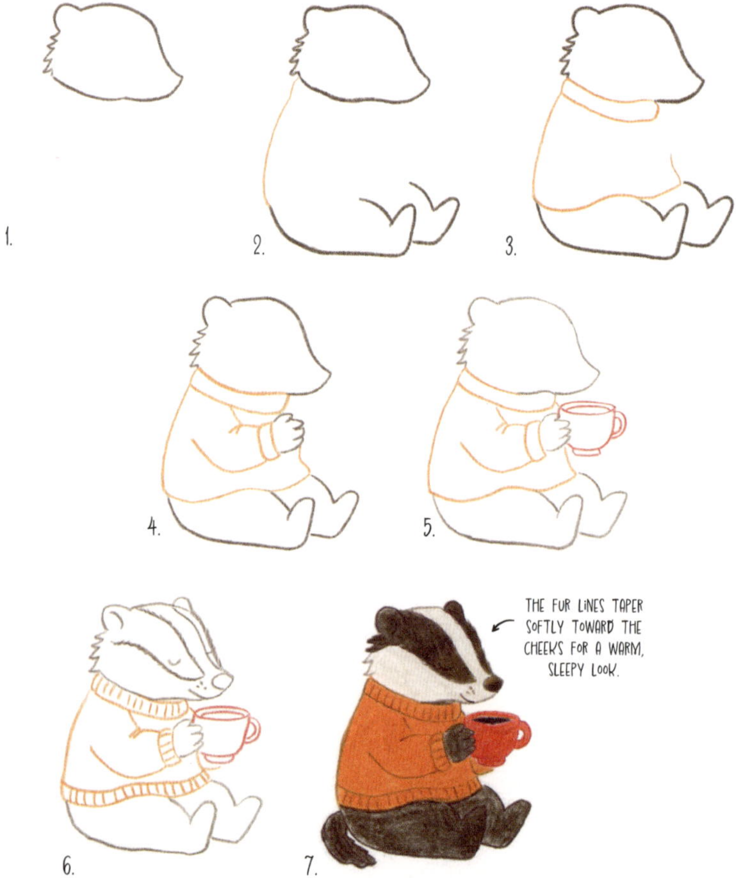

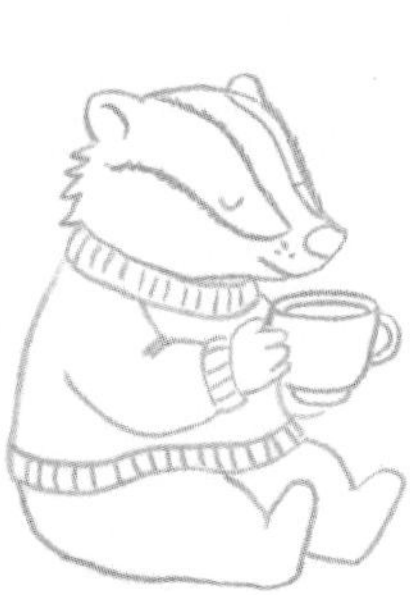

BUBBLE BATH

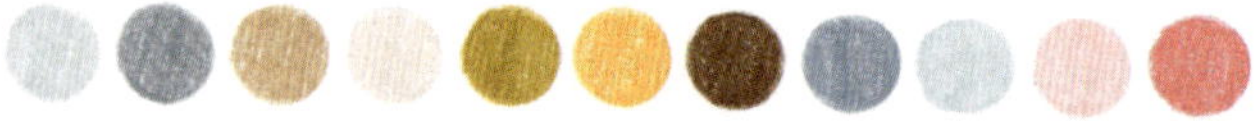

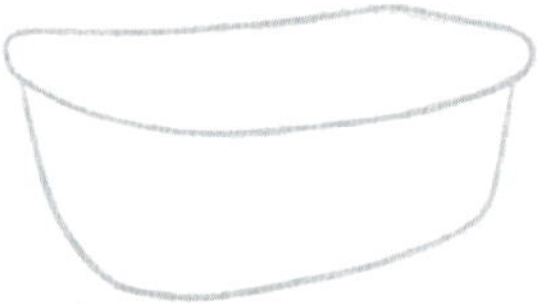

1.

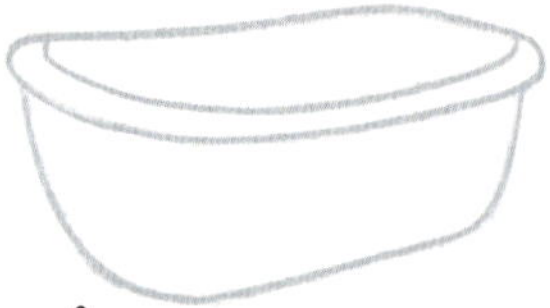

2.

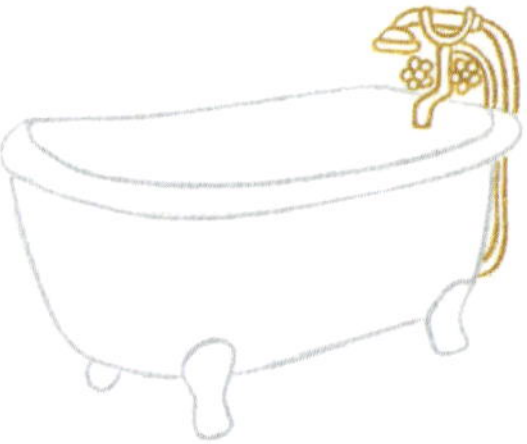

3.

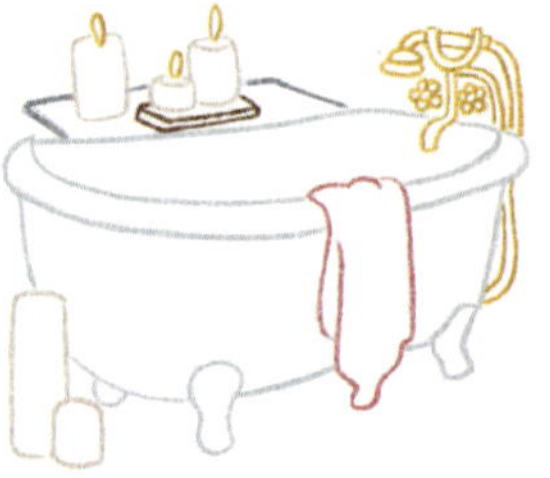

4.

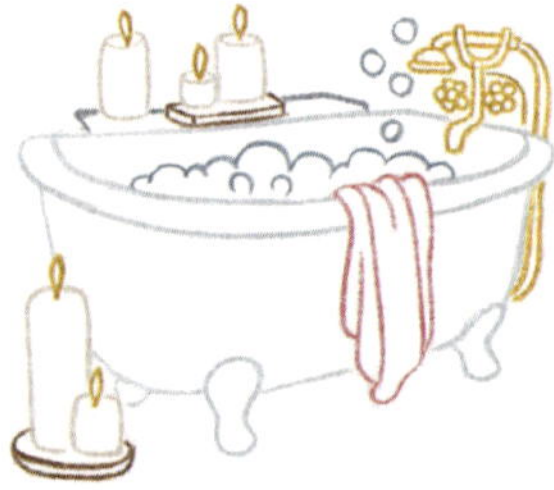

5.

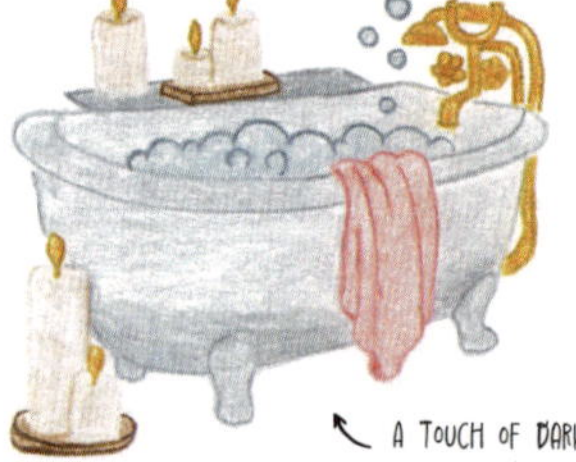

6.

A TOUCH OF DARKER GREY RIGHT UNDER THE TUB'S CURVE ADDS INSTANT DEPTH WITHOUT OVERPOWERING THE SOFT PALETTE.

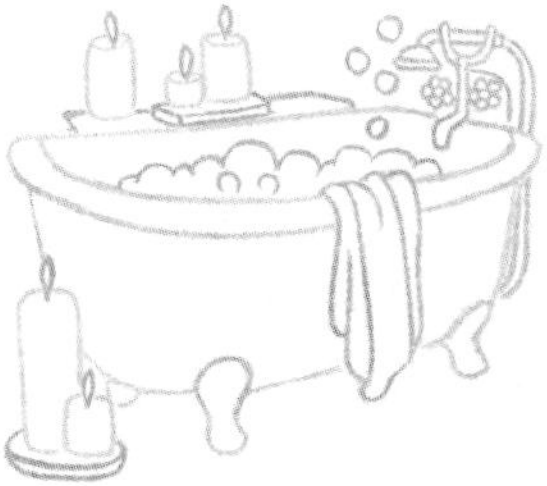

Hiking Badger

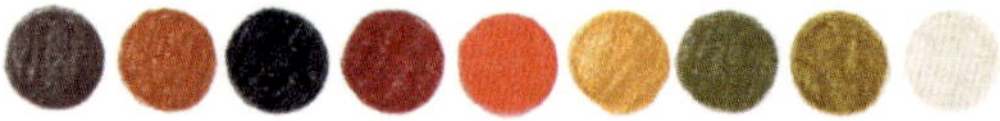

1.

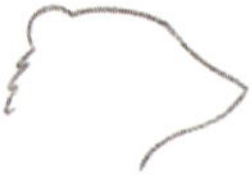

2.

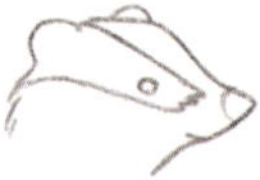

3.

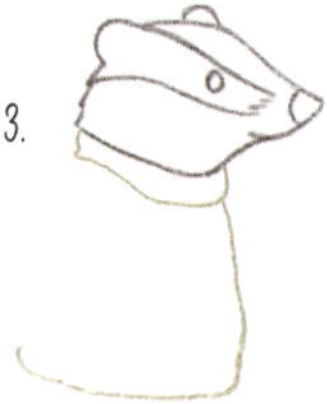

4.

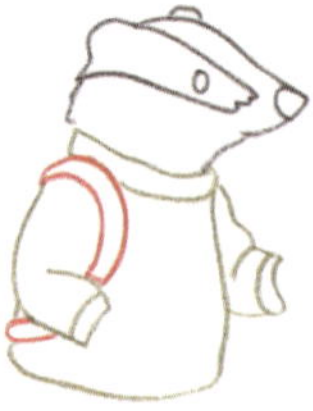

5.

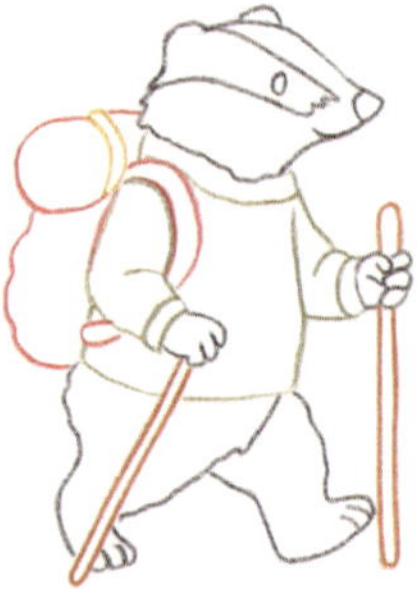

6.

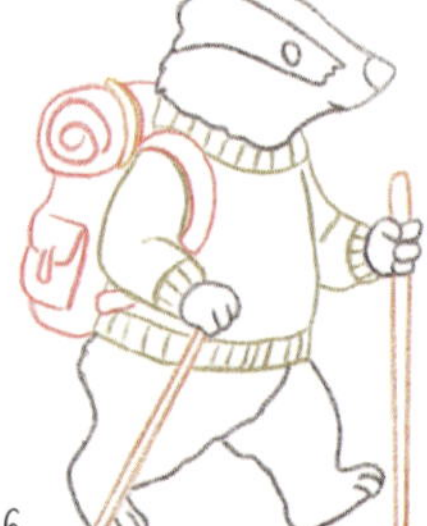

7.

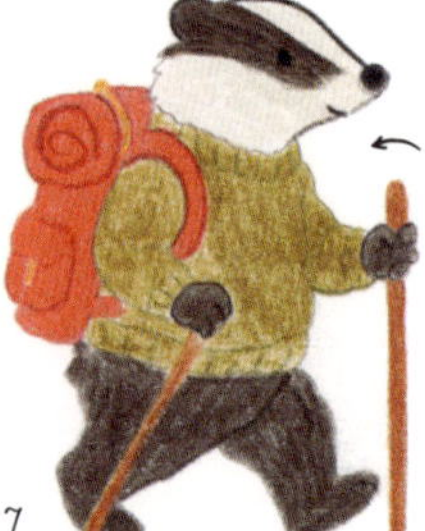

FILL THE SWEATER WITH TINY OVERLAPPING STROKES INSTEAD OF SOLID COLOUR TO GIVE A KNITTED TEXTURE.

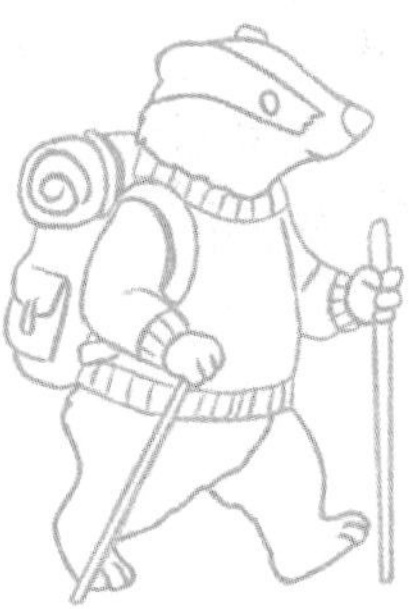

ART SUPPLIES

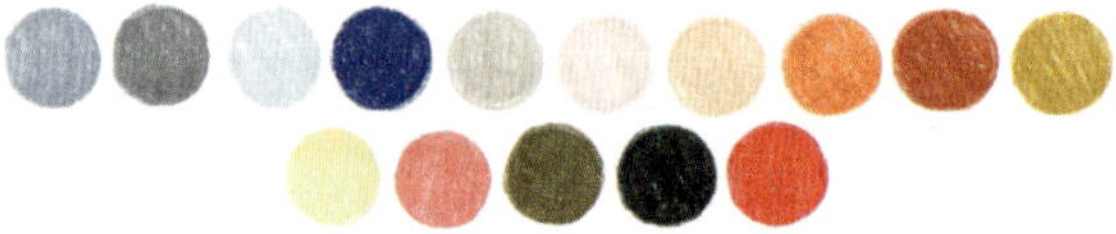

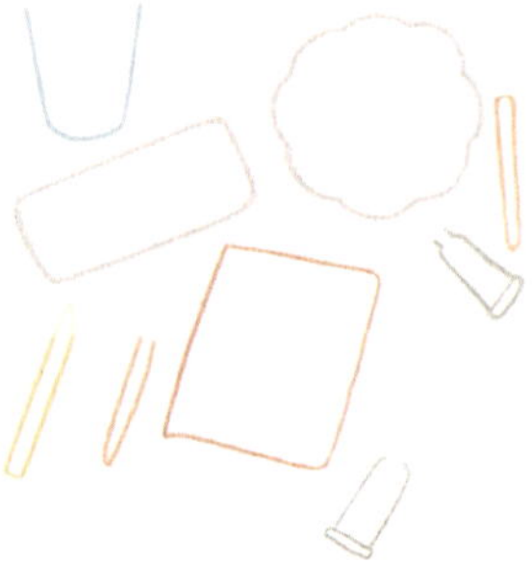

1.

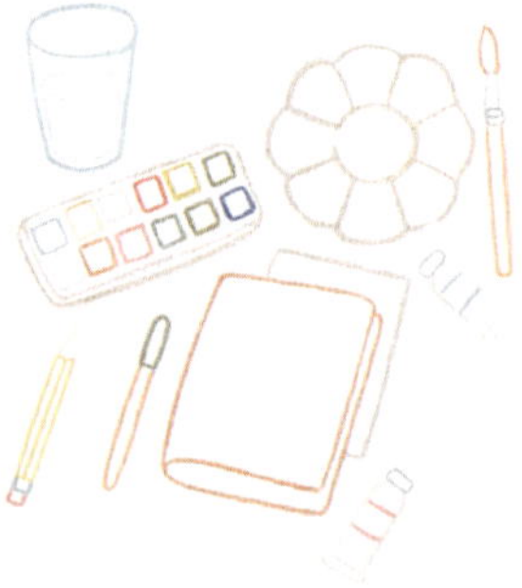

2.

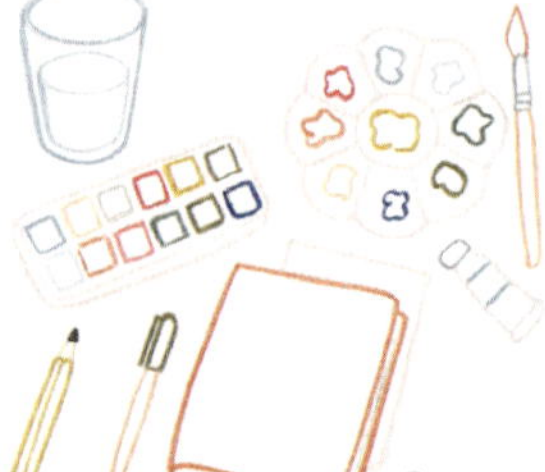

3.

SHADE THE WATER DARKER AT THE TOP AND LET IT SOFTEN TOWARD THE BOTTOM.

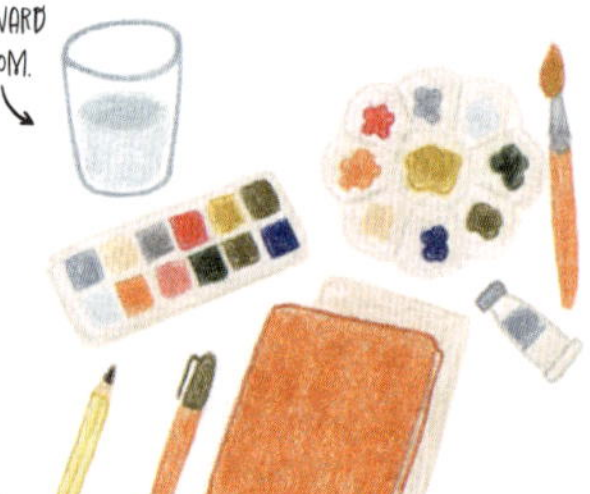

4.

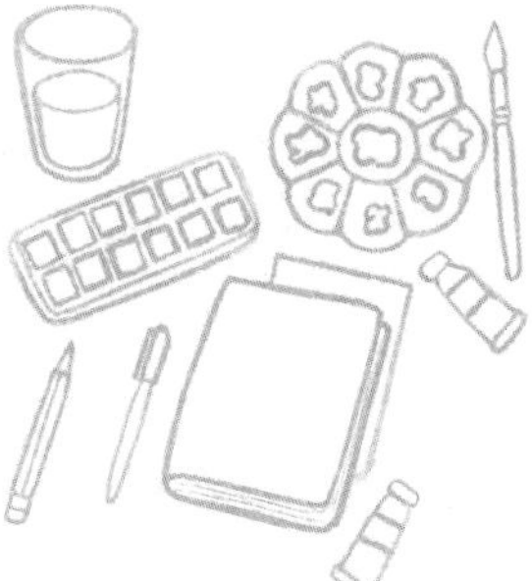

GARDENING HEDGEHOG

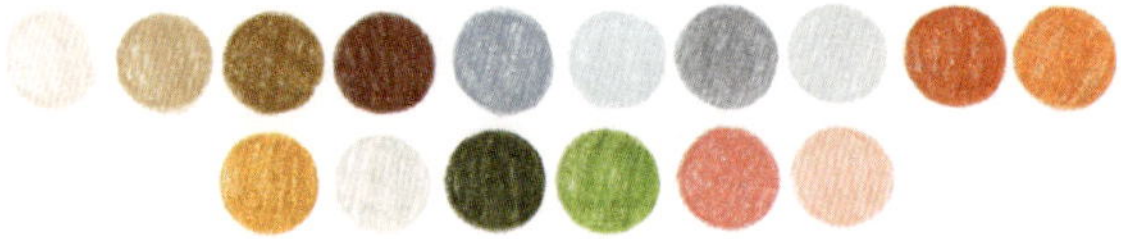

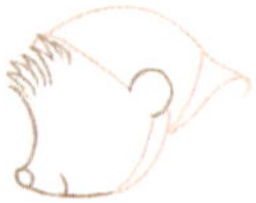

1.

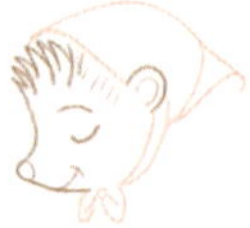

2.

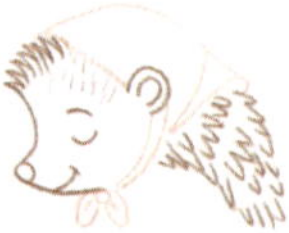

3.

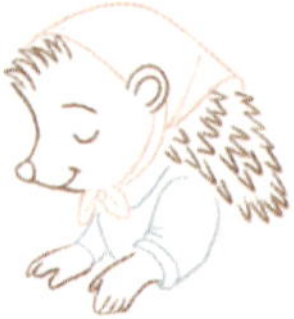

4.

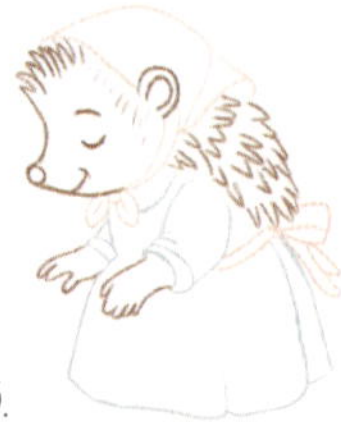

5.

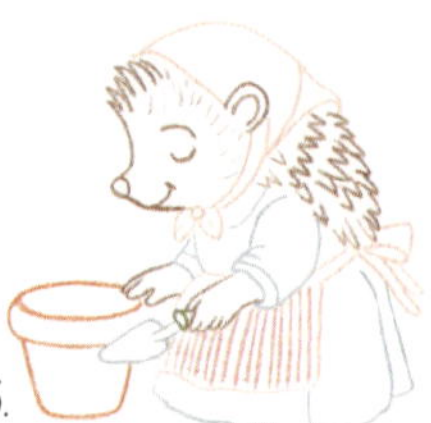

6.

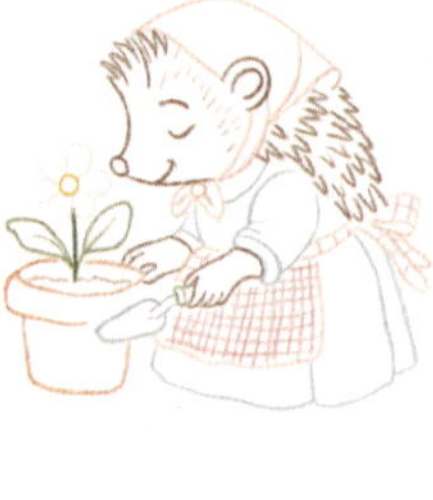

7.

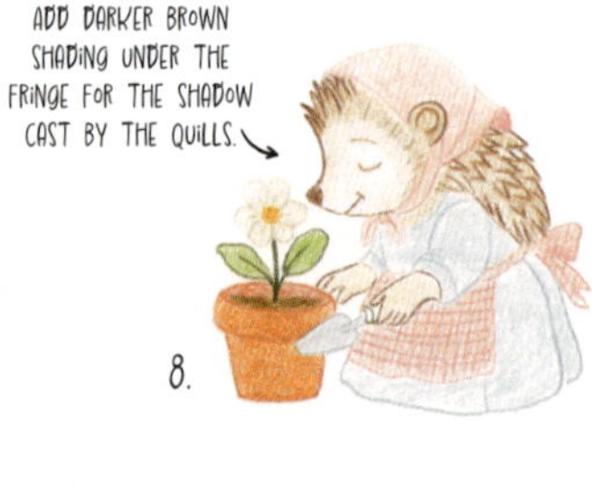

8.

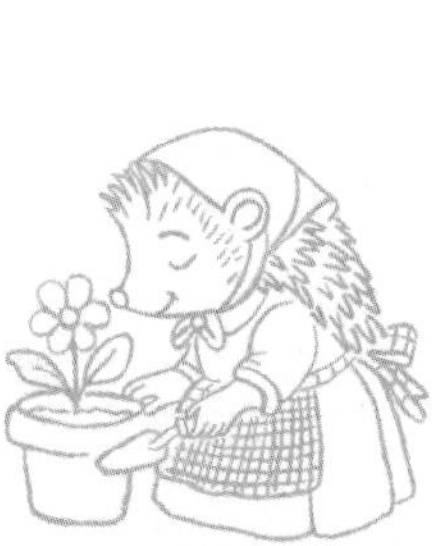

RABBIT WITH A PIE

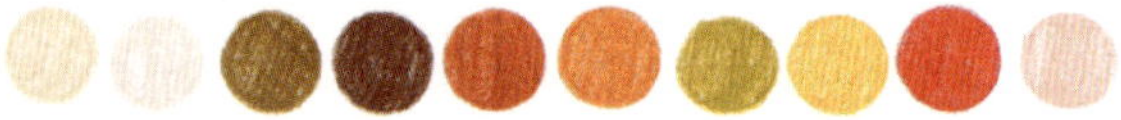

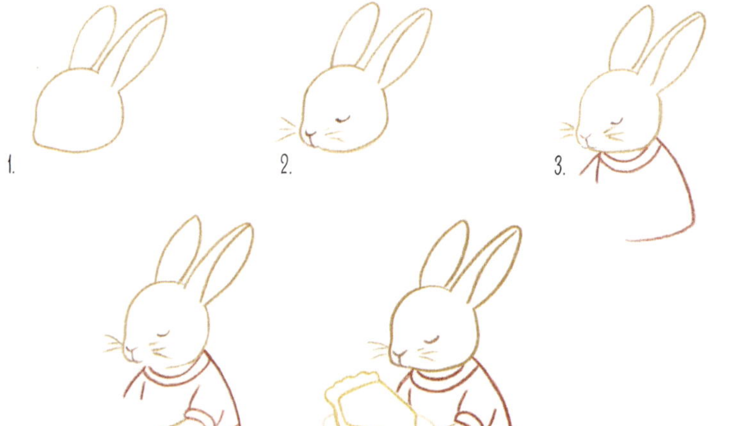

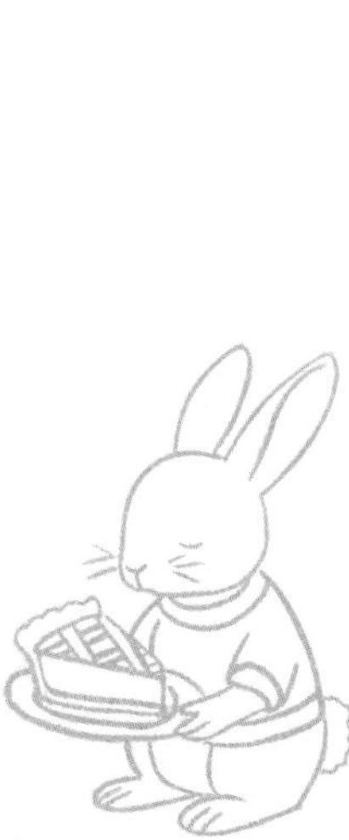

DUCK WITH UMBRELLA

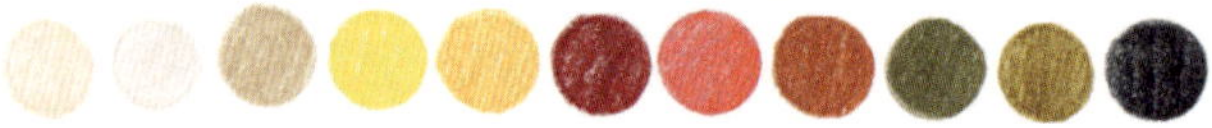

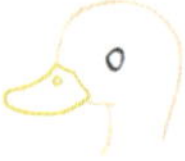

1.

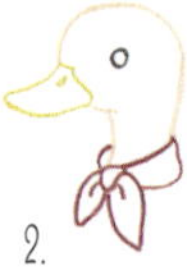

2.

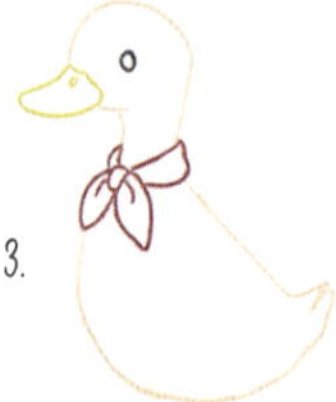

3.

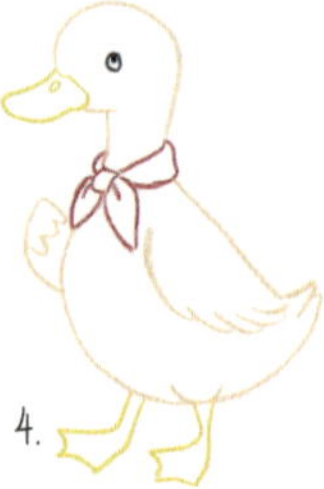

4.

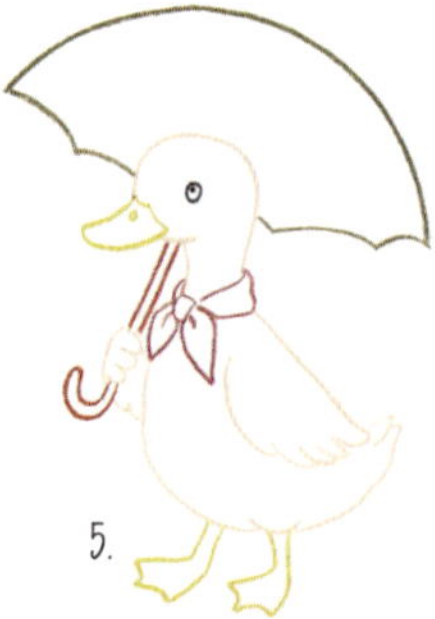

5.

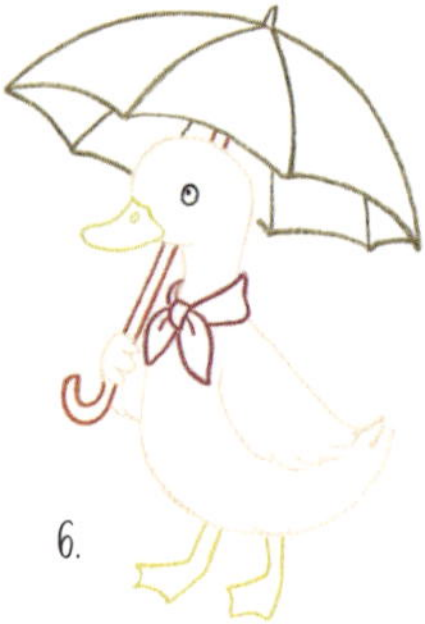

6.

USE MORE PRESSURE ALONG THE RIBS AND EDGES OF THE PANELS SO THE UMBRELLA LOOKS CURVED.

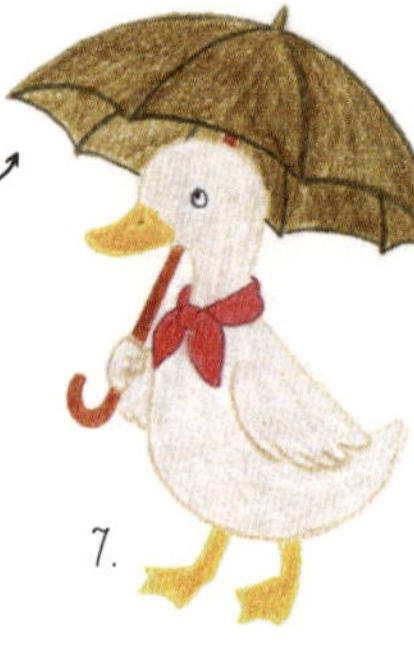

7.

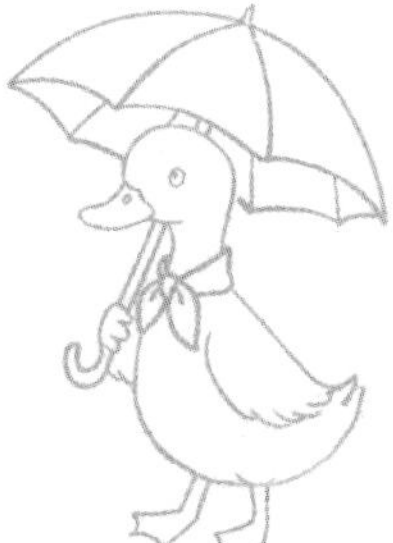

MUSHROOM PICKING

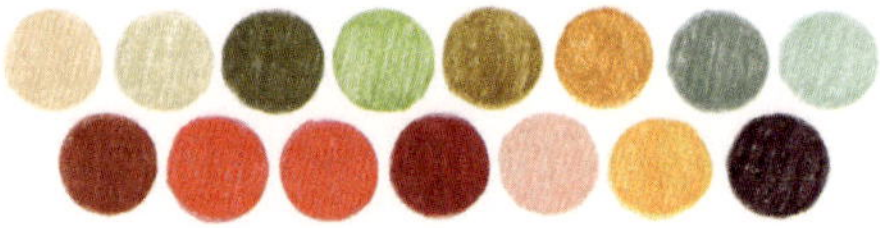

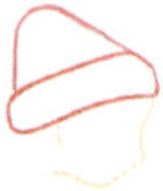

1.

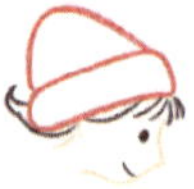

2.

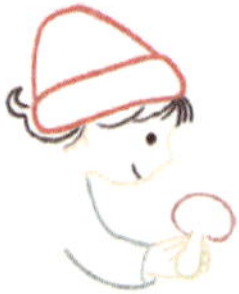

3.

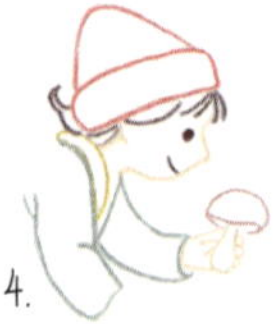

4.

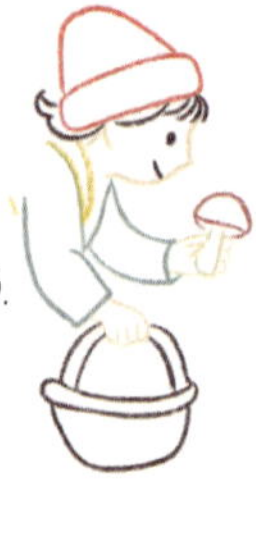

5.

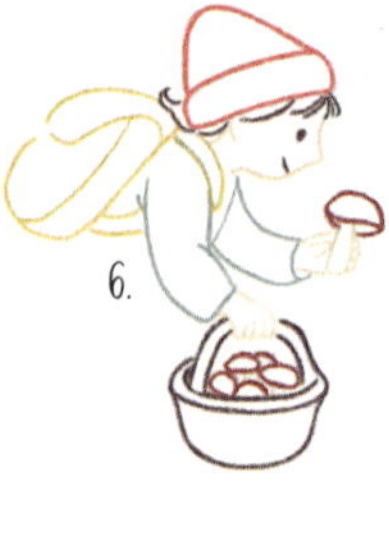

6.

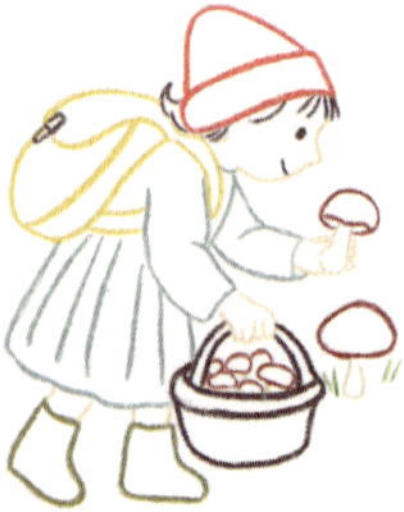

7.

USE DARKER VERTICAL STROKES BETWEEN THE FOLDS OF THE DRESS TO SUGGEST VOLUME WITHOUT ADDING OUTLINES.

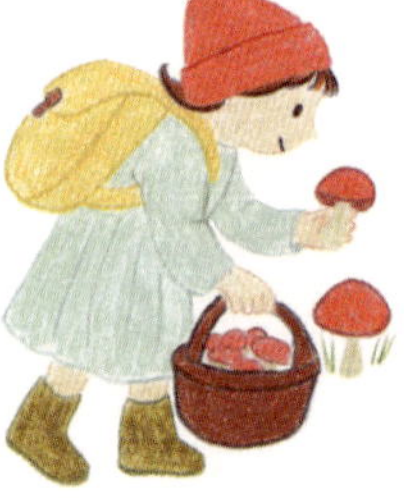

8.

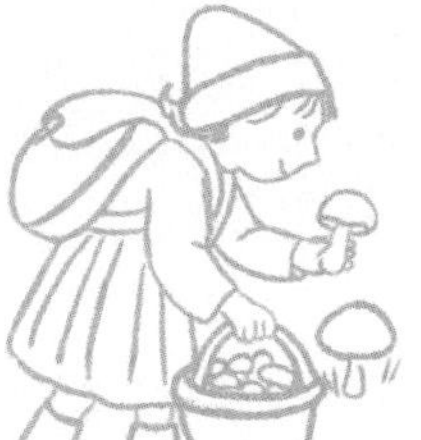

BOOKSHOP

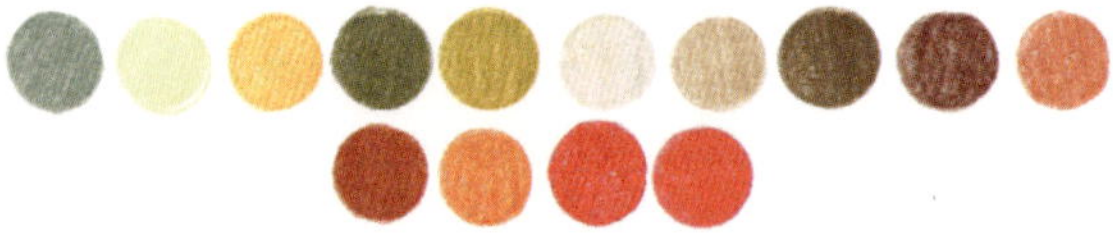

USE SLIGHTLY THICKER LINES FOR THE OUTER FRAME OF THE SHOP.

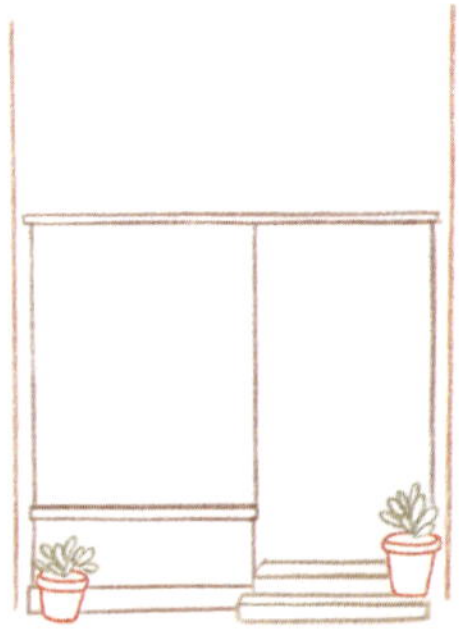

1.

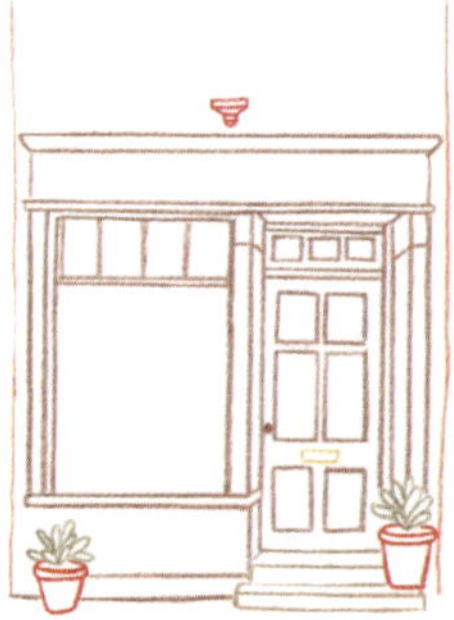

2.

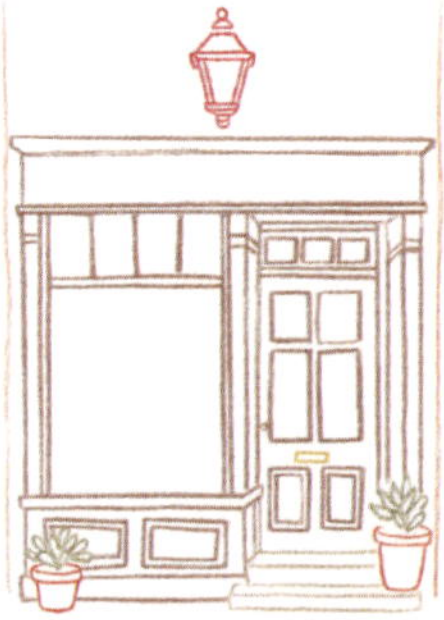

3.

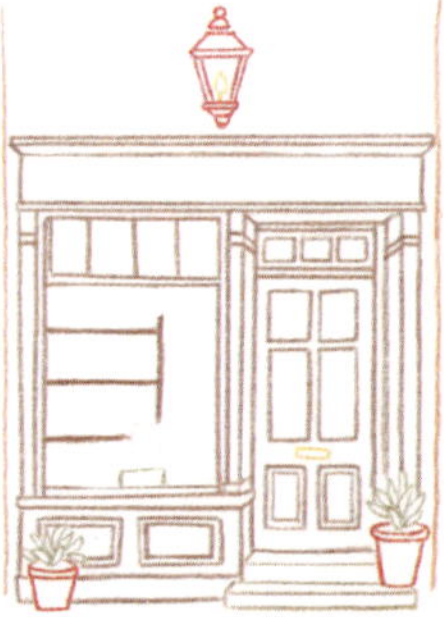

4.

USE LIGHTER STROKES FOR THE INNER WINDOW AND DOOR DETAILS.

5.

6.

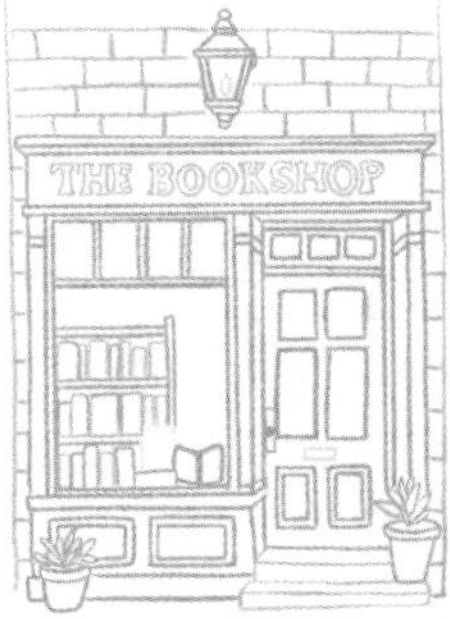
THE BOOKSHOP

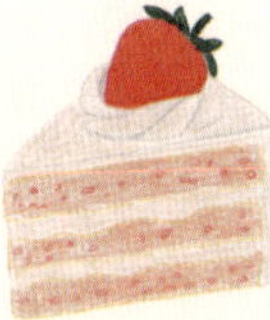

SIMPLE JOYS

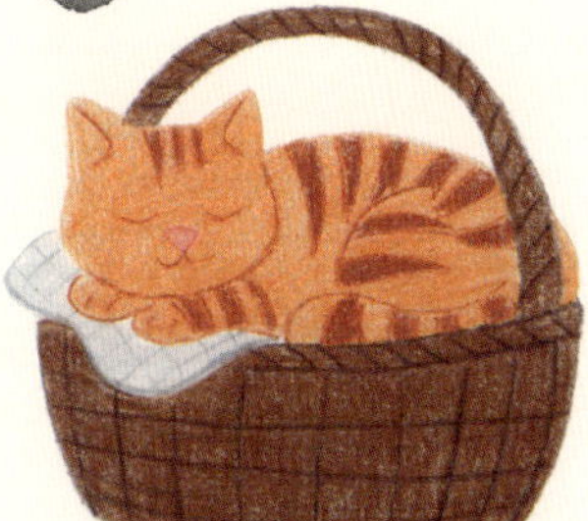

WALL ART

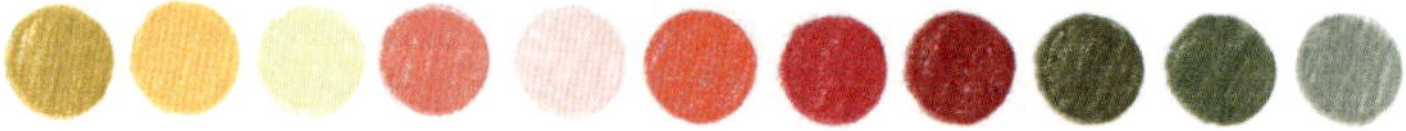

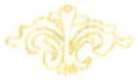

1.

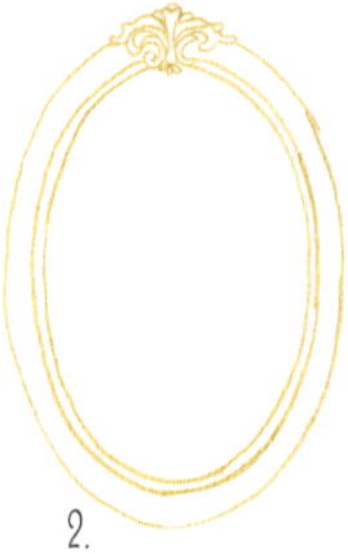

2.

3.

4.

5.

6.

7.

ADD A FEW DEEPER GOLDEN STROKES AROUND THE FRAME'S CURVES TO BRING OUT THE ORNATE DETAILS.

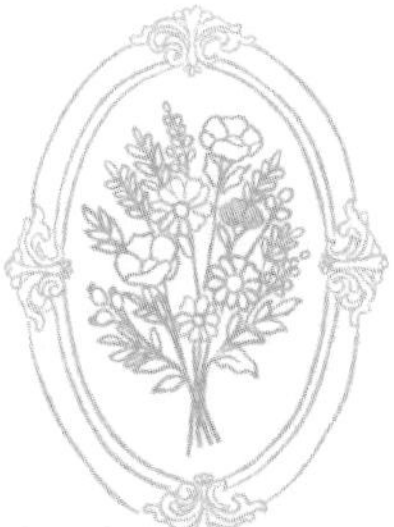

THROW BLANKET

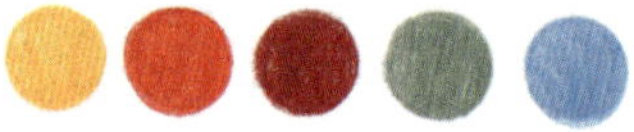

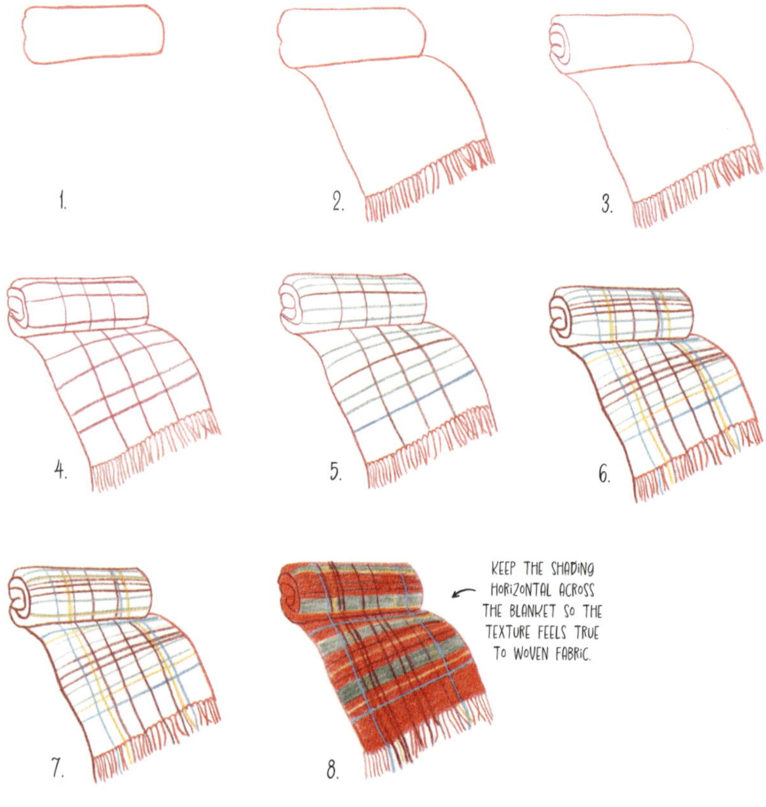

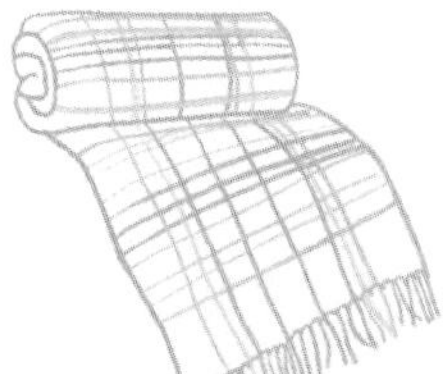

SLEEPY CAT

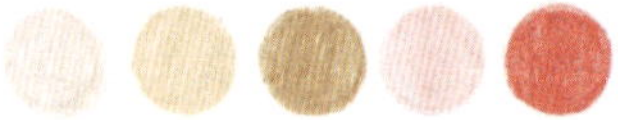

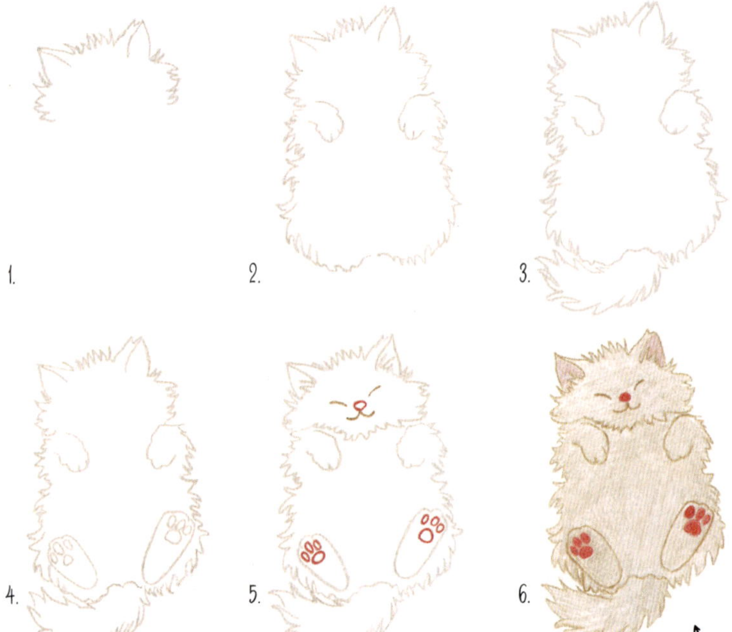

ADD TINY OUTWARD FLICKS AT THE EDGES TO KEEP THE FLUFFY TEXTURE FROM LOOKING FLAT.

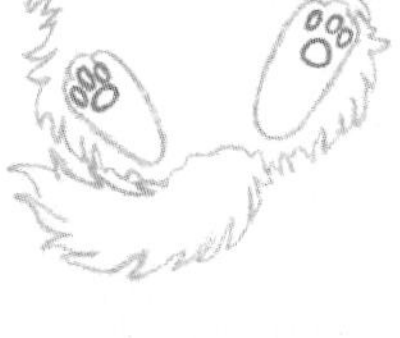

BISCUIT TIN

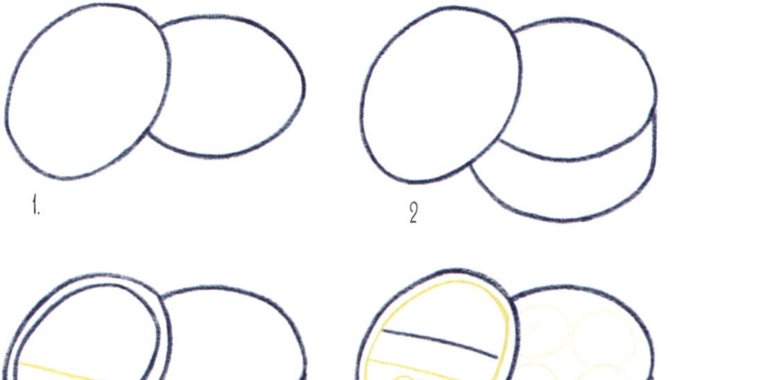
1.
2
3.
4.
A TOUCH OF DARKER YELLOW WITHIN THE BISCUITS HELPS SEPARATE THEM FROM THE BACKGROUND.
5.
6.

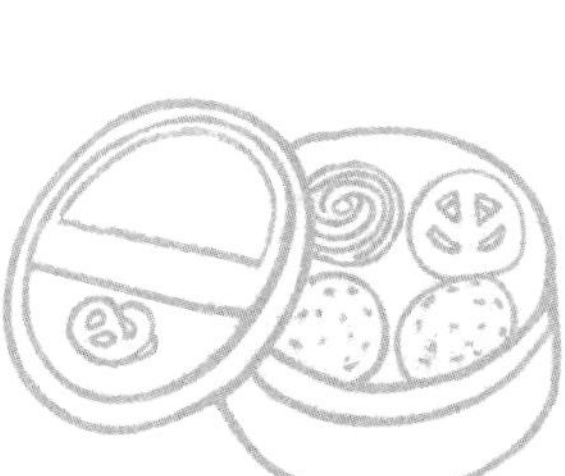

HONEY JAR

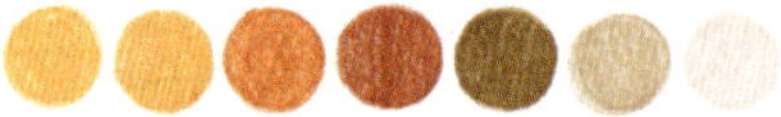

1.

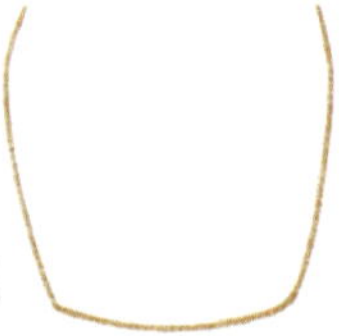

2.

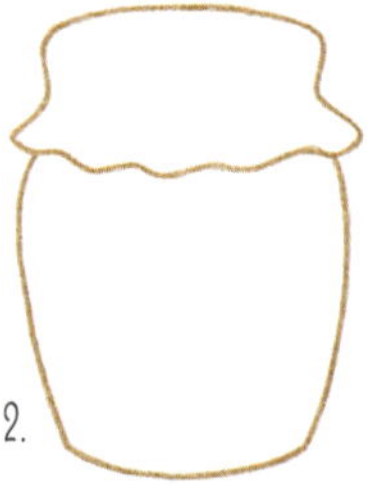

3.

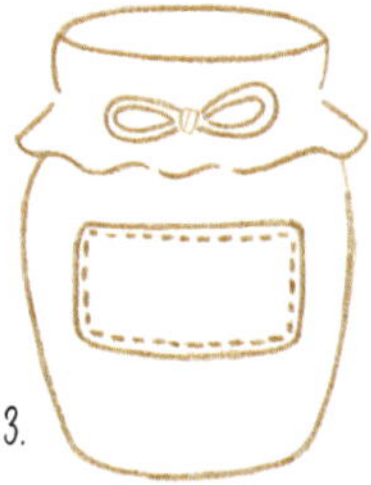

4.

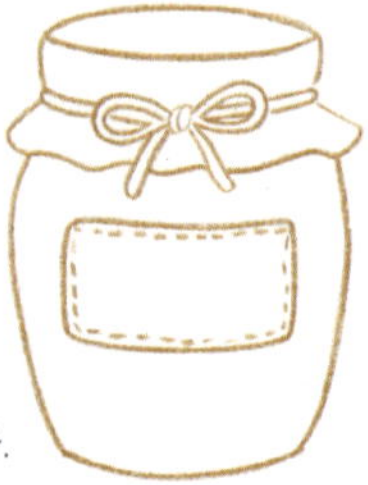

5.

6.

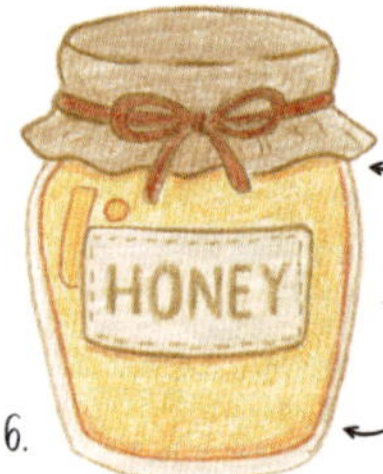

ADD A LINE OF SLIGHTLY DARKER GOLD UNDER THE FABRIC LID...

...AND ALONG THE BOTTOM OF THE HONEY, TO MAKE THE JAR LOOK FULL AND GIVE THE GLASS DEPTH.

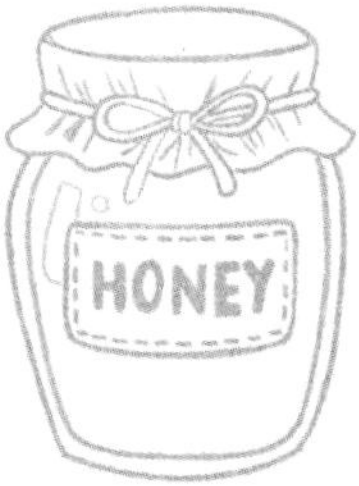
HONEY

APPLE PIE

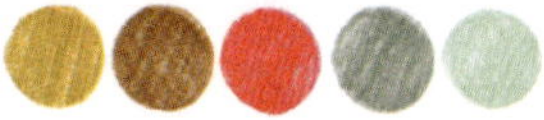

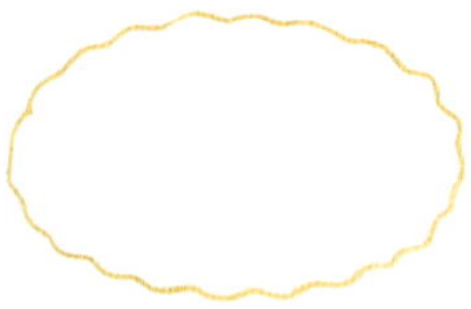

1.

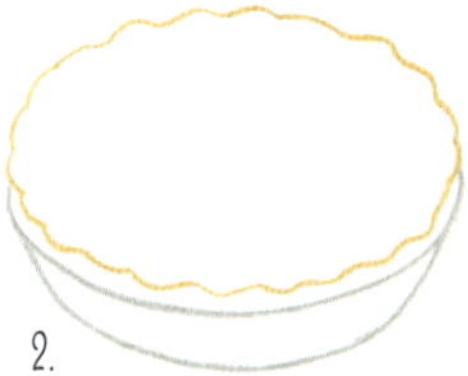

2.

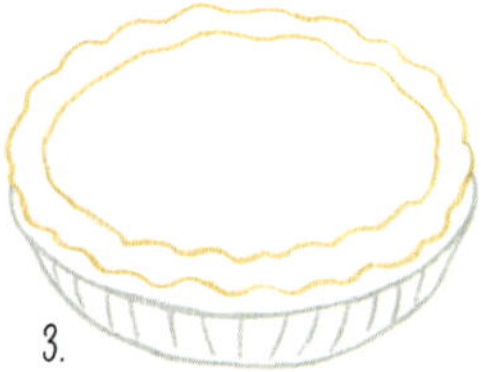

3.

4.

5.

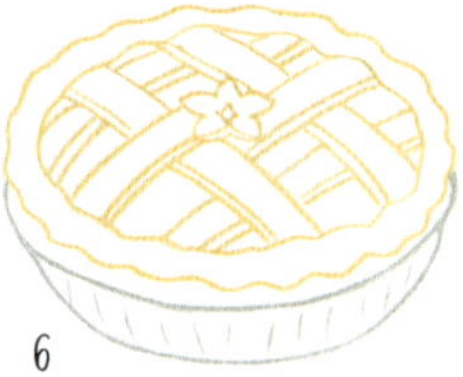

6

DEEPEN THE LATTICE SHADOWS WHERE THE STRIPS OVERLAP TO MAKE THE CRUST LOOK WOVEN INSTEAD OF FLAT.

7.

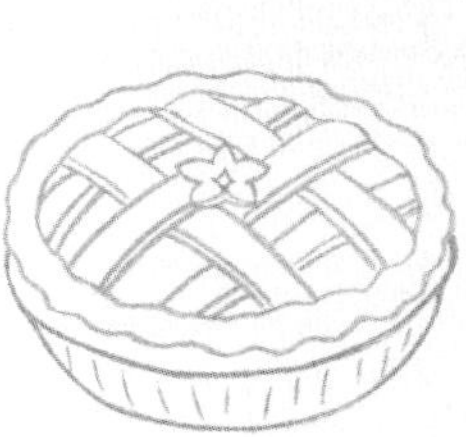

SLICE OF CAKE

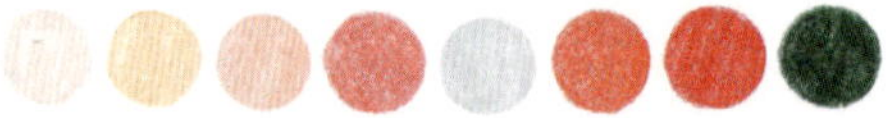

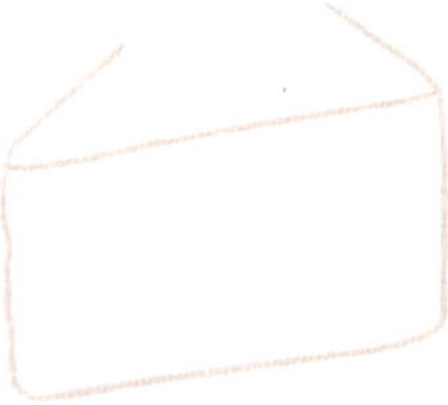

1.

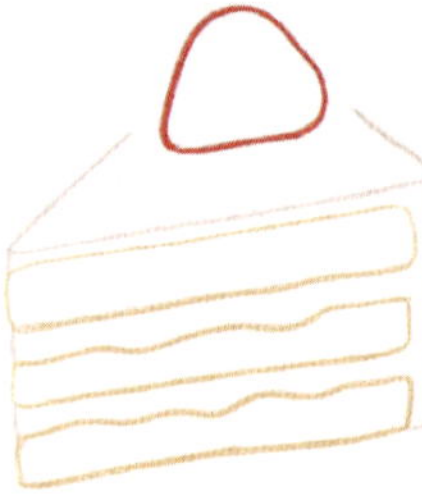

2.

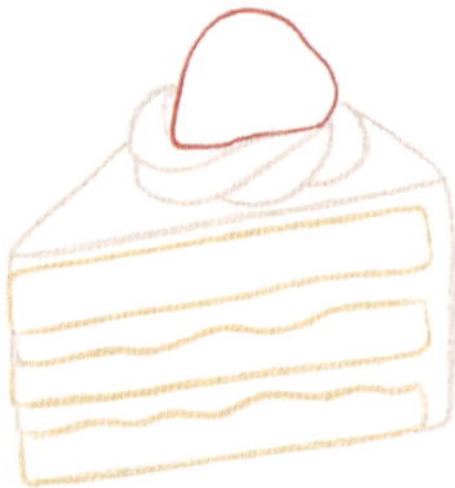

3.

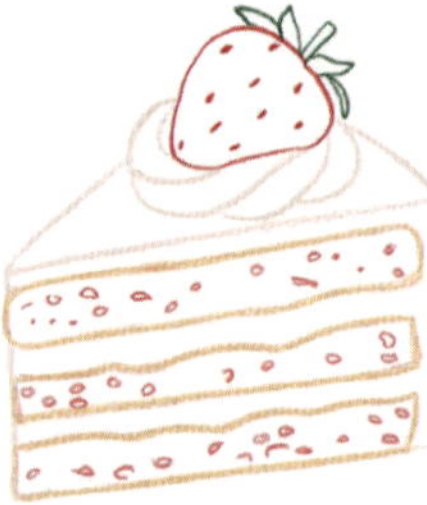

4.

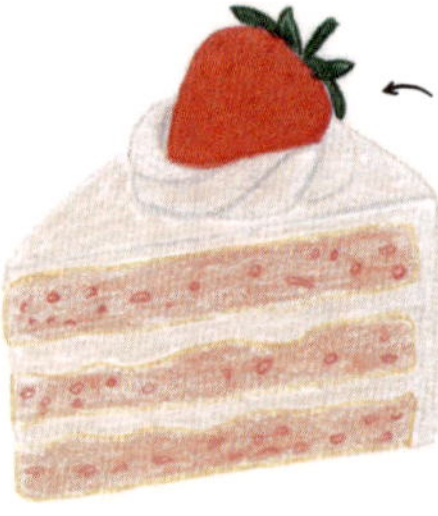

ADD A SLIGHTLY DEEPER RED ALONG THE BOTTOM CURVE OF THE STRAWBERRY.

5.

CAST-IRON STOVE

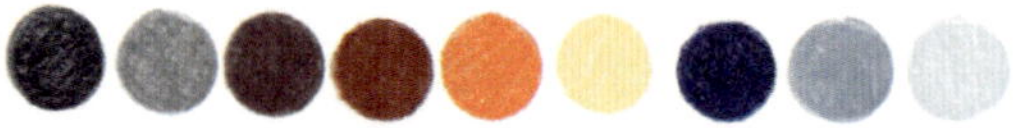

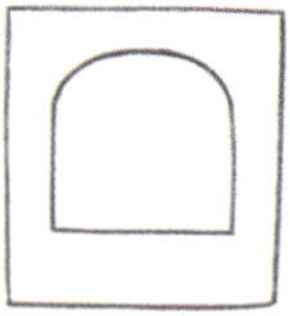

1.

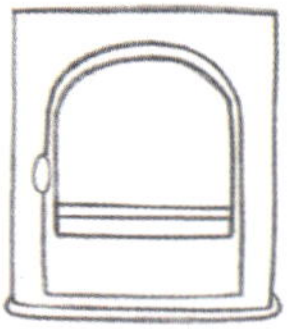

2.

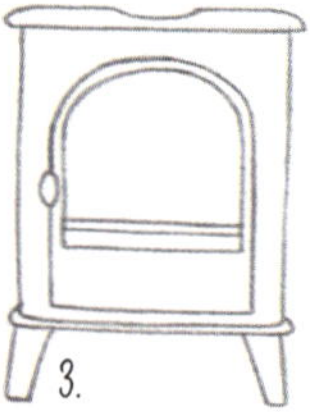

3.

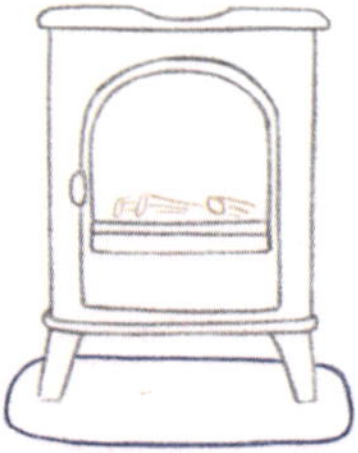

4.

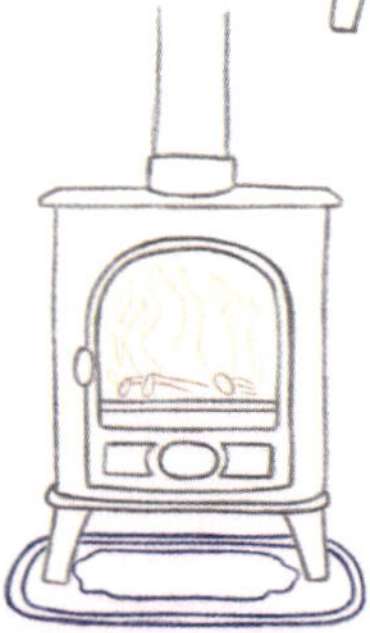

5.

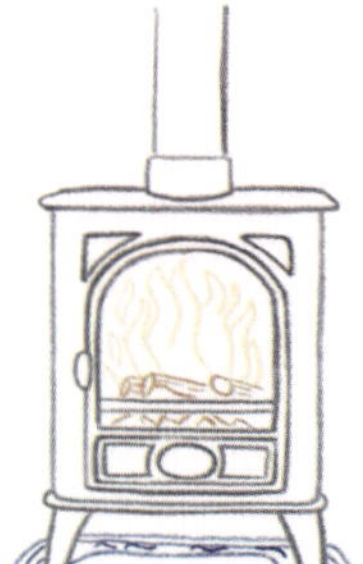

6.

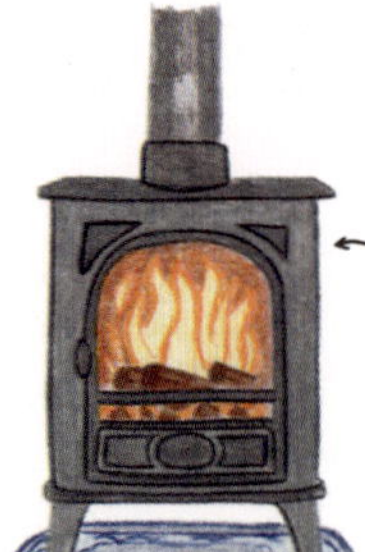

DEEPEN THE GRAPHITE LIGHTLY AROUND THE STOVE'S INNER DETAILS TO GIVE THE CAST IRON A SENSE OF DEPTH.

7.

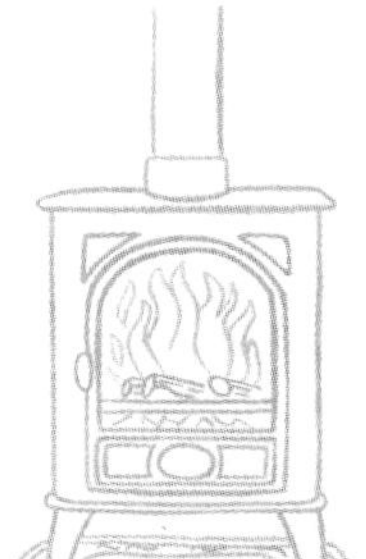

READING BOOKS

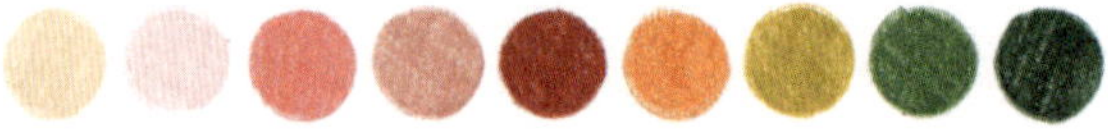

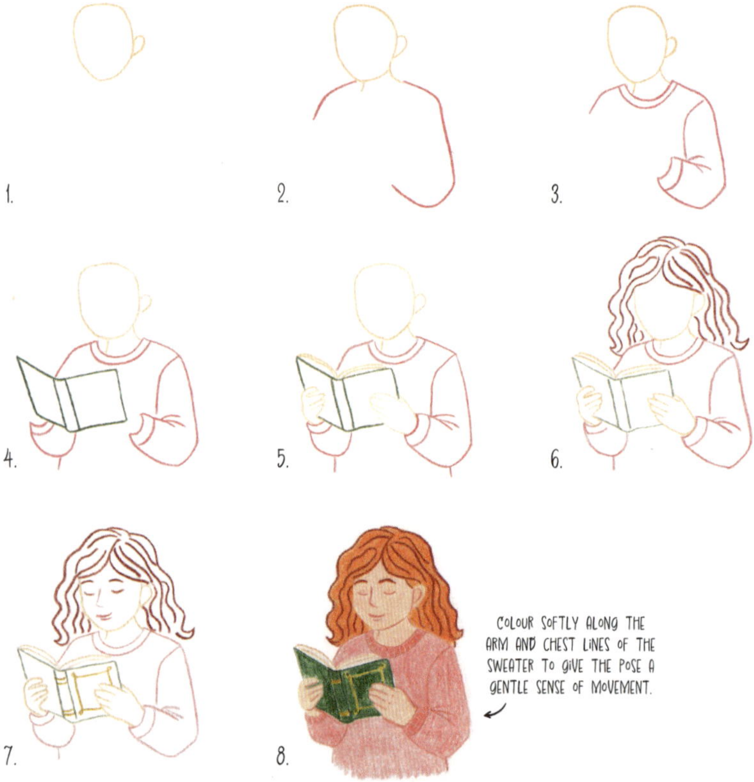

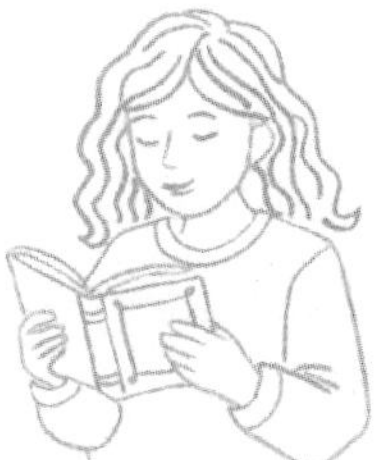

SLEEPY OWL

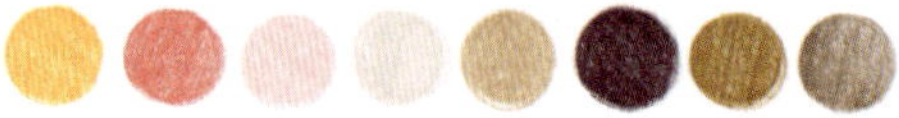

1.

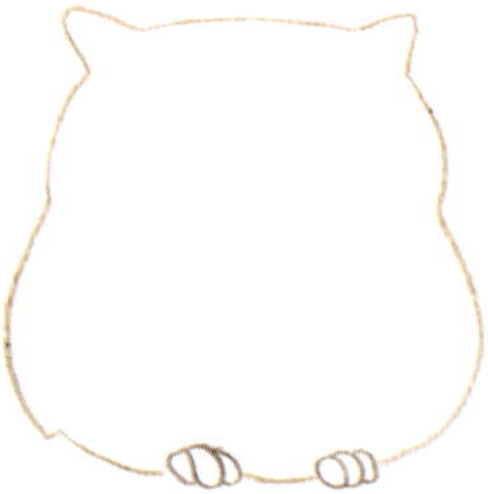

2.

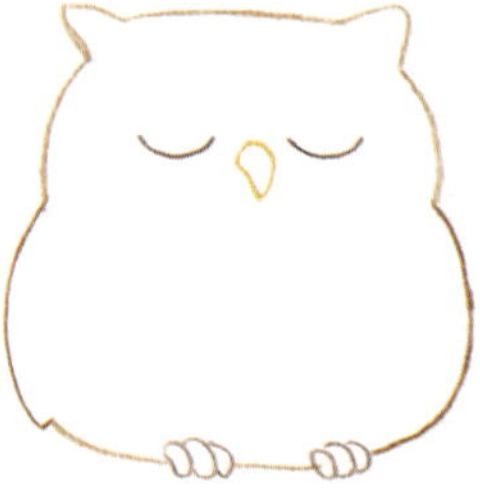

3.

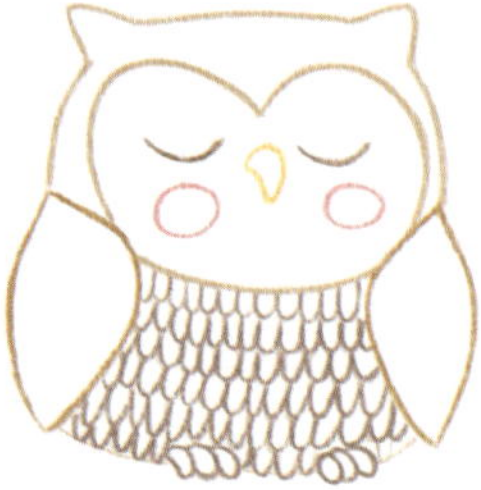

4.

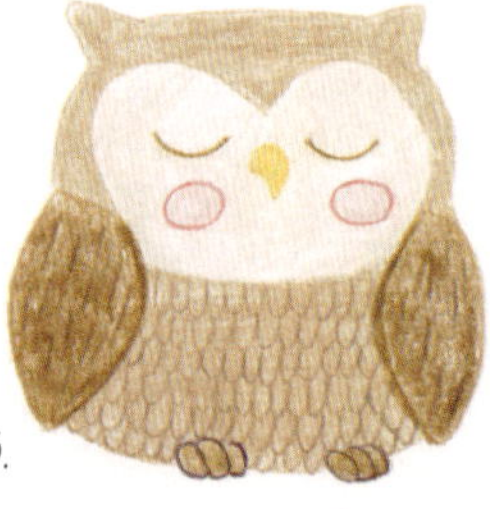

5.

KEEP THE FEATHERS ON THE BELLY SLIGHTLY CURVED IN THE SAME DIRECTION TO MAKE THE OWL LOOK ROUNDER AND SOFTER.

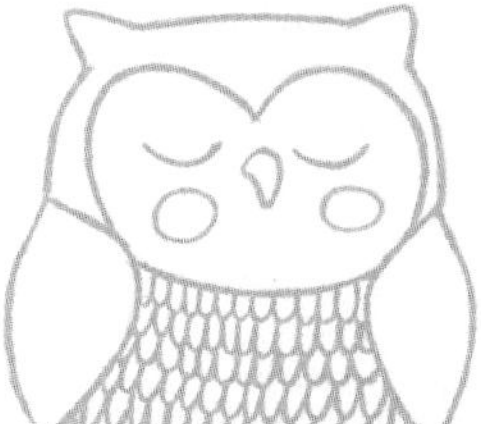

PANCAKES WITH SYRUP

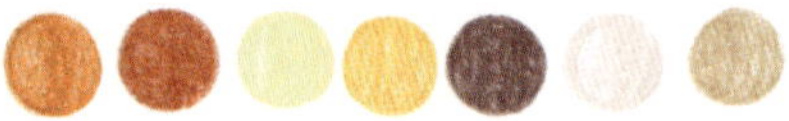

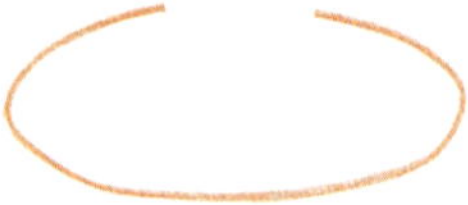

1.

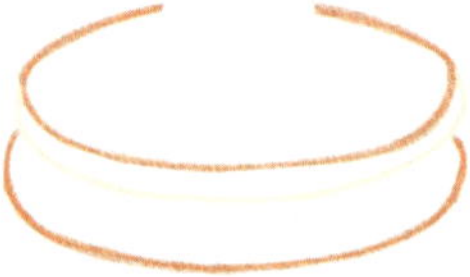

2.

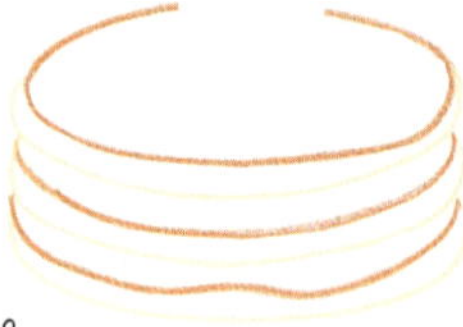

3.

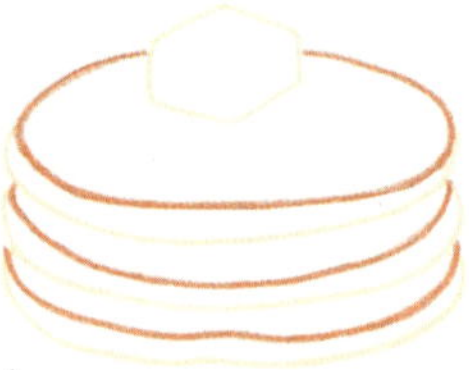

4.

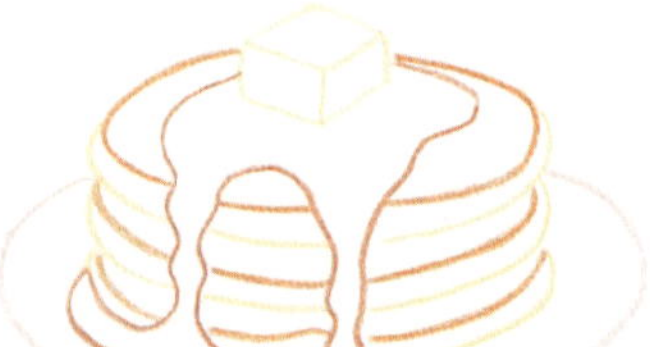

5.

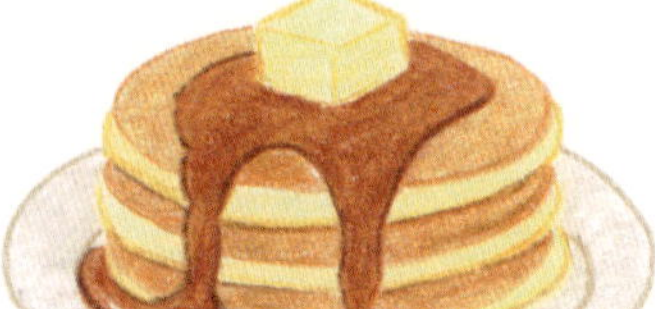

6.

USE THE TIP OF A THIN ERASER TO GENTLY LIFT TINY HIGHLIGHTS IN THE SYRUP, MAKING IT LOOK GLOSSY.

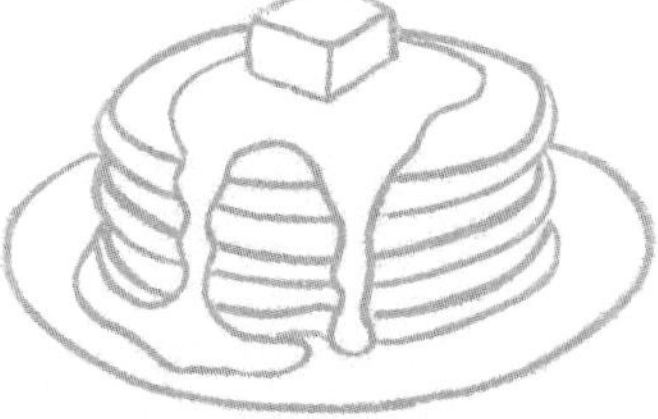

CAT IN A BASKET

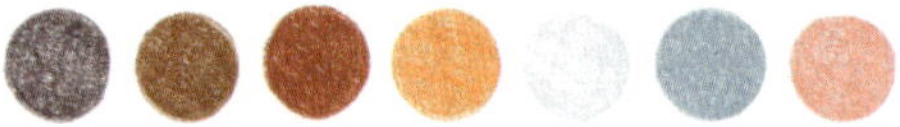

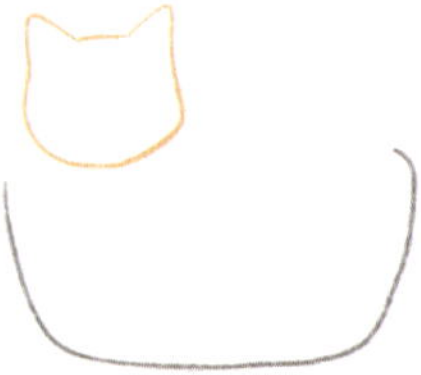

1.

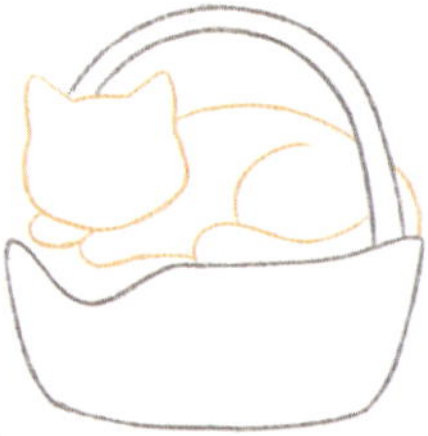

2.

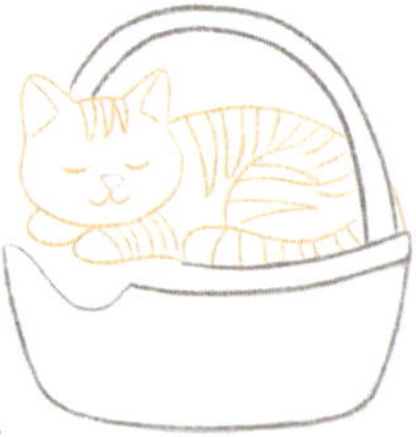

3.

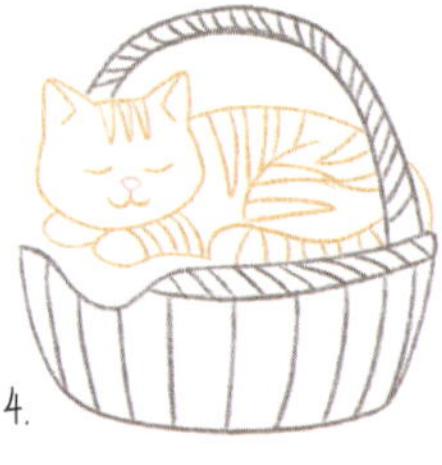

4.

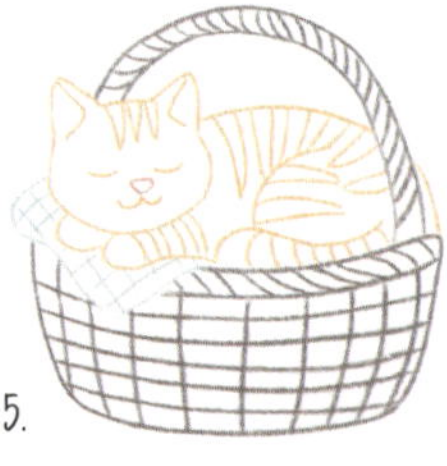

5.

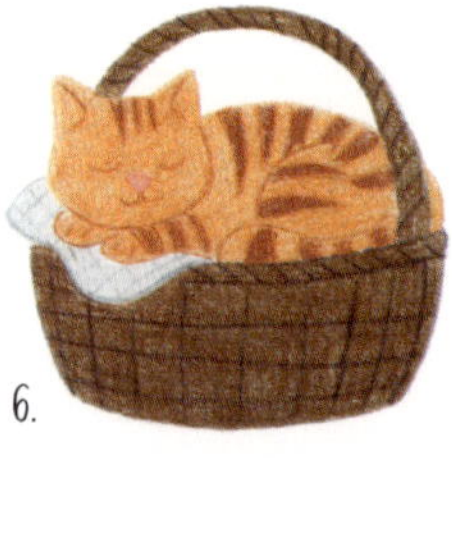

6.

ADDING A FEW EXTRA STROKES OF THE DARKER BROWN INSIDE THE BASKET'S WEAVE HELPS THE PATTERN FEEL MORE TEXTURED.

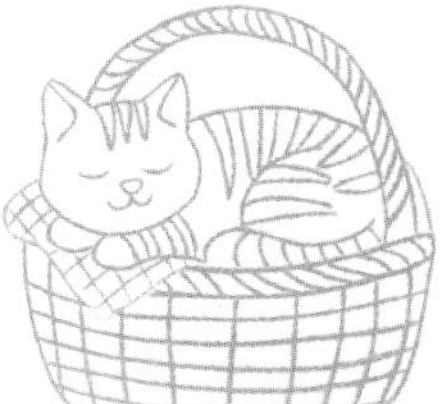

HOMEMADE BREAD

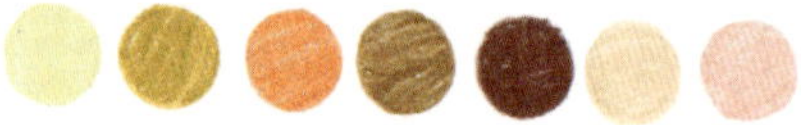

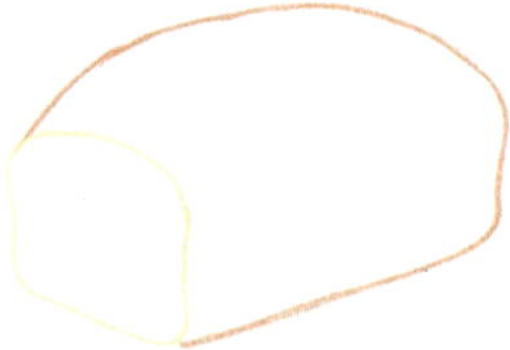

1.

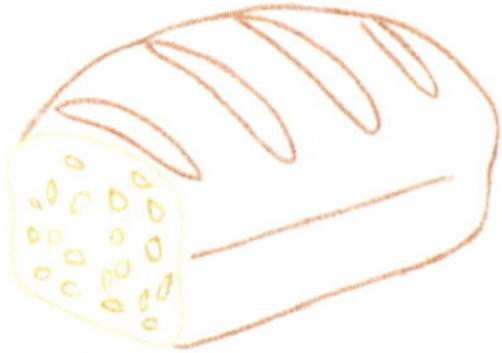

2.

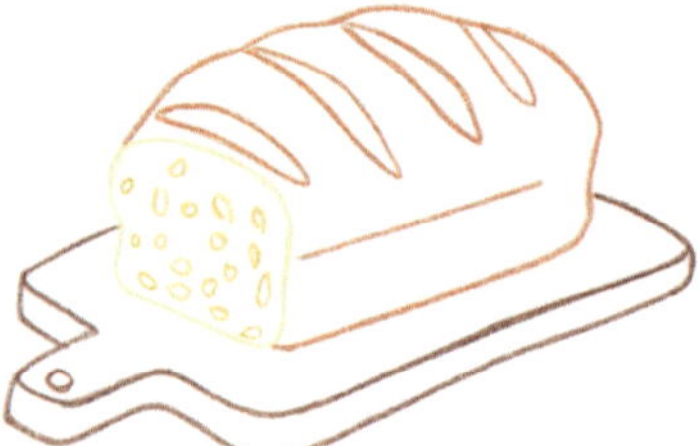

3

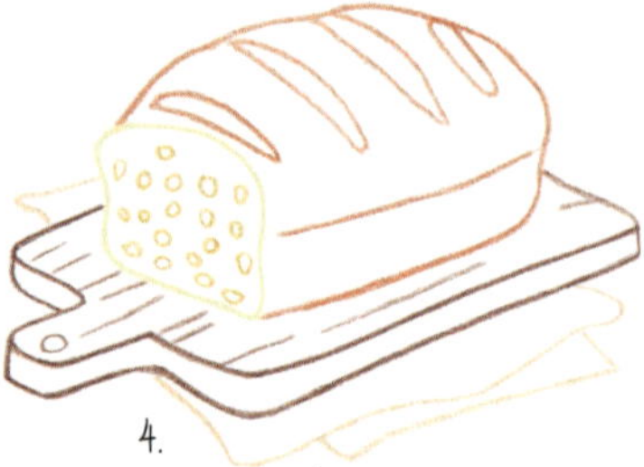

4.

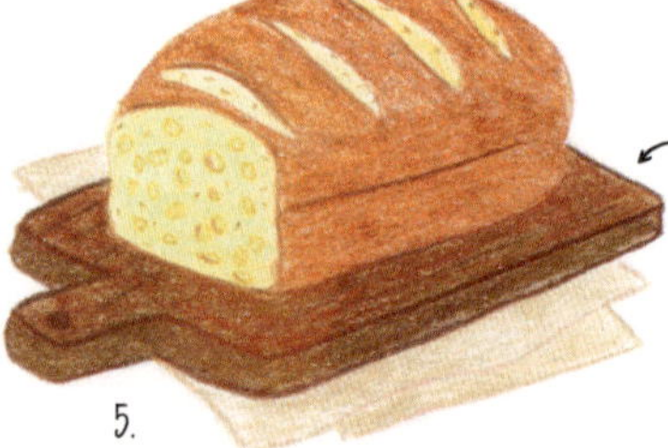

USE A SLIGHTLY COOLER OR DULLER BROWN FOR THE CUTTING BOARD SO THAT THE LOAF STAYS VISUALLY SEPARATE EVEN WITHOUT SHADOWS.

5.

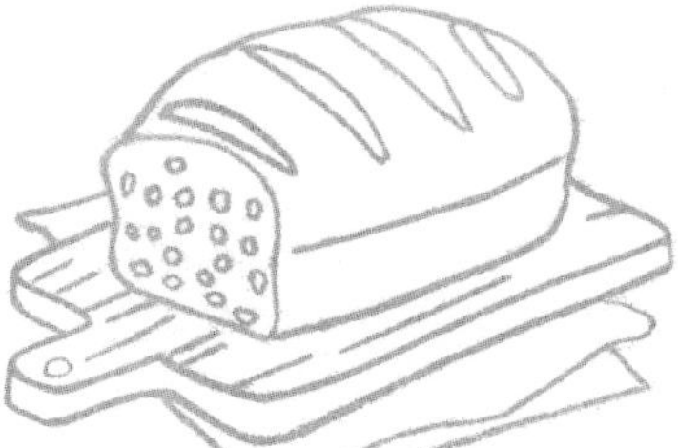

POPCORN BUCKET

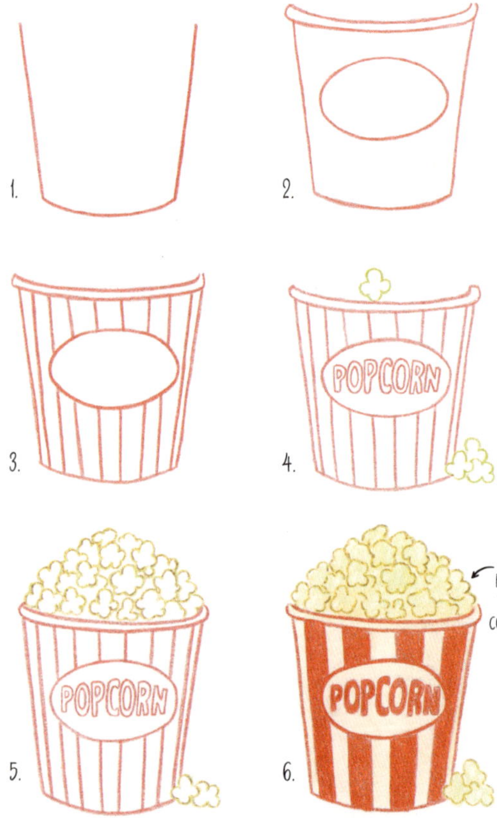

CREATE SMALL PATCHES OF DARKER YELLOW ALONG THE CURVED EDGES OF THE POPCORN PUFFS.

POPCORN

CUTE PLATES

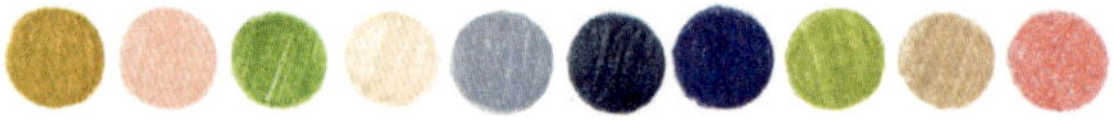

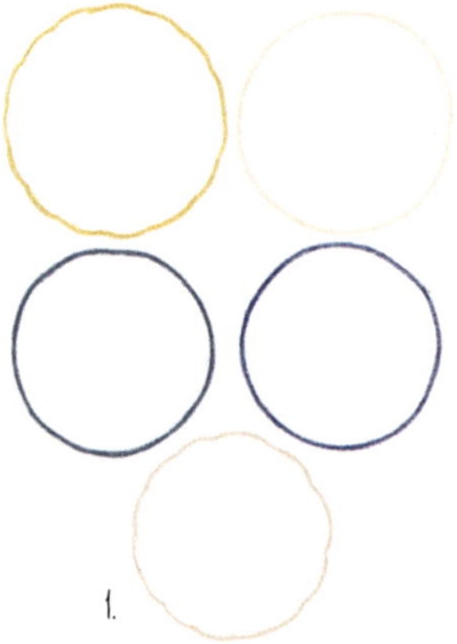

1.

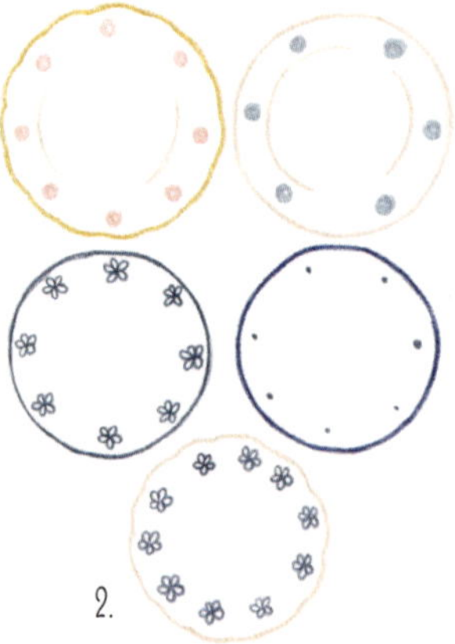

2.

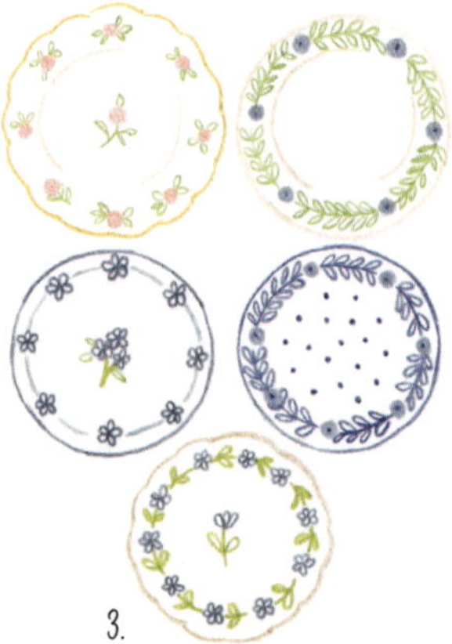

USE SLIGHTLY DARKER SHADES AND A SHARP PENCIL TIP FOR THE TINY DECORATIVE DETAILS SO THAT THEY STAND OUT WITHOUT OVERPOWERING THE PLATES.

3.

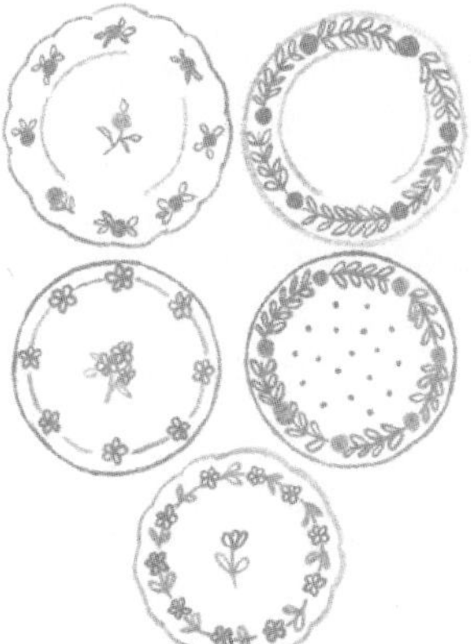

SLEEPY MOUSE

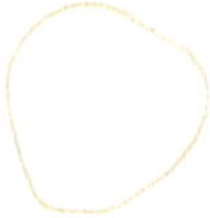

1.

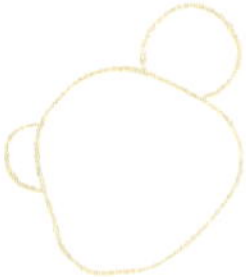

2.

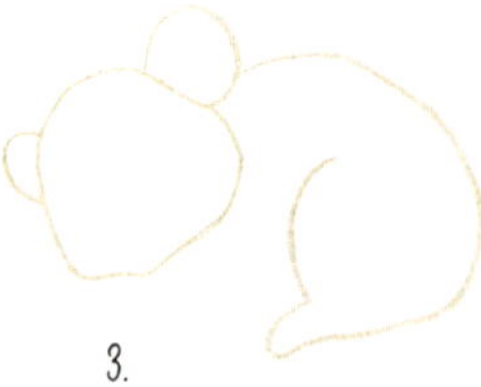

3.

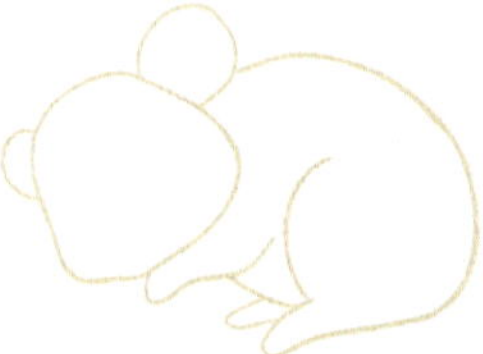

4.

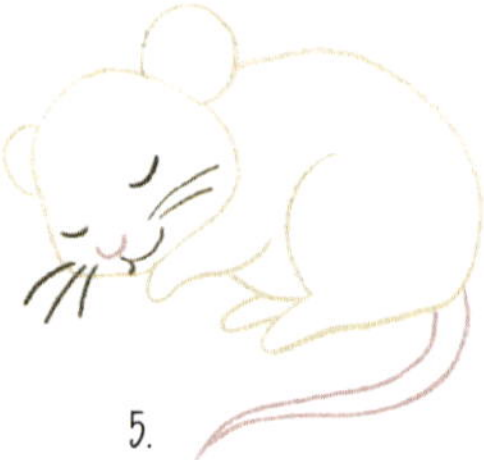

5.

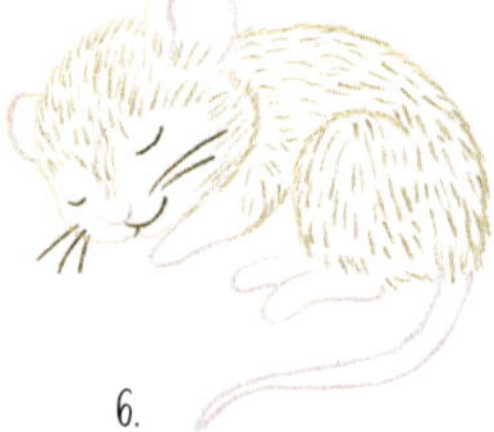

6.

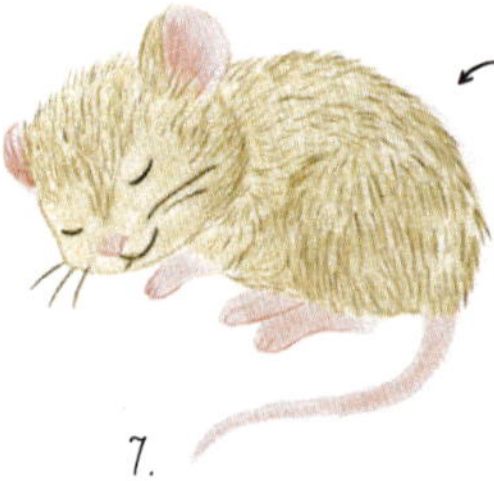

7.

LAYER TINY STROKES ALONG THE CURVE OF THE BODY TO CREATE SOFT FUR WITHOUT FLATTENING THE POSE.

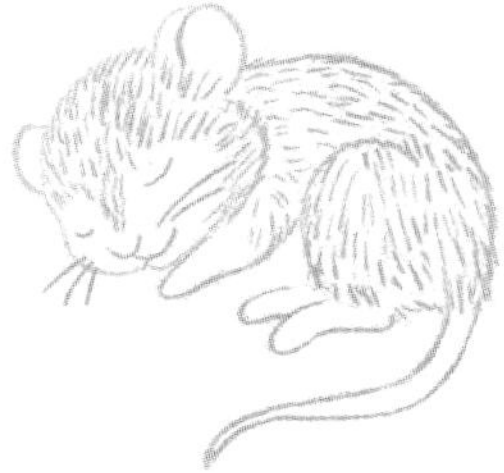

LOST IN MUSIC

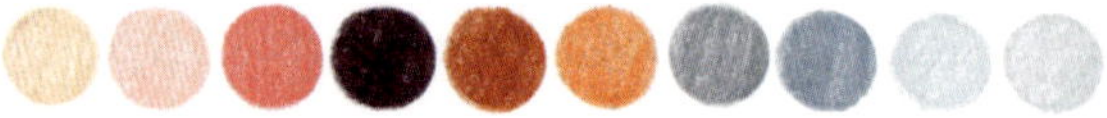

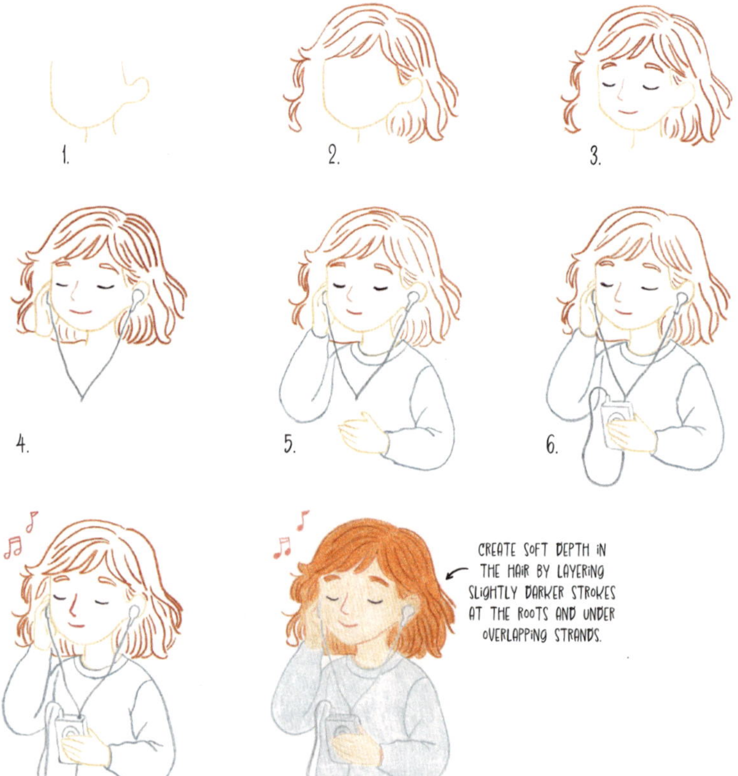

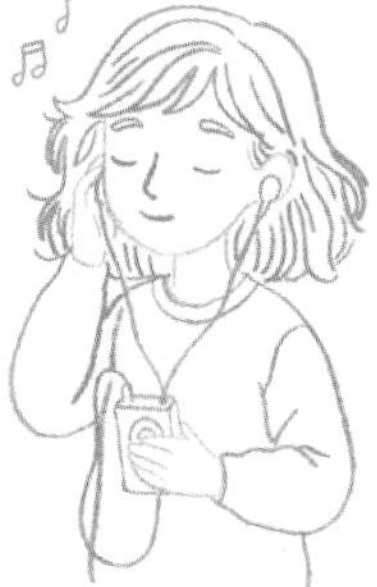

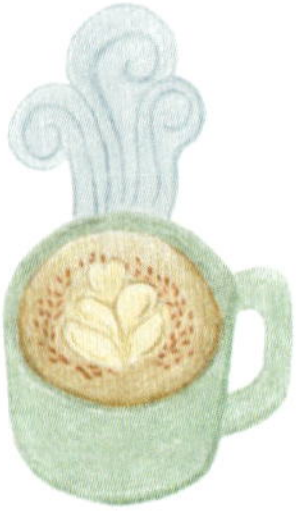

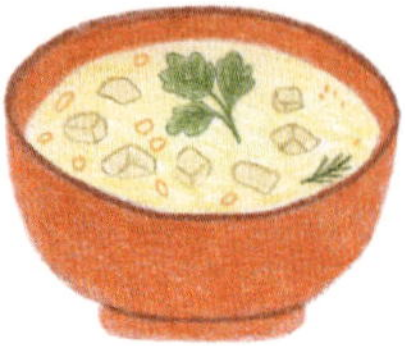

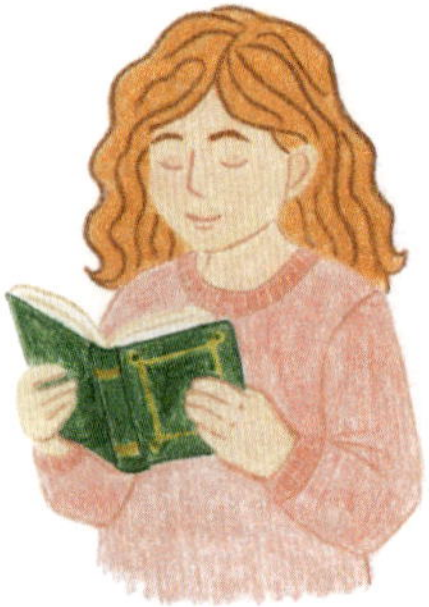

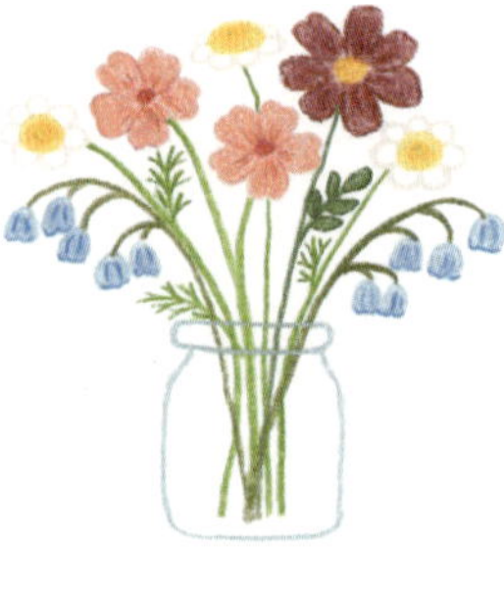

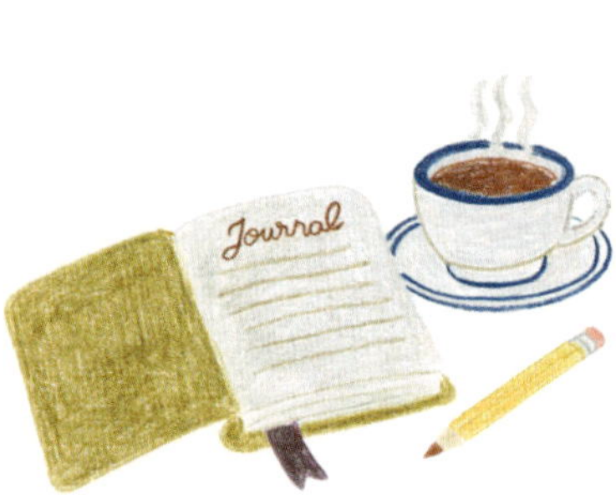
Journal

ABOUT THE AUTHOR

ANALIA FRATTI runs Create and Grow Studio, where she designs hand-drawn stickers for journalling, planners and printables. Her little drawings convey her love of cozy spaces, nature and timeless details. She lives and works in Barcelona.

Instagram: @analiafratti

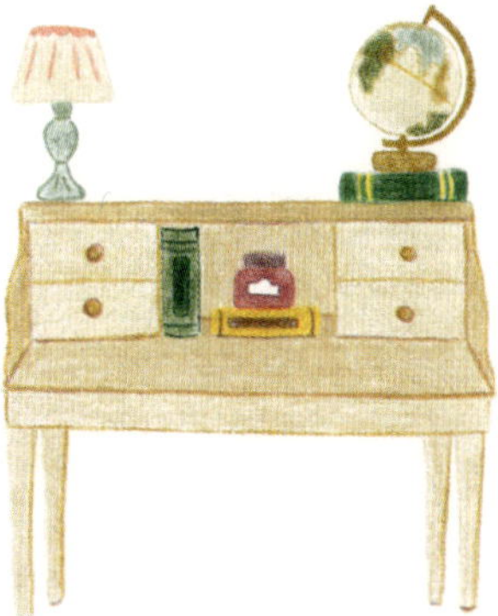

Skittledog

First published in the United Kingdom in 2026
by Skittledog, an imprint of Thames & Hudson Ltd,
6–24 Britannia Street, London WC1X 9JD

Senior Editor: Virginia Brehaut
Cover Designer: Alison Guile
Designer: Masumi Briozzo
Production: Felicity Awdry

EU Authorized Representative: Interart S.A.R.L.
19 rue Charles Auray, 93500 Pantin, Paris, France
productsafety@thameshudson.co.uk
interart.fr

A CIP catalogue record for this book is available from the British Library

ISBN 978-1-83776-097-8
01

Printed and bound in China by C&C Offset Printing Co., Ltd

FSC www.fsc.org
MIX
Paper | Supporting responsible forestry
FSC® C008047